PURE RELIGION

THE STORY OF CHURCH WELFARE SINCE 1930

BY GLEN L. RUDD

Published by
The Church of Jesus Christ of Latter-day Saints
Salt Lake City, Utah

We extend sincere appreciation for the use of photographs in this book. Photographs that are not specifically identified were provided by the LDS Church Archives, the LDS Church Visual Resources Library, Charles M. Knighton, Paul H. Heath, Brent and Helen Lee Goates, Max Bramall, and Jesse M. Drury, Jr. Painting on page 282: *All the City Was Gathered Together,* by James J. Tissot. Painting on page 362: *Christ's Image,* by Heinrich Hofmann, original in Riverside Church, New York City, New York.

PURE RELIGION

*Pure religion and undefiled
before God and the Father is this,
To visit the fatherless and widows
in their affliction, and to keep himself
unspotted from the world.*

JAMES 1:27

CONTENTS

General Welfare Committee members, 1995. Sitting, left to right: Bishop H. David Burton, Bishop Merrill J. Bateman, Bishop Richard C. Edgley, President Thomas S. Monson, President Gordon B. Hinckley, President James E. Faust, Chieko N. Okazaki, Elaine L. Jack, Aileen H. Clyde. Standing, left to right: Elder Henry B. Eyring, Elder Jeffrey R. Holland, Elder Robert D. Hales, Elder Richard G. Scott, Elder Joseph B. Wirthlin, Elder M. Russell Ballard, Elder Dallin H. Oaks, Elder Russell M. Nelson, Elder Neal A. Maxwell, Elder David B. Haight, Elder L. Tom Perry, President Boyd K. Packer

FOREWORD

The Welfare Program of The Church of Jesus Christ of Latter-day Saints has been a vital part of the teachings and practices of the Church since the restoration of the gospel. The program is rooted in holy scripture, is taught by God's prophets, and is timeless in its purpose.

Operating procedures vary to meet current needs, while divine principles endure. The Great Depression of the 1930s provided a stern test of faith as members rallied under the direction of their Church leaders to feed the hungry, provide work for the unemployed, and lift the downtrodden from the depths of despair to a newness of life. The guiding direction of the First Presidency charted the course and led the way.

From the garden project in the Fifth Ward and the modest storehouse on Pierpont Avenue in Salt Lake City, we now enjoy a coordinated system of agricultural projects, processing plants, and bishops' storehouses supplying Deseret brand products throughout the United States and many parts of Canada.

Employment centers dot this and many other lands, placing the unemployed in honorable jobs. Those Church members considered by many as unemployable by reason of age and disability receive work opportunities, training, and job placement through Deseret Industries. LDS Social Services agencies assist members with adoptions and counseling services.

This is not all. The generosity of Church members makes food, clothing, and essential help available to millions of our Heavenly Father's most needy children the world over. These humanitarian efforts provide literacy training, home production skills, medical care, and vital know-how that liberate those who might otherwise remain enslaved by indigent circumstances.

Leaders of nations marvel at the Welfare Program's success and seek to understand how it operates, lifts, and blesses. The future bodes well for Church welfare work.

At long last the epic history of the Welfare Program has been compiled and written in attractive book form by Glen L. Rudd. Born in 1918, Brother Rudd's contact with Church welfare dates from the 1940s when he served as a young bishop of a ward with many welfare challenges. For a quarter of a century spanning the 1950s, 1960s, and 1970s, he served capably as the coordinator of the Salt Lake Regional Bishops' Storehouse, known as Welfare Square. Other positions of responsibility followed, including service as a General Authority of the Church. From his experience and with the help of his remarkable library of historical documents, treasured photographs, and teachings of the prophets on Welfare Program themes, this remarkable and useful volume is published.

Pure Religion will be fascinating reading for all Church leaders and members and will be a treasured addition to every personal library. It will also inspire the thinking and efforts of Latter-day Saints around the world as they consider the admonition from the Apostle James: "Pure religion and undefiled before God and the Father is this, To visit the fatherless and widows in their affliction, and to keep himself unspotted from the world" (James 1:27).

—President Thomas S. Monson

ACKNOWLEDGMENTS

The material in this book has been gleaned from my files and my memories and, for the most part, reflects my own observations of the establishment and growth of the welfare program of the Church. The book does not represent the official position of the Church.

The manuscript of the book was prepared with the encouragement and counsel of Keith B. McMullin, managing director of the Church's Welfare Department, his assistant Frank Richardson, and other members of the department staff. I express my thanks to them.

Ilona Nielsen typed the original dictation and assisted faithfully in many ways over the months of preparation.

Lee Miller, a personal friend for many years, helped me to organize the material and keep my thoughts focused. He was a great asset throughout the entire preparation period.

Bishop Jesse M. Drury, the original storehouse keeper, was my first mentor in welfare work, and I am grateful for his guidance. He related many experiences to me over the years, and I have used some of them in this book.

Stewart Eccles contributed greatly by verifying my notes and memories of events that occurred long ago.

Charles Knighton, former manager of the Salt Lake Bishops' Central Storehouse, assisted in collecting needed photographs.

I am grateful to many other friends and welfare associates who have encouraged and assisted me in many ways.

I appreciate the meticulous editing done by Susan Hainsworth and the fine design work done by Scott Welty, both of the Church Curriculum Department.

President Thomas S. Monson, as a friend, quietly encouraged me in this assignment. We served as young bishops in adjacent wards, and both of us had large numbers of needy people to care for.

Most of all, I am grateful to my wife, Marva, who has encouraged me each day to do my best. I greatly appreciate her patience and encouragement.

—Glen L. Rudd

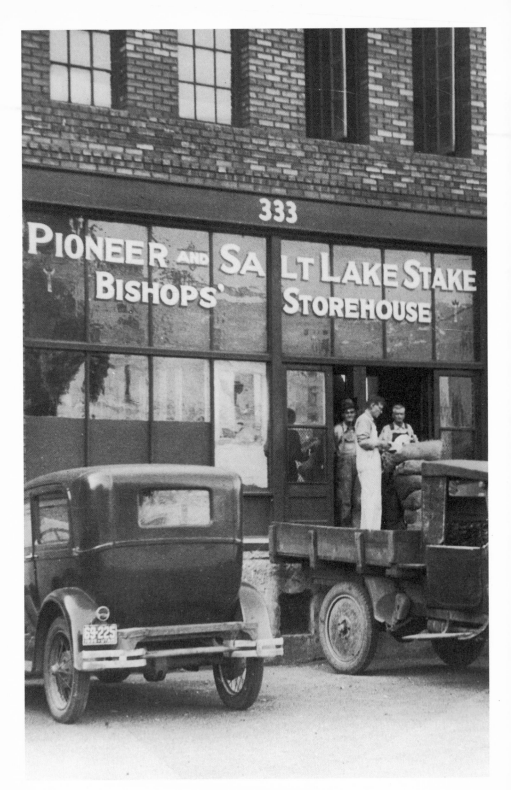

Bishops' storehouse, 1932

CHAPTER 1

HUMBLE BEGINNINGS

In April of 1936, the First Presidency of The Church of Jesus Christ of Latter-day Saints announced the inauguration of a welfare plan to care for the poor and needy of the Church. Since the time of this announcement, the growth and accomplishments of the Church welfare program have been a remarkable and wonderful adventure. The program was instituted to solve the problems of poverty that have plagued worldly societies and governments throughout the history of mankind. Its successes confirm the inspiration of its beginnings and the true, eternal principles upon which it is based.

EARLY HISTORY

Welfare work in the Church didn't begin in 1936, nor did it begin when the Church was restored in 1830. It is an inherent part of the gospel of Jesus Christ and has existed in one form or another whenever the gospel has been on the earth. The Lord has always required his Saints to establish some type of benevolent system to take care of the poor and those who are otherwise unable to care for themselves. The following scriptures, from Old Testament, Book of Mormon, and New Testament times, make this clear:

"Bring ye all the tithes into the storehouse, that there may be meat in mine house, and prove me now herewith, saith the Lord of hosts, if I will not open you the windows of heaven, and pour you out a blessing, that there shall not be room enough to receive it" (Malachi 3:10).

1

"But before ye seek for riches, seek ye for the kingdom of God.

"And after ye have obtained a hope in Christ ye shall obtain riches, if ye seek them; and ye will seek them for the intent to do good—to clothe the naked, and to feed the hungry, and to liberate the captive, and administer relief to the sick and the afflicted" (Jacob 2:18–19).

"Therefore, if ye do not remember to be charitable, ye are as dross, which the refiners do cast out, (it being of no worth) and is trodden under foot of men" (Alma 34:29).

"Neither was there any among them that lacked: for as many as were possessors of lands or houses sold them, and brought the prices of the things that were sold,

"And laid them down at the apostles' feet: and distribution was made unto every man according as he had need" (Acts 4:34–35).

At various times throughout the early history of the latter-day Church, individuals and families were without the necessities of life and in need of assistance. The bishops of the Church, who had a scriptural mandate to seek out the poor, cared for their people in the best way they could with available resources. Many good things were done for the members in a quiet, local manner. In the Salt Lake City area, where the greatest concentrations of Church members lived, much was accomplished by the General Relief Society Presidency, the Presiding Bishopric, and many local bishops. Neither were the poor overlooked by the Presidency of the Church.

Bishops' storehouses have been one way of caring for the poor since the days of the Prophet Joseph Smith. When the Saints migrated west, it wasn't long before small local storehouses were established to help the needy. A general bishops' storehouse and tithing office was located where the Joseph Smith Memorial Building (formerly the Hotel Utah)

Right: Lyman
Wyoming
Bishops'
Storehouse,
1940s

Center:
Evanston
Wyoming
Bishops'
Storehouse,
1940s

Below:
Kamas Utah
Bishops'
Storehouse,
1940s

now stands. This storehouse took care of the needs of the people in Salt Lake City for many years.

In smaller communities throughout Utah, Idaho, Arizona, and in a few other places, bishops received tithing-in-kind and fast-offerings-in-kind as well as small amounts of cash. In order to handle these contributions, small bishops' storehouses and tithing offices were constructed.

Before 1936, there were at least 135 bishops' storehouses throughout the Church. They were not organized by regions nor supervised by Church headquarters, though counsel was given to properly administer them. They were simply local storehouses, from which commodities received from those who were able to give were distributed to those in need. When times were difficult in those early years, bishops, with their storehouses, kept the needy in the communities from suffering. President J. Reuben Clark, Jr., said, "The Church survived; the people prospered. Character endured intact. We took care of our own poor. In times of scarcity neighbors helped one another" (*Church Welfare Plan: A Discussion* [address given at Estes Park, Colo., 20 June 1939], p. 7).

In every bishop's handbook from 1900 to 1923, instructions were given for the proper care of bishops' storehouses. The bishops were to see that the grounds, trees, and shrubbery were kept in good condition. They were taught the principles of handling tithing-in-kind, as well as many other welfare principles. Many bishops helped to organize the Saints so that the storehouses were as important to them in their day as they are to Church members today.

Another aspect of the welfare program in those early years was the employment program. Beginning in the early 1900s, the Presiding Bishopric supervised an employment program called the Deseret Employment Bureau. This bureau operated intermittently during the first three decades of the twentieth century.

Above: St. George Utah Bishops' Storehouse, 1940s

Center: Coalville Utah Bishops' Storehouse, 1940s

Right: Midway Utah Bishops' Storehouse, 1940s

As a result of the serious economic depression that engulfed America in the 1920s, many stakes began organizing stake employment committees. By the late 1920s, the presidents of six stakes in the center of Salt Lake City (Salt Lake, Ensign, Liberty, Pioneer, Granite, and Grant stakes) had organized a committee to manage a regional employment center to supplement the Deseret Employment Bureau. The president of the Cottonwood Stake, Henry D. Moyle, a prominent attorney, asked permission for his stake to join with the other six to help find employment for his members. President Moyle was promptly made chairman of the committee, and he was delighted with the calling. He was a young and vigorous stake president who served with great ability and led out with the full cooperation of the other presidents.

In 1930 unemployment among Church members had become critical. Many prominent and faithful members were

Courtesy of Wide World Photos, Inc.

Unemployed men in Salt Lake City uprooting and sawing old trees to be used for fuel, early 1930s

Brethren cutting wood at Granite Stake wood yard, 1931

without work and therefore without income. For example, in Pioneer Stake about 60 percent of the wage earners were unemployed, and at one point unemployment in the stake reached 70 percent.

The high unemployment caused a shortage of money for buying food and clothing, but the curse of idleness seemed to be the main problem facing members. Elder Harold B. Lee said on a number of occasions that it was idleness that brought about the development of the welfare program. Many men were seeking work, and after long days without success they would return to their homes discouraged and disgruntled. Their wives and families suffered, not only because of the lack of necessities, but because of conflicts brought on by discouragement and low self-esteem. Even families that were committed to the gospel began to have problems they had never had before. Several women went to their bishops to see if they or the stake presidents could help the men find work.

These same challenges were felt throughout the Church. Stake presidents and bishops everywhere were coping with the welfare problems of the Saints.

PIONEER STAKE WELFARE COMMITTEE

Harold B. Lee, president of Pioneer Stake, 1930–1936

In 1924, a twenty-five-year-old man, his brother, and their wives moved from Idaho to the Poplar Grove Ward of Pioneer Stake. Five years later this young man, Harold B. Lee, was called as a counselor in the stake presidency. A year after that he was called by the Lord to preside over the Pioneer Stake—at the age of thirty-one.

President Lee was a very concerned young president. He was keenly aware of the poverty and idleness that existed throughout his stake. He gathered around him able men and discussed the situation with them, praying many times for inspiration to know what to do.

In 1932 President Lee and his two counselors, Charles S. Hyde and Paul C. Child, organized a Pioneer Stake welfare committee. President Child was assigned as chairman. He immediately put his committee to work to develop what was to become the center of welfare activity in the Salt Lake Valley.

The original members of this committee were Paul C. Child, chairman; Jesse M. Drury, Fifth Ward bishop, storehouse keeper; Alfons J. Finck, high councilor, secretary and accountant; Fred J. Heath, high councilor, work and employment director; Edna Madsen, stake Relief Society president;

C. O. Jensen, former bishop; and Thomas E. Wilding, high councilor.

Bishop Jesse M. Drury had lost his job with the railroad, and the position he now took as storehouse keeper began a lifelong involvement with bishops' storehouses. As a bishop, he presided over about 500 members with a spirit of generosity and love. His ward area was along the railroad tracks going south through the city, and the welfare load was heavy because many of the members of the ward were elderly. Bishop Drury learned early that distressed people needed his patience and kindness. He was gifted with the ability to reach out and help them.

Jesse M. Drury,
storehouse keeper, 1930s

Brother Fred J. Heath spent most of his time promoting the collection of available produce from farms in the area. He also encouraged the production of commodities in the stake and on various ward farms. He gave all the time he could to helping volunteers do the work that needed to be done and was always an inspiration to them. During the time the concrete was being poured for the Welfare Square grain elevator and on every other project with which he was involved, he would gather the workers and have a word of prayer before they began their shift. He was a splendid pioneer in the Church welfare program throughout his life, and while he kept himself out of the limelight, without his

Fred J. Heath,
first welfare work
director, 1930s

9

efforts much of the success enjoyed in those early years would have taken longer to achieve.

PIONEER STAKE STOREHOUSE

The Pioneer Stake welfare committee decided to prepare a bishops' storehouse to meet the needs of the stake. Paul C. Child, assisted by Jeremiah Hancock of the stake high council, obtained the free use of a large building at 333 Pierpont Avenue that had formerly housed two businesses. The building was within the boundaries of the Pioneer Stake and became the original storehouse of the stake.

Several members of the high council who were unemployed helped to prepare the storehouse facilities. The welfare committee minutes of 15 July 1932 recorded:

"[Bishop Drury, the storehouse keeper,] reported the conditions of the Storehouse, work done and projects ahead. The Storehouse had been cleaned, whitewashed; shelves had been built, also a counter and fence gate. The sewing room had been cleaned and papered. The office space was being improved. Lighting and plumbing had been overhauled. Lumber for shelves and some cabinets were donated by Bishop [Kaspar] Fetzer. Some of the lumber had to be bought. The elevator had been boarded and made safe; windows and doors had been put in. The stairway had been boarded in and made safe. Sign 'Pioneer Stake Storehouse' had been painted on the outside. Phone number Wasatch 7666 had been put in. Some suitable scales for purchase had been located, and Bishop Drury was authorized to obtain them" (quoted in Jesse M. Drury, *For These My Brethren* [reprint, 1991], p. 27).

Brother Alfons J. Finck recorded his observations about the storehouse and cannery:

"The fitting up of the place required the cleaning up and disposition of several wagon loads of dirt. By the donations

Inside Pioneer Stake Bishops' Storehouse, 1932; foreground: Bishop Jesse M. Drury, Alfons J. Finck, and Phillip Jensen

of lumber for shelves, furniture for office and store, paint and many other things, we were able to open for operation. . . . Among the donations was a two burner gas stove, a washboiler with which to start the canning operations. Among the skilled men were two members of the high council; Brother Frank Fullmer did the plumbing and a lot of similar work, and Brother Joseph Derbyshire did all the electrical work" ("The Early Days of the Welfare Plan in Pioneer Stake," unpublished paper, summer 1966).

Associated with the storehouse was a sewing center, a delivery system, a coal yard, and other services to keep idle people working and to help care for people who could not care for themselves. The stake welfare program, with the storehouse as its center, was designed to lift the members in their hour of need.

Involving the Bishops

The Pioneer Stake welfare committee accomplished much in getting the storehouse established, but President Lee reported at a stake welfare meeting on 17 March 1932 that the bishops in the stake felt they didn't have an important enough part in the establishment of the storehouse.

On 20 June 1932 a special meeting was held in the stake center. President Harold B. Lee presided, and his counselors, President Hyde and President Child, were present. The work accomplished by the stake welfare committee was presented to the bishops. Then the bishops were informed that from that time forward the storehouse was to be a *bishops'* storehouse, under the supervision of a council of all the bishops in the stake. The stake committee moved aside so that the bishops could have the responsibility of owning and operating the storehouse. Bishop Joseph H. McPhee of the Twenty-fifth Ward was appointed to be the chairman of the bishops' council. He was to work closely with the storehouse keeper, Bishop Drury of the Fifth Ward. Besides Bishop Drury and Bishop McPhee, the other bishops in the stake were:

William F. Perschon	Fourth Ward
Richard D. Andrew	Sixth-Seventh Ward
Charles Weed	Twenty-sixth Ward
George Phillips	Thirtieth Ward
Richard F. Nichel	Thirty-second Ward
John Balfour	Brighton Ward
Tracy Y. Cannon	Cannon Ward
Robert Scott	Poplar Grove Ward
Marcena Foster	Mexican Branch

The stake welfare committee was not dissolved. It continued to serve by promoting projects and handling other matters that could best be accomplished at the stake level.

The Storehouse Opening

After months of work, prayer, and fasting and many meetings, the Pioneer Stake storehouse on Pierpont Avenue was ready to open. Brother Drury wrote:

"On the opening day, the store was fully stocked with all the necessary food items and each department had been made ready for operation, being supplied with equipment and personnel selected. The personnel of the Storehouse were selected with great care. Every effort was made to put the right man in the right job. These positions were very responsible and the people to be taken care of would prove to require much tact. Those who had never known want, now were without the barest necessities of life. How to deal with these people would be no easy matter. No one was made to feel that he was at the charitable stage; he was to be accepted as a member of the program, earning that which he received. He would be giving more than he received; he would belong to an organization that turned a life of want into an abundant way of living" (Jesse M. Drury, *For These My Brethren,* p. 8).

The storehouse was officially opened on 19 August 1932, a day set apart as a fast day throughout the stake. The stake members were invited to the opening ceremonies and asked to bring with them their fast-offering contributions, to be received by the bishops of each ward. A substantial sum was collected that day.

President Harold B. Lee explained the stake welfare program and asked the blessings of the Lord upon the project. He said that if the members of the stake would cooperate with the stake presidency and the ward bishops, he knew the program would be a success.

The Cannery

A small cannery was developed as part of the storehouse on Pierpont Avenue. It began operation with about forty workers. Sister Ida Alvord, who worked almost thirty years as a cannery worker and supervisor, said about the opening of the cannery:

"That first year we canned corn, peas, tomatoes, string beans, peaches, apricots and pears. . . . We would shell our own peas and snip our own beans and husk and cut the corn from off the cob. Then we would scald our tomatoes or peaches; we would place them in wire baskets and dip them into boiling water for about one minute until the peeling was loose" (unpublished personal history of Ida Alvord).

Some of the workers were donating their time in order to keep busy. Others were earning commodities as welfare recipients. These people worked unitedly and with a desire to make the storehouse and cannery a success.

Sister Alvord also wrote: "Several times President Grant visited our little storehouse, and I had my picture taken a number of times with him. I especially remember having my picture taken with him while turning the crank of the sealer, which was done by hand. . . .

"One time when President Grant came to visit us we were making pickles. . . . I was so shy in those days and to have a picture taken with President Grant was wonderful" (unpublished personal history of Ida Alvord).

This visit occurred when President Heber J. Grant was investigating the Pioneer Stake storehouse project as a pattern for the entire Church. President Grant visited the storehouse a number of times, as did President J. Reuben Clark, Jr., and President David O. McKay.

Many years later Elder Harold B. Lee spoke of the humble beginnings of the welfare canning effort:

"As I listened to these experts in food production and handling, I thought back to some of the years of my early beginnings with fear and trembling. I just wonder how in the world we ever made it.

"In the early days of the Welfare Program in Pioneer Stake, we set out not knowing where to go; we knew we had to go somewhere because we had reached rock bottom, and

Preparing tomatoes for canning, 1932

we had a great number of apples and onions. I tell you we became one of the strongest stakes in the whole Church, speaking of onions, before the next spring. The apples began to spoil before spring, but our brethren were very frugal and they were of a mind to save everything they could, so they began to peel off the rotted parts and decided to make some cider. I was in the Salt Lake City Commission at that time, and Nephi McLaughlin was in my engineering department as a chemist. He called me one day and said, 'Commissioner, my boys have just brought me some samples of the cider you are making down at your Pioneer storehouse.' And he said, 'We find enough alcohol to make the people drunk if they drink it, and if they don't get drunk they'll get enough arsenic from it to kill them.'

"We did away . . . with the cider; we destroyed it.

"I am thinking of how we cooked the canned peaches down in Zion Park and down in Gridley on open fires and in

President Harold B. Lee's onions

Relief Society sisters preparing applesauce, 1936

Cannery workers in Zion Park Stake, 1940

open tubs, and the only test we had often was when Elmer Christensen, the state chemist, would make a spot check. We would take about one can out of 10,000 and ask him to test it to see if there was any danger of food poisoning. Now that is all the inspection we had in those early days. We thank the Lord for Elmer Christensen because he gave us a little peace of mind that we wouldn't have otherwise had" (Harold B. Lee, "Those Who Know, Do," welfare agricultural meeting, 30 Sept. 1967).

Harvesting Crops

In the early 1930s commodity prices were very low. Farmers were unable to hire any help, and most of them were harvesting what produce they could and letting the rest spoil. Work directors from various stakes contacted these farmers and offered to provide them workers, hoping the workers would receive commodities in return. Men were sent

Alpine Stake preparing and canning corn

out onto the farms in Davis, Utah, and Salt Lake counties and allowed to work all day helping farmers harvest their crops, which were then shared with the volunteers.

It wasn't long before trucks were bringing loads of fine fruits and other produce to the storehouse. Brother Alfons Finck, the account clerk and secretary, said that tomatoes, onions, potatoes, and many different fruits were brought in from as far away as Idaho. The onions and potatoes were stored in large bags in the upper part of the Pierpont Avenue storehouse. The same was done with canned goods as they were processed. (At one time the weight of these stored goods became so great that the ceiling began to sag. Special props had to be placed to prevent the ceiling from collapsing.) The commodities were then distributed to the homes of the needy.

Harvesting crops was not without its problems. Bishop Jesse M. Drury wrote the following account of what was probably the most serious accident:

"On the morning of October 24, 1932, a truck load of approximately 30 men were picked up at 7:00 A.M. in a covered truck at the Fifth Ward Chapel. The morning was foggy and damp and the visibility was poor. At Eighth North, in crossing the Bamberger Railroad, the truck was struck by a South bound Bamberger passenger train and was completely demolished and thrown a considerable distance.

"The men were on their way to the beet fields to top beets and the bottom of the truck contained a large number of beet knives which were razor sharp. Twenty-four of the men were badly injured. Some of them were so seriously hurt that it was believed that they would die. Ambulances were rushed to the scene and the men were taken to St. Marks and Emergency Hospitals at the Police Station. From there, they were moved to the L.D.S. Hospital.

"When word of the disaster was received, Fred J. Heath and myself rushed to the scene. Just before we reached there,

Harvesting 700 acres of dry farm,
Dog Valley Farm, Juab Stake, Nephi, Utah, 1937

19

Thinning sugar beets on a welfare farm, 1933

Brother Heath stopped the car and fell upon the steering wheel. It seemed that he could go no further, for he was completely overcome with grief. 'To think that this could happen to our men,' he wept. Knowing the task which lay ahead of him, he became more composed and started the car again.

"First we went to St. Marks Hospital where we saw Christof Langhorst, who was suffering from a broken hip, broken pelvis bone and other injuries. Brother L. R. Thorne, the truck driver, had a number of injuries, the most serious being a broken hip. We could not help but share the pain of their injuries.

"We administered to them and they seemed to be in high spirits. We bade them good-bye, telling them that we were going to the L.D.S. Hospital to see the other men. Here we met President Lee and his counselors, Paul C. Child and Charles S. Hyde. Immediately we formed partners and went about administering to the men who had been injured. They were cut up and bleeding profusely; doctors were attending to their wounds. Abraham Breur, August H. Michaelis, and Horace Leonard seemed to be the most seriously injured. One of the men from the Twenty-fifth Ward, whose back was believed broken, was administered to by President Lee and myself. This Brother left the hospital within three days completely healed. That night a prayer circle was held in one of the hospital wards where many of the men were confined. This was held under the direction of President Lee. Throughout the Stake people said their prayers for their beloved brethren. Despite the seriousness of the injuries of the men, none of them died. It was a wonderful manifestation of the power of the Priesthood in administering to these men.

"Many thought that this would be the end of our work and activities, but there rose a greater spirit of determination to carry through this program. The accident was looked upon as an unavoidable incident. Everything which could

Welfare workers after harvesting sugar beets, 1932

Regional sugar beet and vegetable field, 1937

possibly be done for the injured was done for their comfort and needs. Most of the men were able to return to work within a short time, all being fully compensated" (Jesse M. Drury, *For These My Brethren*, pp. 67–68).

OTHER STAKES' EFFORTS

Not all of the welfare work in the early 1930s was being done in one stake. While the Pioneer Stake was "pioneering" its welfare system, other stakes were also becoming involved. At first they worked independently, with their bishops trying to assist the poor as conditions worsened and needs of the members increased.

The Salt Lake Stake joined with Pioneer Stake in the Pierpont storehouse a few months after the storehouse opened. The sign on the building was changed to show the joint ownership.

Hugh B. Brown, the president of Granite Stake, organized a small storehouse about the time the Pioneer Stake storehouse was established, in addition to being involved in the employment bureau. President Brown's counselors were Marvin O. Ashton and Stayner Richards. All three of these brethren later became General Authorities.

President Joseph Daynes and his counselors, of Grant Stake in the southern part of Salt Lake City, directed that many parcels of farmland in the stake be used as projects to produce vegetables for the needy. The stake was able to send surplus vegetables to the other stakes' storehouses and also handled some commodity orders from those storehouses.

President Bryant S. Hinckley of the Liberty Stake fully realized the problems that existed in his stake. He organized the priesthood brethren and Relief Society sisters to try to handle the situation. The following summary was written by Bishop John Fetzer of that stake:

"As Bishop of the 8th Ward from 1919 to 1942 we had many problems in regard to the Welfare of the members of this Ward. On account of being a low rental district, with most of the homes being old Pioneer homes, we had many old people and many widows with their families. At one time we had 96 widows and their families. As times became more difficult the Welfare problem also became more difficult and we had to build up an Employment office for the Stake to find work in 1930 for the unemployed. Also our Ward and the 3rd Ward got land for raising vegetables and potatoes, etc. and we also built a Root Cellar for storing our crops; but we found that our Ward did not have the means to raise sufficient amounts for everyone's needs. The Liberty Stake then came to the rescue in organizing the Stake Welfare project in 1932 and it became a wonderful help to

Inside a bishops' storehouse, 1936

the poorer wards as the better off were able to help the Wards in need. The Liberty Stake found a Store Building on 7th East and 7th South with a large adjoining lot. The Storehouse became [one of] the first L.D.S. Bishops' Storehouses in the Church. . . . As the 8th Ward had the largest need in the stake I was requested and appointed manager of the Bishops' Storehouse with several fine Assistants: Eric Rosenval, Rose Woodruff, Charley Latham, Karl Weiss as Welfare Directors. . . . We also had a Women's Sewing Center at the L.D.S. Business College large Basement Room led by the Stake Relief Society directed by Sister Romney, to provide clothing, etc. for all our needy. We also contacted the farming communities north and south to find work and food for our needy families and the Lord was with us. As the farmers had no money to pay laborers for harvesting we arranged with them to harvest on shares of their crop which worked out wonderful and made the farmers

24

and us happy and they gladly turned one-quarter and on some crops even one-third of the harvest over to the Welfare. . . .

"Brother Sims and others who had trucks helped in taking our Brothers and Sisters to the farms and in the evening brought them home and also our shares of the harvest. Our supplies received this way were given out to the families of our workers and other families in need. The families received their share according to the size of the family. The fruit and vegetables left over were canned in the cannery set up in the 31st Ward kitchen. The canned food was then also divided out to the families and we also had one storage room and basement filled with supplies. All men workers also received each month one dollar cash for each day worked and all women workers received each month 50 cents cash for each day worked in harvesting, sewing center or cannery in order that they would be able to pay their rent. This Welfare work was a wonder and we also used all skilled Painters to decorate

**Inside the Salt Lake Regional Bishops' Storehouse
(the old Salt Lake Knitting Factory)**

all the Chapels in the Stake and we also improved the homes of the aged. We also bought at Fort Douglas shoes and blankets and clothing all woolen at a very low sales price of surplus U. S. material. We also set up a shoe repair shop with one of our deaf and dumb members, Bro. Mills, one of our first Adult Aaronic Priesthood Members, and helpers resoled all shoes in need. . . . We came together each morning at 6:45 at the Bishops' Storehouse at 7th East and 7th South and we had a short spiritual talk by the Stake Presidency or High Councilors or Bishops and then any questions were answered as needed and then a prayer for the Lord's blessings for the day was asked and we were blessed as no accidents occurred during the difficult work done. This experience was the most blessed experience in my life and we all came so close to each other with love and humility. . . .

"In 1936 the General Church Welfare for the whole Church was organized by the First Presidency and I was called by the Church as the architect for the General Church

President George Albert Smith, Thomas Towler, President Rudger Clawson, Elder Joseph Fielding Smith, Elder Joseph F. Merrill, and others in Salt Lake Regional Bishops' Storehouse, September 1937

Welfare building and the cannery building and root cellar and grain elevator at 7th South and 7th West, and also called by the General Church Welfare Committee to plan and build Bishops' Storehouses all over the Church" (John Fetzer, "Liberty Stake Welfare: Golden Jubilee History of Liberty Stake of The Church of Jesus Christ of Latter-day Saints, 1904–1954" [Salt Lake City], pp. 41–42).

In the Liberty Stake Third Ward, with the permission of the stake presidency, Bishop Sheldon R. Brewster purchased a small home near the corner of Seventh South and Second East. A family lived in the home, but the two front rooms were set up as a ward storehouse. A refrigerator, tables, racks, and shelves were put into the rooms and in no time were loaded with food, clothing, shoes, and household items. This small ward storehouse met the needs of the members of the Third Ward for many years.

The Cottonwood Stake was also severely affected by unemployment. Its members were dependent upon two activities that were devastated by the Depression—agriculture and mining. Farmers lost most of their markets, and serious drought added to their burden. Many stake members worked in the smelters in Murray and lost their jobs. By 1930 only one blast furnace was in operation. The unemployment required the stake to organize to care for those who needed help. Henry D. Moyle, president of the stake, effectively led his bishops in caring for distressed members. He established a storehouse on State Street just south of the center of Murray, organized a stake security committee, and built a small cannery.

President Lee, President Moyle, and other stake presidents in the Salt Lake Valley became good friends and began to trade commodities to balance the surpluses and needs of each stake. (See appendix A for a listing of stake presidents in the Salt Lake area, 1930–1936.)

First regional bishops' storehouse in Salt Lake City
(the old Salt Lake Knitting Factory)

Salt Lake Regional Bishops' Storehouse workers, 1937;
front row, left side: President Charles Fagg,
President Thomas Towler, Bishop Jesse M. Drury

**Inside the Salt Lake Regional Bishops' Storehouse, 1937;
Bishop Jesse M. Drury and others**

SALT LAKE REGIONAL STOREHOUSE

Harold B. Lee realized that one or two stakes in Salt Lake City were not capable of moving the storehouse work forward by themselves. In 1937 all of the stake storehouses in the Salt Lake Valley were combined into the first regional storehouse. It was located on Second West across from West High School in the old Salt Lake Knitting Factory. This building was large and could accommodate the needs of the bishops better than any of the individual stake storehouses. The regional operation was more efficient in taking care of the needs of the people.

WARD AND STAKE WELFARE FARMS

Ward welfare farms began to arise throughout the West as bishops used small parcels of property in their ward areas to grow crops for their people in need. These commodities were

Harvesting peas on Grant Stake Farm, 1940

given directly to the needy or to a bishops' storehouse for distribution.

The Pioneer Stake allowed members to plant crops on a large piece of property within its boundaries. Members planted sugar beets, potatoes, tomatoes, onions, and other crops. The project became known as the Pioneer Stake welfare farm.

Many other stakes also developed vacant properties for the raising of vegetables and fruits for their people.

PIONEER STAKE GYMNASIUM

In 1933, unemployment was still a serious problem in Pioneer Stake. The stake presidency felt the need to start a building project to give the men something to do. They decided to build a recreational center, or gymnasium, for their people. President Harold B. Lee said of the effort:

"The Pioneer Stake gym was undertaken as a work project under our Pioneer Stake relief program. The First Presidency gave us $4,500, the unemployed of the stake furnished us with carpenters, masons, painters, bricklayers, and laborers, and the balance of the cost was taken from funds earned in produce the previous summers. The work on the gymnasium was directed by T. T. Burton and the laborers were organized by Fred J. Heath. Both of these brethren were unemployed and were members of the high council of the stake. When completed, a fine opening social was held, at which President Heber J. Grant and Bishop Sylvester Q. Cannon, Presiding Bishop of the Church and native of our stake, were present. All the rough lumber for the building and all the bricks were secured from old dilapidated buildings which were obtained from the owners for the tearing down and cleaning up the premises. Bishop Nicholas G. Smith, of the 17th Ward, donated an old building that provided most of our large timbers" (quoted in L. Brent Goates, *Harold B. Lee: Prophet and Seer* [Salt Lake City: Bookcraft, 1985], p. 99).

Charles Worthen, former bishop of the Fourth Ward and an excellent brick mason, was in charge of the masonry work. Many otherwise unemployed men and older boys

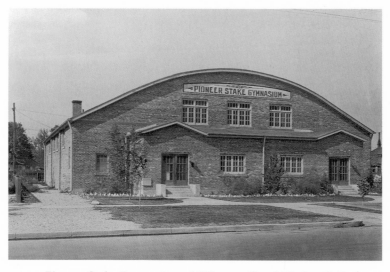

Pioneer Stake Gymnasium, 1933; now Harold B. Lee Hall

worked on the building and received many rewards for their efforts. By August of 1934 the building was completed and ready for dedication.

President Lee reported that the men who worked on the building donated their time at no cost to the stake. The building, although approved as a work project, was erected without the aid of public funds. It was built entirely by men and women living within the boundaries of the stake.

This project gave the people of Pioneer Stake the finest gymnasium in Salt Lake City at that time with the largest basketball court.

When the gym was finished in 1934 it was valued at $30,000, a lot of money during the Depression years. The building is still standing and is now known as the Harold B. Lee Hall. It is located on Ninth West between Fifth and Sixth South in Salt Lake City. It is used for all types of recreational activities. An addition was later built for offices so the facility could be used for more purposes. Stake conferences were held in the building for some time.

ADDITIONAL WORK PROJECTS

The efforts of the Pioneer Stake presidency to combat idleness continued with many wonderful benefits. Almost every ward meetinghouse was renovated or rebuilt.

After the Thirtieth Ward meetinghouse was condemned, unemployed men demolished the building, and much of the material was salvaged to construct a new meetinghouse.

The Fifth Ward building was completely remodeled, including a new addition and a new furnace room. It was also rewired. Most of this work was done by unemployed ward and stake members.

The Thirty-second Ward meetinghouse was rebuilt, with almost all of the labor being donated by the members of the ward. A brief history of the Pioneer Stake recorded that the newly rebuilt meetinghouse was "a most imposing building which will always stand as a monument to the great Church Welfare plan and show what can be accomplished by united effort" ("Pioneer Stake of Zion," author unknown, 1938).

During the construction and remodeling of these buildings, the stake also sponsored a project to make 30,000 concrete and cinder blocks, which were the equivalent of 150,000 regular-sized bricks. These were used as inner walls in the construction.

The Fourth Ward meetinghouse was built and finished by a hired contractor in 1934 and 1935, but much of the labor was donated by unemployed and other volunteer workers from the ward. Quite likely stake members have never been as unified as they were during the great war on idleness waged by Pioneer Stake.

CONCERNS OF THE PRESIDING BRETHREN

The Pioneer Stake presidency met with President Heber J. Grant and his Counselors, J. Reuben Clark, Jr., and David O. McKay, on several occasions to let them know what the stake was doing and to ask for direction in their work. They also met with Presiding Bishop Sylvester Q. Cannon and his Counselors several times, and many problems were worked out. Even though there were some stresses and strains in the process, everyone involved had a great desire to take care of the members and bless their lives.

During the Depression years, the First Presidency was aware that all stake presidents and bishops were faced with problems and were generally doing the best they could to help their people. Many stake presidents were in contact with the First Presidency and the Presiding Bishopric to keep them apprised of the great demands being made upon them to help the poor and needy.

Presiding Bishopric, 1936. Left to right: Second Counselor,
Bishop John Wells; Presiding Bishop, Sylvester Q. Cannon;
First Counselor, Bishop David A. Smith

President Heber J. Grant became personally involved with helping members to survive the Depression. Whenever President Grant met with priesthood leaders, he urged them to reach out and take care of the people. He had no fear of the Church's ability to care for those in desperate need. He was confident that the Lord would provide if proper direction were given to the bishops and stake presidents.

When President Harold B. Lee and his counselors met with President Grant on one occasion, President Grant made a strong declaration of what the Church policy should be in taking care of the people. He said that the Church leaders would not allow the people to suffer. If necessary they would close the seminaries, shut down missionary work for a period of time, or even close the temples, but they would not let the people go hungry. Fortunately, none of this happened. President Grant and his Counselors were anxious to set up a system that would allow the Church to reach out and take care of the people no matter what the cost.

Heber J. Grant had been President of the Church since the end of 1918 and was recognized as an expert in financial affairs. He was a very kind and compassionate person and was greatly concerned about the poverty of Church members. President J. Reuben Clark, Jr., had been ambassador to Mexico and was recognized as an outstanding international lawyer before being called to the First Presidency in 1933. President David O. McKay was an educator who had been in the Council of the Twelve since 1906. He became the Second Counselor in the First Presidency in 1934. It was upon the shoulders of these three men that the development of a modern-day Church welfare program rested.

President Harold B. Lee mentioned on several occasions that President McKay provided tremendous leadership in getting things organized and moving before President Grant changed the assignments of his Counselors and President Clark took over the supervision of welfare work. Many people are not aware of this important contribution by President McKay. When President Clark picked up the reins, he became the dominant welfare leader for the next several years.

GEMS OF PURE RELIGION

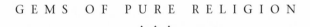

The Beet Thaw of 1934

"One year we harvested all but seven acres of our beets, but due to the lateness of the season and the early snow storm accompanied by severe cold which had frozen the ground, it was impossible to harvest the remainder of the beets. We were faced with the total loss of the beets and we had little hope of a change of weather, let alone any thaw.

"On the first Sunday in December, the Stake Presidency and the High Council held their regular prayer meeting at the Salt Lake Temple. We were advised by our Stake work director, Fred J. Heath, of the seriousness of the loss of the sugar beets as the sugar factory was to close on December 15.

"Not only the loss of the beets was involved, but the untiring labors of the two Ward projects which had been undertaken by the Priesthood groups would have also been in vain. These men and boys had worked so hard and felt very discouraged to think that all the work they had put in was to be to no avail.

"Brother Heath had been selected to give the special prayer, and he asked permission to lay this matter before the Lord and ask that we join in his faith for the answer to the prayer. Seldom had I heard a more beautiful prayer which was caressed with simple words of humility and earnest appeal. His every word was etched in faith and we felt the depth of his words.

"That very afternoon a Chinook thawing wind came up and by Monday morning all of the snow had disappeared and the ground was thawed out. Despite the mud, we were able to put a number of boys and men to work and they harvested approximately seventy-five tons of sugar beets and hauled them to the factory by Saturday. Just as they took the last load in, another snow storm set in.

"We knew that the Lord surely did answer the prayers of his servants when asked in faith and especially in so good a cause as we had undertaken to do."

Jesse M. Drury, *For These My Brethren* (reprint, 1991), pp. 68–69

◆ ◆ ◆

At the Welfare Cannery

The vines went in and the peas came out,
And the boys measured tons with a whoop and a shout;
They were rushed to the canning room, dumped in a vat;

We were working so fast they scarce knew where they
    were at.
With quick nimble fingers and infinite care,
The ladies picked out all the leaves lurking there.
Then into the blanching bin, scalded they were,
And escalated upward to the brine and a stir.
The peas went up and the cans came down,
And our next winter's dinner went round and round.
A second per can and each lid was sealed tight,
While swift moving hands packed each kettle just right.
Then into the cooler so quick like a flash,
The canned peas were ours, for a few cents in cash.

Now that's how the canning went, so it is said,
With everything profit and nothing in "red."
But that's just half the story I'd say,
For more than the canning was doing that day.
Of course, the men were perspiring, and the women were
    warm,
And the bending and steaming were doing no harm;
But more than all that—in each true worker's heart,
Was the keen satisfaction of doing one's part,
And a feeling of brotherhood thrilled everyone,
Of sharing together the toil and the fun.
Yes, Jefferson Ward learned in canning that day
That whatever the future holds—let come what may,
The people are unified—hand, heart and soul,
And each one will work for the good of the whole.

So hail to the canners, who worked mighty hard,
And hail, proudly hail, to dear Jefferson Ward.
Mabel Jones Gabbott, 8 July 1943

First Presidency, 1936: President J. Reuben Clark, Jr., President Heber J. Grant, and President David O. McKay

CHAPTER 2

THE CHURCH WELFARE PLAN

As various stakes developed ways to provide for their needy members, many Church leaders and members began to anticipate that one day the First Presidency would announce a general Church program to help the poor and needy. For three or four years the First Presidency and other general Church leaders had been carefully watching the work that went on in Pioneer and other stakes.

One of the concerns of the First Presidency was the increasing numbers of Church members receiving relief through public funds. While many of those on public relief rolls may not have been active members (and thus may not have sought out the Church for help), the Brethren felt it necessary to move forward more quickly in addressing the problems of unemployment and idleness.

President Harold B. Lee recorded in his journal that one year before the Church announced the establishment of what was then called the Church Security Plan, he was invited to meet with the First Presidency. This meeting was lengthy, and welfare activities were thoroughly discussed. President Lee wrote:

"On April 20, 1935, I was called into the office of the First Presidency, where with President Heber J. Grant and President David O. McKay (President Clark then being in the East, but they had had some communications with him so that all members of the Presidency were in agreement) I discussed the relief situation in the Church and various methods of handling the same. President Grant said he wanted to take a 'leaf out of Pioneer Stake's book' in caring for the people of the Church. He expressed dissatisfaction with the then existent program of social service investigations. He said that there was nothing more important for the Church to do than to take care of its needy people and that so far as he was concerned, everything else must be sacrificed [so that] proper relief [could be] extended to our people. I was astounded to learn that for years there had been before them, as a result of their thinking and planning and as a result of the inspiration

Harold B. Lee, managing director of the welfare program, and President Heber J. Grant, 1936

of Almighty God, the genius of the very plan that was waiting and in preparation for a time when, in their judgment, the faith of the Latter-day Saints was such that they were willing to follow the counsel of the men who lead and preside in this Church. My humble place in this program at that time was described" (quoted in L. Brent Goates, *Harold B. Lee: Prophet and Seer* [Salt Lake City: Bookcraft, 1985], pp. 141–42).

President Lee, under the direction of the First Presidency, spent the following days and weeks praying and thinking through his experiences with welfare work and the great challenge that was now before him to be part of a welfare plan for the entire Church.

In the ensuing year President Lee and others held many meetings with General Authorities, businessmen, and other people to help work out the numerous details and challenges of adapting a local program to meet the needs of the entire Church.

THE ANNOUNCEMENT

In the April 1936 general conference, President Heber J. Grant publicly announced the establishment of a centrally directed welfare program called the Church Security Plan.

Elder Albert E. Bowen of the Quorum of the Twelve later commented on the announcement:

"Among other things the message of the Presidency urged upon the Saints the importance of and the necessity for a revival in observance of the law of tithing and of fast offerings, this as a means of providing revenue in the manner established by the Lord for the needs of the poor and for the incidental spiritual benefit to all who conform. The concept of universal brotherhood was remembered in that bishops whose wards had few or no needy, were yet to fulfil the law and send surpluses to others less fortunate. It was declared to be fundamental that opportunities for work must be provided so that, the sick and infirm excepted, all who received aid should have the privilege of rendering service in return. Work was to be found in private industry if possible; if not, work projects were to be established to provide it that relief might so far as possible be taken out of the realm of charity. Solicitude for the sensitivities and the well being of all recipients was evidenced in these noble words:

" 'No pains must be spared to wipe out all feeling of diffidence, embarrassment, or shame on the part of those receiving relief; the ward must be one great family of equals. The spiritual welfare of those on relief must receive especial care and be earnestly and prayerfully fostered. A system which gives relief for work or service will go far to reaching these ends. . . .

" 'Whether we shall now take care of our own Church members in need and how fully, depends wholly and solely upon the faith and works of the individual Church members. If each Church member meets his full duty and grasps his full opportunity for blessing, full necessary relief will be extended to all needy Church members; insofar as individual members fail in their duty and opportunity, by that much will the relief fall short' " (Albert E. Bowen, *The Church Welfare Plan* [Gospel Doctrine course of study, 1946], pp. 27–28).

On 18 April 1936, Harold B. Lee was called as the managing director of the new program. At that time he was also a Salt Lake City commissioner, and he was asked to resign from that position to spend his full time in his new priesthood calling. He was also released as president of the Pioneer Stake and was succeeded by his counselor, Paul C. Child.

Two days later, on 20 April, Elder Melvin J. Ballard was named by the First Presidency as the chairman of the welfare program. Bryant S. Hinckley wrote of Elder Ballard and this new plan:

"This great movement, which was the outgrowth of a prolonged and bitter depression, was a history-making movement. Men everywhere during the depression were out of employment, almost destitute of clothing, and threatened with hunger. It was estimated that 80,000 were on relief even in the Church. The Church rose magnificently to this great emergency and put into operation a welfare program which at once attracted the attention and favorable comment of the entire nation. Nothing else has ever brought to this Church so much favorable publicity as has this program.

" . . . No other man labored with greater zeal; no one put forth a more constant effort to establish it and to put it into operation than [Elder Melvin J. Ballard] did. He traveled almost day and night over the Church, meeting with stake presidents—sometimes three and four in a day—organizing and motivating the whole plan. . . .

"May 22, 1936, while touring the Eastern States Mission, he met Elbert Thomas, Senator from Utah, who took him to the White House in Washington, D.C., and introduced him to President Franklin D. Roosevelt, where he talked for fifteen minutes with the President about the welfare plan. He said: 'I told him our program. The President said that the Mormon Church could do it. They have something that no other Church has' " (*Sermons and Missionary Services of Melvin Joseph Ballard* [Salt Lake City: Deseret Book Co., 1949], pp. 118–19).

President Harold B. Lee, while he was a member of the Council of the Twelve, also paid tribute to Elder Ballard:

"When the First Presidency issued a proclamation to the Church at the April Conference, in 1936, entitled 'An Important Message on Relief,' outlining what has since been called the Church welfare plan, there was set in motion a movement that was to become a tremendous challenge to the loyalty of the entire Church membership. . . . No mistake

Left to right, seated, 1937: Elder Albert E. Bowen, adviser to the
welfare program; Elder Melvin J. Ballard, chairman; Elder John A.
Widtsoe, adviser. Left to right, standing: Harold B. Lee, managing
director; and Henry D. Moyle, general committee member

had been made in the selection of Elder Melvin J. Ballard to
lead the way. . . . He traveled more than fifty thousand miles
by auto and by train each of those first years, carrying to the
members and non-members of the Church the message of
this new movement pertaining to their temporal salvation"
(quoted in *Sermons and Missionary Services of Melvin Joseph
Ballard,* pp. 119, 122).

THE OBJECTIVE

No finer statement concerning the objectives of the
Church welfare plan can be found than one given by
President J. Reuben Clark, Jr., in behalf of the First Presidency,
to a special meeting of stake presidents on 2 October 1936:

"The real long term objective of the Welfare Plan is the
building of character in the members of the Church, givers
and receivers, rescuing all that is finest down deep inside of

them, and bringing to flower and fruitage the latent richness of the spirit, which after all is the mission and purpose and reason for being of this Church."

The First Presidency also made a powerful statement that has been used widely throughout the Church, in all the handbooks, and in most other printed welfare documents since the beginning of the welfare program. They said:

"Our primary purpose was to set up, in so far as it might be possible, a system under which the curse of idleness would be done away with, the evils of a dole abolished, and independence, industry, thrift and self respect be once more established amongst our people. The aim of the Church is to help the people to help themselves. Work is to be reenthroned as the ruling principle of the lives of our Church membership" (in Conference Report, Oct. 1936, p. 3).

President David O. McKay elaborated on the spiritual objectives of the plan:

"The development of our spiritual nature should concern us most. Spirituality is the highest acquisition of the soul, the divine in man; 'the supreme, crowning gift that makes him king of all created things.' It is the consciousness of victory over self and of communion with the infinite. It is spirituality alone which really gives one the best in life.

"It is something to supply clothing to the scantily clad, to furnish ample food to those whose table is thinly spread, to give activity to those who are fighting desperately the despair that comes from enforced idleness, but after all is said and done, the greatest blessings that will accrue from the Church Security Plan are spiritual" (in Conference Report, Oct. 1936, p. 103).

WELFARE PROGRAM GIVEN BY REVELATION

The welfare program was given to the Church by direct revelation from the Lord. Elder Henry D. Moyle stated:

"When the Lord speaks through his servants, as he did in 1936, there is no room left for any doubt in the minds of true Latter-day Saints. We believe in the words of Amos which have been quoted here before today, that 'Surely the Lord God will do nothing, but he revealeth his secret unto his servants the prophets.' (Amos 3:7.)

"In this respect we reaffirm our ninth article of faith: 'We believe all that God has revealed, all that he does now reveal, and we believe that he will yet reveal many great and important things pertaining to the Kingdom of God.'

" . . . Had it not been for the inspiration of the Almighty, President Grant and his Counselors would not have foreseen as they did the future requirements to meet the changing conditions in the world in which we live. Their prophetic foresight made it possible for the people to anticipate and prepare for the future" (in Conference Report, Apr. 1956, pp. 59, 61).

President David O. McKay, at a regional meeting in February 1937, said: "The Church Security Plan has not come up as a mushroom over night. It is the result of inspiration, and that inspiration has come from the Lord. . . . Those who have selfishness in their hearts would like to see it fail, but it is not going to fail" (quoted in Albert E. Bowen, *The Church Welfare Plan*, p. 3).

President J. Reuben Clark, Jr., testified at the close of a special welfare meeting held on 3 August 1951:

"So I hope that nobody will go from this meeting feeling in his heart, or having in his heart any doubt but that the Welfare Plan came through revelations that began in Adam's time and that have continued on until the present, and that the revelation which came to President Grant, in setting up the Welfare Plan, was merely to set up an organization which should be able to bring together, the United Order having passed away, the resources of the people to care for those who are in need.

" . . . I have tried to indicate, so that there would be no doubt left in your minds, that the Welfare Plan is based upon revelation, that the setting up of the machinery is the result of a revelation by the Holy Ghost to President Grant, that it has been carried on since that time by equivalent revelations which have come to the brethren who have had it in charge" ("Testimony of Divine Origin of Welfare Plan," *Church News,* 8 Aug. 1951, pp. 13, 15).

President Harold B. Lee explained in the October 1972 general conference that he had received clear and direct guidance from the Lord about how to organize the new welfare program:

"I had a lesson years ago as to the greatness of priesthood. It had to do with the call of the First Presidency for me to come to their office on a day that I shall never forget—April 20, 1935. I was city commissioner in Salt Lake City. I was a stake president.

"We had been wrestling with this question of welfare. There were few government work programs; the finances of the Church were low; we were told that there wasn't much that could be done so far as the finances of the Church were concerned. And here we were with 4,800 of our 7,300 people who were wholly or partially dependent. We had only one place to go, and that was to apply the Lord's program as set forth in the revelations.

"It was from our humble efforts that the First Presidency, knowing that we had some experience, called me one morning asking if I would come to their office. It was a Saturday morning; there were no calls on their calendar, and for hours in that forenoon they talked with me and told me that they wanted me to resign from the city commission, and they would release me from being stake president; that they wished me now to head up the welfare movement to turn the tide from government relief, direct relief, and help to put the Church in a position where it could take care of its own needy.

"After that morning, I rode in my car (spring was just breaking) up to the head of City Creek Canyon into what was then called Rotary Park; and there, all by myself, I offered one of the most humble prayers of my life.

"There I was, just a young man in my thirties. My experience had been limited. I was born in a little country town in Idaho. I had hardly been outside the boundaries of the states of Utah and Idaho. And now to put me in a position where I was to reach out to the entire membership of the Church, worldwide, was one of the most staggering contemplations that I could imagine. How could I do it with my limited understanding?

"As I kneeled down, my petition was, 'What kind of an organization should be set up in order to accomplish what the Presidency has assigned?' And there came to me on that glorious morning one of the most heavenly realizations of the power of the priesthood of God. It was as though something were saying to me, 'There is no new organization necessary to take care of the needs of this people. All that is necessary is to put the priesthood of God to work. There is nothing else that you need as a substitute.'

"With that understanding, then, and with the simple application of the power of the priesthood, the welfare program has gone forward now by leaps and bounds, overcoming obstacles that seemed impossible, until now it stands as a monument to the power of the priesthood, the like of which I could only glimpse in those days to which I have made reference" (in Conference Report, Oct. 1972, pp. 123–24; or *Ensign,* Jan. 1973, p. 104).

President Marion G. Romney, at the dedication of the Welfare Square Bishops' Storehouse on 25 May 1976, testified: "I know that President Clark felt that the Welfare

Program was a revelation. I heard him declare it in a Welfare meeting down in Orem when we had the stake presidents of that whole area together. He said without any reservations that the Welfare Program began by direct revelation from the Lord to President Grant. And he knew that it was of the Lord. So did President Lee. I believe those men are here today and that they are pleased with this work, as is President Grant and the other presidents of the Church down to today."

Brother Lauritz George Petersen, who worked in the Church Historian's Office for many years, wrote an account of a conversation he had with Elder John A. Widtsoe about the beginnings of the welfare program. He said:

"I asked Elder John A. Widtsoe if the Welfare Program was a revelation from the Lord given through President Heber J. Grant. Brother Widtsoe called me into his room and we sat down upon the leather couch, and he told me that when he was coming from Europe, in the fall of 1933, after having served six years as mission president, upon reaching New York he was called to Washington, D. C., where the Brethren were dedicating the chapel. A brother met him at the station and took him to where they were to stay. While there he was told by Brother J. Reuben Clark, because John A. Widtsoe was a member of the Council of the Twelve, that he felt that Brother Widtsoe should know that President Heber J. Grant had received a revelation telling them to prepare the Welfare Plan, and [it] was to be taken from out of the Doctrine and Covenants. He said that he was not surprised when the Church announced the Welfare Plan to the Church three years later (1936). He said that some say that it was the plan of Brother Lee and some said that [it] was from him (Brother Widtsoe). Brother Widtsoe said that they may have contributed to it, but that the Welfare Plan was a revelation from the Lord.

"I then asked Brother Widtsoe if this had been recorded in history and he said that he didn't think so, so I am taking the liberty of writing it down so that it may be available in the future."

There can be no question that the Lord gave President Heber J. Grant a revelation. Time and again over the years, living prophets have testified to this reality. The growth and success of the welfare program is in itself a testimony that the Lord has established and guided it through his living prophets and will continue to do so.

GENERAL WELFARE COMMITTEE

At the 1936 October general conference, the First Presidency presented for a sustaining vote the members of the General Welfare Committee. They were Elder Melvin J. Ballard, chairman; Harold B. Lee, managing director; and other members of the committee: Mark Austin, Campbell M. Brown, Stringham A. Stevens, and Henry D. Moyle.

At the April 1938 general conference, the name Church Security Plan was changed to Church Welfare Plan. The Presiding Bishopric was changed to include Presiding Bishop LeGrand Richards and Counselors Marvin O. Ashton and Joseph L. Wirthlin. Changes were also made in the General Welfare Committee. Henry D. Moyle was sustained as chairman of the committee, with Robert L. Judd as vice chairman and Harold B. Lee as managing director. Other members of the committee were Mark Austin, Campbell M. Brown, William E. Ryberg, Stringham A. Stevens, J. Frank Ward, and Theodore DeBry as secretary.

The Church created fourteen welfare regions through which the welfare work would be directed and managed (see appendix B). Each region had a council composed of all stake presidents in the region. One of the stake presidents was chosen by the General Welfare Committee to be chair-

General Welfare Committee and advisers, April 1938. Left to right: Theodore DeBry, J. Frank Ward, Mark Austin, Stringham A. Stevens, Campbell M. Brown, Harold B. Lee, President J. Reuben Clark, Jr., President Heber J. Grant, President David O. McKay, Elder Melvin J. Ballard, Elder John A. Widtsoe, Elder Albert E. Bowen, Bishop Sylvester Q. Cannon, Henry D. Moyle, Robert L. Judd

Presiding Bishopric, 1938: Bishop Marvin O. Ashton; Bishop LeGrand Richards, Presiding Bishop; and Bishop Joseph L. Wirthlin

man of the regional council. He was also assigned to be chairman of an executive committee with two other stake presidents assisting.

Members of the General Welfare Committee accompanied General Authorities to stake conferences to hold special welfare meetings with bishops and other welfare workers in the stakes. They also spoke on welfare subjects in one of the general sessions of the conferences. In this way the members of the Church were taught the principles of the welfare program and the basic needs of the poor and needy began to be met.

The General Welfare Committee members were sustained as general officers of the Church in the October 1940 general conference. Over the next few years, committee members were sustained and released as the work increased. These people were chosen for their outstanding abilities in their fields of labor as well as for their deep religious convictions.

General Welfare Committee members, 1946. Sitting, left to right: Belle S. Spafford, Bishop LeGrand Richards, Elder Marion G. Romney, Elder Albert E. Bowen, Henry D. Moyle, President David O. McKay, President George Albert Smith, President J. Reuben Clark, Jr., Alice Rentmeister, Elder Harold B. Lee, Elder John A. Widtsoe, Mark Austin, Clyde J. Brown. Standing, left to right: Lorenzo Hatch, Elder Thomas E. McKay, William E. Ryberg, Elder Clifford E. Young, Clyde C. Edmonds, President Antoine R. Ivins, Elder Alma Sonne, Marvin O. Ashton, Paul C. Child

Among them were specialists in a number of professions, including agriculture. Committee members spent many hours each week filling their assignments. Many members served for several years.

In addition to the visits made to conferences by committee members, members of the First Presidency traveled to many areas of the Church to introduce the new program of Church welfare.

Committee members continued visiting stake conferences until the position of Regional Representative was established in the fall of 1967. Regional Representatives were given the responsibility to teach and promote all priesthood principles, including Church welfare. The members of the General Welfare Committee were released, and some of them were called as Regional Representatives.

In 1941 Harold B. Lee was sustained as a member of the Quorum of the Twelve and President Marion G. Romney, of the Bonneville Stake, was made an Assistant to the Quorum

Elder Marion G. Romney, assistant managing director of the welfare program, and Elder Harold B. Lee, managing director, late 1940s

President J. Reuben Clark, Jr., in Washington D.C. to introduce the welfare program, 1940. Left to right: Edgar Brossard, Ezra Taft Benson, Robert L. Judd, President Clark, Louise Bennion, Abram H. Cannon, Samuel R. Carpenter

President J. Reuben Clark, Jr., officially introducing the welfare program to Washington D.C. stake priesthood and Relief Society leaders, 1940

of the Twelve. Two months later Elder Romney was appointed to be the assistant managing director of the General Welfare Committee. He immediately took over the day-to-day operations of the general Welfare Office, which was located in the Union Pacific Building on the corner of South Temple and Main Streets.

In 1947, Brother Henry D. Moyle was called to be a member of the Quorum of the Twelve. At that time, Elder Lee, Elder Moyle, and Elder Romney were charged with leading the Church's welfare work under the direction of the First Presidency, primarily President J. Reuben Clark, Jr.

Elder Romney was ordained to the Quorum of the Twelve in 1951. He became chairman of the General Welfare Committee in 1959. In 1963, the Presiding Bishop, John H. Vandenberg, became the chairman of the General Welfare Committee, and Elder Lee and Elder Romney became advisers. Today, the General Welfare Committee is comprised of the First Presidency, Quorum of the Twelve, Presiding Bishopric, and General Relief Society Presidency. (See appendixes C and E for more information about the members of the General Welfare Committee.)

MANAGING DIRECTOR OF THE WELFARE DEPARTMENT

The managing director of the Welfare Department is a key position in the Church's welfare work. On 7 July 1959 Elder Henry D. Taylor, an Assistant to the Quorum of the Twelve, was called to serve in this position. Elder Taylor served faithfully until 6 April 1972. He guided the staff of the Welfare Department to greatly enhance the work of the general committee. He was able to follow the direction of those above him and work effectively with his staff and field workers. He was an obedient leader, and he made friends because of his kindness.

Elder Taylor was succeeded as managing director by Junior Wright Child on 6 April 1972. Brother Child's ability in financial matters was extremely important in this position. He was very successful in working with the men who managed the various operations of welfare. He served for approximately three years and was succeeded by Dr. James O. Mason. Dr. Mason served for only a few months and was appointed as deputy director of health services for the state of Utah. Dr. Mason was later made a member of the Second Quorum of Seventy.

R. Quinn Gardner became the managing director of the Welfare Department in the summer of 1975. Brother Gardner was a vigorous leader, and welfare work made tremendous advances during the approximately six years he served as managing director. The First Presidency and the Presiding Bishopric directed him to expand welfare facilities to areas throughout the United States and Canada. He was released to assume another Church assignment on 29 June 1981.

Original Welfare Office staff, 1937: Harold B. Lee, managing director, and Theodore DeBry, secretary

Members of the Welfare Office staff, 1963. Left to right: William M. Walsh; Lionel Dredge; Donald M. Bagley; Henry D. Taylor, managing director; Irvin B. Nydegger; James E. Larsen; Alfred W. Uhrhan

Welfare Department leadership, 1977. Left to right, seated: Glen L. Rudd; R. Quinn Gardner, managing director; Keith B. McMullin; Larry Whiting. Left to right, standing: Martin Zackerson, C. Scott Grow, Edward Soper, David Albrecht, Clair Bishop, Curtis E. Ravsten, Julian Kau, D. Weston Thatcher

Welfare Department leadership, 1986. Left to right, seated: Lowell D. Wood; Dexter Davis; John H. Cox; Keith B. McMullin, managing director; Karl Keeler, Curtis E. Ravsten. Left to right, standing: Roger Elkins, Allen Litster, Edward J. Bishop, J. Patrick Reese, Dennis R. Lifferth, James B. Holm, Loy Despain, Michael Robbins, Oliver McPherson, Isaac C. Ferguson, Gary L. Winters, Victor L. Brown, Jr., Dale Payne

Welfare Department leadership, 1994. Left to right, seated: Lyle J. Cooper; William S. Bush; Keith B. McMullin, managing director; F. Earl Matheson; Larry L. Whiting. Left to right, standing: John H. Cox, Frank D. Richardson, Dennis R. Lifferth, Curtis E. Ravsten, Ronald B. Garrison, Harold C. Brown, Isaac C. Ferguson

Luncheon for former Welfare Department administrators,
November 1993. Sitting, left to right: Lionel Dredge, Stewart B. Eccles,
James E. Larsen, Arben O. Clark; standing, left to right: Irvin B.
Nydegger, William M. Walsh, President Thomas S. Monson,
Glen L. Rudd, Charles M. Knighton

Glenn L. Pace, who later served as a member of the
Presiding Bishopric and a member of the First Quorum of
Seventy, followed Brother Gardner as managing director and
served from 1 July 1981 until May of 1985. He directed an
extensive study of the appropriate role of welfare projects in
a Church that was becoming much more urbanized, and
he recommended that the handling of welfare projects be
modified.

In 1985 Keith B. McMullin, who had been a director in
the Welfare Department, was selected as the new managing
director. Under Brother McMullin's administration, welfare
has moved away from a trend toward headquarter's management back to more local priesthood leadership. Brother
McMullin has a vision of bishops and stake presidents taking

a greater part in directing the present-day welfare program to better meet their local needs. He is constantly aware of the problems of people in need. His greatest desire is to have local priesthood leaders once again be the primary welfare leaders they once were during the early years of the Church welfare program.

GEMS   OF   PURE   RELIGION

◆ ◆ ◆

President McKay's Parable of the Light

At the October 1962 general conference, Elder Harold B. Lee made the following statement:

"President McKay, . . . I am reminded of something you said when you came to the first regional meeting of the church welfare plan held in 1936 down in the old Pioneer Stake Hall where all the stake presidents of this area were called together. . . . At the conclusion you made this statement in something of a parable. . . .

" 'An engineer pulled his train into a station one dark and stormy night, and while the engineer was out oiling his engine and getting ready for the next run, a timid passenger left his place in the train and walked up to the engineer and asked, "Aren't you afraid to pull your train out into the dark tonight, raining and storming like it is?" Without looking up, the engineer replied, "I am not pulling my engine out into the dark tonight." "Why," said the passenger, "it's pitch dark outside the lights of the station. I should think that with the responsibility of these four or five hundred passengers depending upon your handling of the train, you would be a nervous wreck."

" 'For an answer the engineer pointed up to the bright headlight and he said, "Do you see that light up there? That

61

throws out an intense white light a thousand yards ahead on the track. When I pull out of the station tonight, I will be running my engine only to the first circle of that light, a thousand yards away, and when I get to the outer circle of that light it will still be out another thousand yards in front of me. All through this dark night I will not be running in one foot of darkness all the way." '

"Then President McKay said, 'Now, brethren, . . . all through this night of uncertainty when we are trying to establish the security of our people in a temporal way, this Church will be running in light of the revelations that come from God, all the way.' "

Harold B. Lee, in Conference Report, Oct. 1962, pp. 79–80; or *Improvement Era,* Dec. 1962, pp. 939–40

First load of potatoes for the root cellar, 1938

CHAPTER 3

WELFARE SQUARE, 1938–1959

When the Church welfare program was in place, the General Welfare Committee turned its attention to planning a much needed large welfare center in Salt Lake City. The Pioneer Stake storehouse on Pierpont Avenue and other small stake storehouses had taken care of the needs of some stakes from 1932 until about 1937. Then the stake storehouses were consolidated into a regional storehouse, but a larger facility was soon needed.

The Church obtained a valuable piece of property for the new center, mainly through the efforts of Brother Henry D. Moyle. It was purchased from Bonneville on the Hill, a Utah corporation. The property included most of the block between Sixth and Seventh West and Seventh and Eighth South on the west side of Salt Lake City. (The streets west of Main Street were later renumbered, and Sixth and Seventh West became Seventh and Eighth West.) It was determined that on this property would be built the operations headquarters for the general Church welfare program and a storehouse for the Salt Lake Valley. The facilities would be called Welfare Square.

In April 1938 eight buildings in the central part of Salt Lake City had been condemned by the city. They were owned by the Clayton Investment Company and were located on Regent Street and Plumb Alley between First and Second South and Main and State Streets. One of the build-

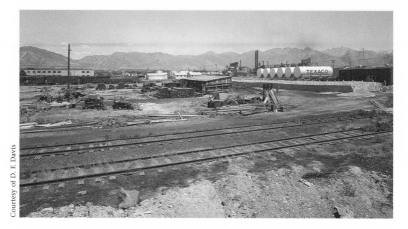

Courtesy of D. F. Davis

Courtesy of D. F. Davis

Above: 1.5 million bricks stacked on Welfare Square (to the right) before construction began

Left: Beginning construction on Welfare Square, 1938

ings was four stories high, three buildings were three stories high, and one was a two-story structure. The Church offered to demolish these buildings for the salvage materials. The offer was accepted. Volunteer workers from the wards and stakes in the valley were called upon to accomplish the sometimes hazardous work of demolition. The project was directed by Brother William E. Ryberg of the General Welfare Committee. He was a general contractor, and one of his employees was in charge of all the demolition.

Salvaged from these eight buildings and transported to Welfare Square were more than 1,500,000 bricks, 200,000 board feet of rough lumber, 50,000 board feet of one-inch lumber, and 40,000 square feet of flooring material. Also salvaged were a hand-operated elevator, an electric-powered elevator, 750 square feet of standard strength plate glass, 4,000 square feet of window glass, 150 doors, and 1,500 pounds of electrical wire and fixtures. The value of all this recovered material in 1938 dollars was about $20,000.

A private professional wrecking firm had previously estimated that they could demolish the buildings in three months. The volunteer Church workers took just five days longer.

The only expenses to the Church were the wages of one paid supervisor and the cost of hauling the materials to the new location. Hundreds of Latter-day Saint men and boys, most of them financially distressed, worked over 14,000 hours to accomplish this huge demolition assignment. There were no serious accidents of any kind, and all the medical costs were less than three hundred dollars. (Taken from a report by William E. Ryberg, member of the General Welfare Committee, to President David O. McKay, 14 June 1938.)

Root cellar under construction on Welfare Square, 1938

Courtesy of D. F. Davis

Courtesy of D. F. Davis

Interior of root cellar, July 1938

Stewart B. Eccles, long-time manager of welfare facilities, said that when he first went to Welfare Square, the construction had not started. There was a large sign on the front of the property which said, "Future Home of Salt Lake Regional Bishops' Storehouse." Large piles of bricks, lumber, doors, glass, and other materials were scattered all over. Men and women were knocking the mortar off of bricks, pulling nails out of lumber, and otherwise cleaning up the material so that it could be used in the construction of the buildings.

Root Cellar

The first structure to be built on Welfare Square was a root cellar. It was built under the direction of the General Welfare Committee and local priesthood leaders, using volunteer workers. When it was finished, it was one of the most modern root cellars in the area. It was large enough to store fifty railroad carloads of potatoes and other commodities. It was possible to drive trucks down into one end of the root cellar, half of which was underground, and then out the

Above: Preparing corn for the welfare program, 1940s

Right: Original cannery on Welfare Square, early 1940s

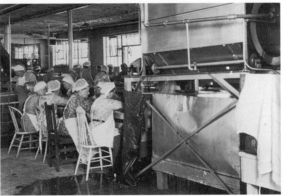

other end after being emptied. Almost before the cellar was completed, potatoes by the truckload were arriving for storage. These would be distributed later to various storehouses throughout the West.

CANNERY

At the same time the root cellar was being built, workers began construction of a modern cannery with sufficient capacity to process fruits and vegetables for the welfare needs of the entire Church. This building had three floors, two above ground, and a full basement for storage of

69

Left to right: Elder Harold B. Lee, President George Albert Smith, Elder Marion G. Romney, and Stewart B. Eccles inspecting meat in cooler in bishops' storehouse, March 1946

processed commodities. It was completed in November 1938. For a time the front part of the main floor was used as a bishops' storehouse and the rear part contained the cannery facilities. A sewing department was located upstairs.

A heating plant was built at the same time as the cannery for the purpose of supplying heat for all of the buildings to be erected on Welfare Square.

The cannery was in almost daily operation for the next twenty-two years. It is interesting to remember that when the cannery was built it was constructed of materials that were already old. Even though the building is now used for other purposes, it still stands. It is well constructed and will probably be around for many years to come.

BISHOPS' STOREHOUSE

The construction of the first storehouse on Welfare Square began in early 1939 and was completed on 16 April of the same year. Bishop John Fetzer, of Liberty Stake, was the architect. The building was 80 feet wide and 140 feet long, with a total of three floors, a basement and two above-ground floors. Most of the basement was used to store items to be distributed from the storehouse. Also in the basement were two large walk-in freezers, a large vault for valuable papers, an egg candling and packaging room, and several other miscellaneous rooms, one of which was later converted into a barber shop. An elevator in the building served all three floors.

The main floor housed the distribution storehouse. On this floor was a meat department, where several butchers and their helpers cut and packaged meat. There were also two walk-in coolers, one for meat and one for eggs, fruit, butter, and vegetables. The greater part of this floor was the grocery department, where food and other items were stocked and displayed as they are in a supermarket. Shopping baskets were provided, and people were encouraged to do their own shopping. There was an area at the rear of the storehouse where an assembly line of welfare workers prepared orders for delivery to those unable to do their own shopping.

Interior of bishops' storehouse, 1950s

Above: Butcher shop in bishops' storehouse, 1950s

Left: Clarence O. Worthington, one of the original meat cutters, who served faithfully for 25 years

Also on the main floor was a clothing department, where persons with bishop's orders could select their clothing.

The Welfare Square management offices were all located on the main level of the building. They were used by the manager, his secretary, the assistant manager, storehouse keeper, and clerks. Windows extended around the first floor, and a large dock ran along the entire south end of the building.

Inside the building near the entrance was an area for a receptionist and telephone operator. The supervisor over the

Welfare Square guides, the bookkeepers, and the secretaries had their offices in this location also.

The second floor had a large chapel which held about 200 people. It was designed to handle an overflow so that large welfare meetings could be held there. Also on this floor were a sewing center, furniture department, print shop, shoe repair shop, kitchen, and cafeteria for the workers. There were also several storage areas for maintenance supplies.

An interesting feature of the storehouse basement was a tunnel, approximately 100 feet long, that went from the storehouse to the cannery and to the milk plant. The tunnel allowed commodities to be transported to and from different buildings, thus making storage more efficient.

Left: Print shop at Welfare Square, 1950s

Below: Roscoe Eardley in sewing center on second floor of the storehouse, 1940

Courtesy of Hatch & Hatch Photographers

**First Presidency visiting the Welfare Square storehouse, 1940;
Presidents David O. McKay, Heber J. Grant, and J. Reuben Clark, Jr.**

This storehouse served the needy for several years, but eventually its storage space became inadequate because of the Church's growth in the Salt Lake Valley and the resulting increase in the number of bishop's orders.

Bishop Jesse M. Drury served as the manager of this storehouse for many years, just as he had done for the storehouse on Pierpont Avenue and the one in the Salt Lake Knitting Factory, making thirty-one years of service in all. During this time he helped many bishops as they learned their responsibility to care for those in need, and he personally gave kind and understanding care to many hundreds of needy people.

MILK-PROCESSING PLANT

As early as 1938 the members of the General Welfare Committee began discussing the need for including milk products in the storehouse system of the welfare program.

A local stake was assigned to study the possibility of processing milk for the storehouse system. After a period of time the stake reported that operating a milk-processing plant would be too difficult for one stake. In a General Welfare Committee meeting held 5 December 1940, Elder Harold B. Lee reported that the responsibility of establishing a milk-processing plant might be given to the General Welfare Committee. He suggested that this idea be studied to determine its feasibility.

The general committee formed a subcommittee, with J. Frank Ward as chairman and Lester F. Hewlett, Dr. L. R. Curtis, W. Tenney Cannon, and Soren Jacobsen as additional members. Brother Ward was an expert in the dairy industry, and the other members were familiar with milk processing. After meeting once a week for a period of time, they determined that a small milk-processing plant was feasible for Welfare Square. The committee completely designed and organized a milk-processing plant and purchased the neces-

Courtesy of Deseret News

President Alex F. Dunn presenting a gift to Bishop and Sister Jesse M. Drury at the time of Bishop Drury's retirement from Welfare Square, 27 April 1959. Elder and Sister Harold B. Lee look on.

sary equipment. They contacted many people in the dairy industry and made arrangements to purchase surplus raw milk from those dairymen who were willing.

Because of the hard work of this subcommittee, the Church was able to enter the milk-processing business and serve the welfare needs of the entire Church.

The milk plant itself was a small building erected on the west side of the Welfare Square cannery. It began operation on 20 April 1941. Its main purpose was to produce canned evaporated milk and bottled grade A pasteurized milk. The building had a main floor and a basement, with a total of 5,400 square feet. The first superintendent of the plant was J. W. Barnett, followed by Alva Duvall, who stayed with the program for many years.

Grain Elevator

For sixty-four years the sisters of the Relief Society, obedient to a charge from President Brigham Young, had been storing wheat. With the advent of a general Church welfare program, Church leaders felt that a large grain elevator was needed to consolidate the storage of the wheat supply.

With the approval of the First Presidency, work was begun on erecting a grain elevator at Welfare Square. William E. Ryberg of the General Welfare Committee was appointed as the project supervisor, and Roscoe Eardley became the coordinator. Blain C. Glenville was the construction superintendent.

The excavation work was begun on 6 March 1940 and completed two days later. The land at Welfare Square is at a low elevation and has a high water table. It was therefore necessary to prepare a stable support to carry the weight of the large concrete elevator. Workers drove 627 forty-foot logs, nearly five miles in total length, as pilings into the

Grain elevator under construction, 1940

ground. On these pilings they poured a reinforced concrete slab, 27 inches thick by 48 feet wide and 92 feet long.

Slip forms were erected on the slab so that concrete could be poured for the walls of the big tanks. On 6 May at 6:00 A.M., the "big pour" of concrete began. It continued day and night until 14 May. The concrete was poured in one continuous operation, with three shifts of men working twenty-four hours a day for eight and one-half days. It was anticipated that the pouring would take fifteen days, but because of the loyalty and enthusiasm of the brethren who worked, the job was completed in much less time.

The elevator used the largest amount of concrete poured in one operation in the state of Utah at that time. William E. Ryberg reported that nearly 15,000 bags of cement and more than $12,000 worth of reinforcing steel were used. Brother Ryberg said, "Not a single accident serious enough to report occurred during the construction." He also said that the grain elevator is "one of the most modern and best equipped in the country" (*Deseret News*, 26 Aug. 1940, pp. 1, 9).

77

Setting forms for the grain elevator, 1940

Forms moving upward on the grain elevator, 1940

**Grain elevator nearing completion and completed
grain elevator, summer 1940**

Facilities for loading and unloading grain and a track spur for railroad cars adjoin the elevator on the west side. Similar facilities for truck operations are situated on the east side of the elevator. Large amounts of structural steel and machinery were also installed.

Construction of the elevator was possible because the stakes and wards of the Salt Lake Region generously contributed labor and supplies, under the direction of the General Welfare Committee. As far as can be determined, 640 men worked on the project and contributed 70,151 hours of labor. Elder Henry D. Moyle stated that 90 percent of the labor was Church welfare labor and the other 10 percent was specialized work requiring trained experts.

The towering structure, 178 feet high, is clearly visible from most places in the Salt Lake Valley. It has become the

President
David O.
McKay at the
dedication
of the grain
elevator, 27
August 1940

symbol of the welfare program of the Church, representing storage of food in times of plenty for times of want. It is an emblem of preparedness and provident living, the basics of Church welfare philosophy.

The elevator can hold 318,000 bushels (over nineteen million pounds) of wheat. If loaded in standard-size railroad boxcars, the wheat would fill 191 cars, forming a train one-and-one-half miles long. The wheat is continually rotated through use and replacement.

Dedication of the Grain Elevator

On 27 August 1940, dedicatory services were held for the new grain elevator, arranged by Bishop Joseph L. Wirthlin of the Presiding Bishopric. Henry D. Moyle, chairman of the General Welfare Committee, conducted, and LeGrand Richards, Presiding Bishop of the Church, gave the opening prayer. President J. Reuben Clark, Jr., and William E. Ryberg were speakers, as was Amy Brown Lyman, General President of the Relief Society. President David O. McKay of the First Presidency spoke and offered the dedicatory prayer. Almost all of the General Authorities were present. President Clark broke the seal on the first carload of wheat, which was then loaded into the new structure.

At the dedication President Clark said: "This building represents above all else, the spirit of cooperation. . . . I wish that all of us could really appreciate what united effort could mean if we should cooperate in all things as we have in this enterprise. . . . Our fathers and grandfathers, our mothers and grandmothers were fashioned in heroic molds; they were built of the virtues that make mighty empires. It is not too much to hope and pray that we of our day may measure to their stature" (quoted in Cecil McGavin, "Grain among the Latter-day Saints," *Improvement Era,* Mar. 1941, p. 186).

The grain elevator on Welfare Square is not large compared to some others in the country, but it was the largest one in the Church welfare program for a long time. It is an example of what can be done by dedicated volunteers under inspired leadership.

Bishops' storehouse, cannery, grain elevator, heating plant, and root cellar on Welfare Square, 1940

Brother Harold B. Lee reflected: "Why should the Grain Elevator be built? To me there is only one answer. The elevator stands as a prophecy of a time when we will need wheat; of a time when, perhaps, money cannot buy food. Thank the Lord for the wisdom and the foresight of the men who guide this Church!" (minutes of Salt Lake regional welfare council meeting, 21 Aug. 1940).

One of the volunteer workers, now in his eighties, expressed his appreciation for the experience of working on the grain elevator:

"My roots go deep in Pioneer Stake and I have a vivid memory of the trying times during the Great Depression when such a program was sorely needed.

" . . . It has been my privilege and blessing to participate over the years in many welfare projects until the present time when at age eighty my use in such activity is very limited.

"I like to think that the crowning point in these varied activities came when I volunteered to work on the construction of the grain elevator erected on Welfare Square. As you know, it was an around-the-clock project for a full week so that the cement could be poured without a cold seam. As I recall I worked a graveyard shift for almost the entire time. Brother [Fred J.] Heath was one of the foremen and a great motivator. I recall his telling us to give a full 100 percent of our energies the same as if we were being paid four dollars a day. At that time four dollars was considered a fair wage.

"I am pleased that the grain elevator still towers above any building on the Square. As I commute back and forth to the city on the freeway, the structure always stands out as a welcome beacon to the poor and underprivileged. As I do so, I never hesitate to let my children and our extended family know that I had a part in its erection" (a letter from William F. Gygi to the author, 22 Oct. 1993).

Above:
Alfons J. Finck
and Otto P.
Hunger, store-
house workers
for over 40
years

Right:
Johnny, faith-
ful Welfare
Square worker
for 25 years,
with Glen L.
Rudd

Since the grain elevator was built on Welfare Square, the Church has constructed several other grain elevators of varying capacities throughout the United States and Canada. In every bishops' storehouse now in service, wheat is stored in connection with the storehouse and cannery operation.

Relief Society Wheat Program

Most of the wheat stored in the new grain elevator came from the Relief Society wheat program. At the dedication of the grain elevator, Sister Amy Brown Lyman, General President of the Relief Society, was asked to speak. She outlined some of the history of how the Relief Society sisters got into the business of storing wheat:

"The storing of grain in the L.D.S. Church was inaugurated by President Brigham Young in 1876. It was given as a special mission to the women of the Church.

"For a number of years the brethren had been advised to save and store grain against a day of need. They had been told that in this isolated region grain was of more consequence even than gold or silver. But each year they had put the matter off, no doubt feeling the need in this new developing country for any cash they were able to raise by selling surplus grain and other produce.

"In late September of 1876, President Young sent for Mrs. Emmeline B. Wells to come to his office as he had something of importance to discuss with her. When she arrived he told her he wanted the women of Zion to gather and store grain against a time of need or famine, and that he desired her to lead out in the movement. He spoke of drought, crop failure, and the tolls often taken by grasshoppers, and emphasized the fact that the wheat would be held as a reserve and constant protection" (*Deseret News*, 7 Sept. 1940, p. 1).

Sister Wells was the associate editor of the *Women's Exponent,* and she wrote a series of articles to convince the

women of the Church to
assist in the collection of
wheat for storage. Women
everywhere cooperated in
this great effort.

Sister Wells became the
fifth General President of
the Relief Society, and she
regarded her assignment to
lead the sisters in storing
wheat as one of the most
important undertakings of
her life.

During 1877, the women
of the Church were responsible for gathering 10,465
bushels of wheat. By the end
of the following year they

Freida Mount weaving a rug at
Welfare Square, 1950s

had gathered more than 25,000 bushels to be put into storage.

The proper storage of this much wheat became a problem. Bishop R. W. Burton, a Counselor in the Presiding
Bishopric, offered to have grain stored in the general tithing
office. Many ward bishops followed this example and offered
space in their tithing granaries. In addition, small granaries
were built by many ward Relief Society organizations. All the
troubles incident to the storage of grain, such as mice and
weevil damage and mold infestation, were experienced in
those beginning days.

By the early 1900s, steel bins were provided, and later the
grain was stored in small grain elevators. In 1940, the wheat
began to be stored in the grain elevator on Welfare Square.

Twenty-five years after the dedication of the grain elevator, Sister Belle S. Spafford, General President of the Relief
Society, talked about the Relief Society wheat program:

Elders Henry D. Moyle, chairman; Harold B. Lee, managing director;
and Marion G. Romney, assistant managing director of the
welfare program, late 1950s

"I remember my mother telling of gleaning in the fields. Granaries were built all over the Church to store this wheat. . . .

"The granaries became filled. Then when the war came, the First World War, the Government did not have sufficient wheat for the soldiers. They learned of the Relief Society wheat and approached the Relief Society to see if they would sell it to the Government.

"The Relief Society offered to give it to them, but they said they would pay for it, which they did; and it was in excess of $412,000.

"Following that, President Wilson made a trip to Utah to thank the Sisters for the wheat" ("Sister Belle Spafford Tells of Wheat Storage in the Relief Society," unpublished article, 27 July 1965).

Relief Society wheat was used to help many other people in need. In 1898 wheat was sent to the people in Parowan,

Utah, and to other districts that were drought stricken. In 1906 when an earthquake and the resulting fire devastated San Francisco, a train carload of flour from Relief Society wheat was sent. In the same year another train carload of flour was sent to China to relieve suffering from famine. The Relief Society wheat sold to the government during World War I amounted to 200,000 bushels.

On 1 October 1978, Sister Barbara B. Smith, General President of the Relief Society, officially placed the Relief Society wheat and wheat assets in the grain storage program of the Church. In a general conference session, she proposed that 266,291 bushels of Relief Society wheat be made part of the Church welfare program for the benefit of all the members of the Church and that the wheat fund be used exclusively for the purchase of grain. She said that the Relief Society General Presidency had prayerfully considered the matter of their wheat stewardship and had decided that their responsibility had been filled. Sisters in attendance at the conference were given the privilege of sustaining this action.

President Spencer W. Kimball replied, "Sister Smith, in behalf of the brethren of the Church and the Church in general, we accept this great gift that you have given to us from the Relief Society with gratitude and appreciation for its deep significance" (in Conference Report, Oct. 1978, p. 78).

TRANSIENT PROGRAM

In the late 1950s, Welfare Square became the site for another type of service. At this time, many transients were visiting the Relief Society social services office, the Church Administration Building, and Temple Square seeking help. In the administration building, they would go to the offices of General Authorities, some of whom would take out their billfolds and give the transients some money.

Glen L. Rudd, the manager of Welfare Square, realized that the loitering and constant interruption of the schedules of the Brethren were creating a serious problem. He met with the Presiding Bishopric and suggested that the needs of the transients be cared for at Welfare Square. He suggested that a certain amount of fast-offering funds be allocated to Welfare Square. The transients could be carefully interviewed to determine their real needs, and, as appropriate, they could be given assignments at Welfare Square since there was always enough work to do there. They would be assisted first with commodities and then, if needed, with cash from fast offerings. At the end of each month a report would be submitted to the Presiding Bishopric showing the number of transients interviewed, the number of hours they worked, the amount of commodities distributed through the storehouse, and the amount of fast-offering funds expended. This report would be a requisition for the Presiding Bishopric

Aerial photograph of Welfare Square, 1957

to reimburse the fast-offering account with the amount of money expended during the month.

Bishop Joseph L. Wirthlin and his Counselors were very agreeable to the proposition. Since Glen Rudd was a former bishop, they authorized him to be the bishop in charge. He was provided with fast-offering funds and allowed to prepare bishop's orders on the storehouse.

This was an immediate solution to the problem, and the practice has continued to this day. While it has increased the responsibilities at Welfare Square, it has been a great blessing to have a place to send transients in Salt Lake City.

Several other storehouse managers in locations where there are many transients have also been authorized to assist in the same way.

This help has been provided according to correct welfare principles. Except for an occasional emergency or serious health problem, transients have been able to work for what they have received. Many have worked long and hard hours. Some have received more than they could have otherwise earned. In most cases, they have had an opportunity to contribute to the solution of their problems. No attempt is made to put these destitute people on a Church dole. They work for what they receive. Some transients have excuses for not being able to work and say they will come back later, but they don't. It is surprising how many appreciate the opportunity to earn what they receive.

The transient program at Welfare Square is very successful. During 1990 more than 14,500 transients were interviewed for work and assistance.

Use of the Name Deseret

The word *Deseret* is a Book of Mormon word (see Ether 2:3) that has been used as the brand name on all Church welfare products. The question of using this brand name was considered in the General Welfare Committee meeting held on 24 November 1943. The minutes record: "On motion of Brother [Thomas E.] McKay and seconded by Brother [William E.] Ryberg, it was decided to recommend . . . that we adopt the name 'Deseret' as soon as it could be cleared with the Kaysville Canning Company [a private business using the name], and that it be registered in all states in which we intend to use it."

There were seventeen present in the meeting, including Elder Harold B. Lee, Brother Henry D. Moyle, Elder Marion G. Romney, Bishop LeGrand Richards, and President Belle S. Spafford. Apparently the Kaysville Canning Company was willing to give up the use of their brand name to the Church, and Deseret has been used on welfare products ever since.

GEMS OF PURE RELIGION

◆ ◆ ◆

The Red Shoes

"One evening just after the Storehouse was closed, two little girls about thirteen years of age came with an order for shoes for one of them. The little girls were to take part in the Beehive Song Festival. They were to be dressed in white with colored shoes. I waited upon them, and as I took the order the Bishop had written, I noticed that he had prescribed a certain type of shoe on the order.

"The little girl was very disappointed when she saw the shoes that I tried on her, but she was well aware of what the order called for. I was almost glad when I could not fit her in these particular shoes and brought out a pair of red shoes. Her eyes grew wide with admiration and then she sadly said, 'Oh, I could not have those shoes. My Bishop told me that I would have to get some that would do for every day. These are much too fancy. I could not have them.'

"I urged her to try them on just the same, if only to see how they fit. They were a perfect fit and the other little girl said, 'Now you will be dressed just like the rest of us.'

"I told the girl that I was sure her Bishop would not object to her having these shoes—in fact he would be very happy to know that she had been able to be fitted so well.

"She was reluctant and still said that neither her Mother nor the Bishop would like her to get them. Once again I told her that it would be all right. Then I took her to the counter and picked up a box of anklets. I told her that she would need some new anklets to wear with the new shoes.

" 'My Bishop did not say that I could have the anklets.' But as she let her fingers rest upon the bright colors, I told her to pick out three pair. She was close to tears now, so great was her joy. But in that moment she picked out her anklets, she felt that she was almost exalted. Her morale was lifted and instead of being a little girl with an inferiority complex, she was just the same as any other little girl picking out her anklets to her heart's content.

"I knew that the little girl had come from a poor family. The mother was a widow with twelve children and her only means of support was through the Welfare Plan.

"I watched the little girls leave the Storehouse; both were laughing and talking. Under one arm was a box of red shoes and her hand clasped tightly on a small sack which contained her anklets; her joy was complete."

Jesse M. Drury, *For These My Brethren* (reprint, 1991), pp. 55–56

President Henry D. Moyle at the dedication of the new cannery,
15 May 1963. Left to right: Elder John Longden, Elder ElRay L.
Christiansen, President Moyle, President C. Leland Davey

CHAPTER 4

WELFARE SQUARE
AFTER 1960

By 1960 leaders and members of the Church had been greatly strengthened through their involvement in welfare activities. Their dedication and willingness to serve had increased. President Bryant S. Hinckley wrote:

"This undertaking has increased the fast offerings and the payment of tithing; unified the Church, strengthened the morals and stimulated spiritual growth all down the ranks. It is a shining example of practical religion—of Christianity in action. It stands as an additional proof that Mormonism is in reality true Christianity.

"Aside from all the possibilities of providing adequate relief and employment for our people, the finest opportunity provided for the Church is that of leadership, in a world floundering and gradually burying itself in the sea of distress, poor leadership, and destruction" (quoted in M. Lynn Bennion and J. A. Washburn, *History of the Restored Church* [Sunday School course 11, 1955], p. 119).

In 1960 the welfare program was twenty-four years old, and the facilities on Welfare Square had been in heavy use for twenty-one years. It should be remembered that most of the materials used to build the cannery, storehouse, root cellar, and other buildings, except the grain elevator, were materials that had been salvaged from the demolition of old buildings in the central part of Salt Lake City. The time had come to increase the capacity of the original buildings and equipment.

In the early 1960s, an opportunity arose to increase the size of Welfare Square. At this time, the state of Utah was building a freeway through Salt Lake City. State leaders came to the Church and asked to buy a small portion of the northeast corner of Welfare Square. President Moyle discussed this request with the Welfare Square manager, who was not anxious to sell any of the property. He felt that the increased operations on the square required every inch of ground. However, President Moyle, in his wisdom, felt that the Church should cooperate with the state. As a result, a corner of the property was sold.

The manager asked President Moyle what the Church would do with the money received for that piece of property. President Moyle immediately said, "You can have it if you need it." When the manager explained that it was possible to buy five or six houses across the street on Seventh South,

Exterior of the new milk plant, 1960

on the north of Welfare Square, President Moyle felt it was a great opportunity and authorized him to use the funds for that purpose.

The process of purchasing the property began immediately. Seventh South going east was being closed off by the freeway, and the Church purchased all of the north side of this street, the part that adjoined Welfare Square. The city deeded to the Church the portion of Seventh South Street itself that was immediately north of Welfare Square. Today, about one half of the entire block north of the square is owned by the Church, and Welfare Square is about half again as large as it was originally. This is because of President Moyle's willingness to sell the small corner of the square for the construction of the freeway.

NEW MILK PLANT

The milk-processing plant was the first building to be rebuilt. The original plant built in 1941 prepared condensed and bottled milk for a few of the existing storehouses. It handled a little over 100,000 pounds of milk a year. By 1952, with more milk coming in from welfare projects and a greater need, it processed 1,600,000 pounds.

In 1954 it became evident that the needs of the Church welfare program had outgrown the capacity of the milk-processing plant. Fred W. Schwendiman, regional welfare chairman, and Alex Dunn and Henry A. Smith, his assistants, felt that the manager of Welfare Square should begin planning for a larger and more modern processing plant that could meet the growing needs of the Church.

In 1957 a committee was organized to study the possibility of building such a facility. The manager met with engineers and businessmen in the dairy industry, including representatives from Highland and Winder Dairies, to discuss the kinds of equipment and processes that would enable

Courtesy of Hal Rumel

Above: Bottling milk in the new milk plant, 1960. Left to right: Reed Durfey, Morris Shapiro, Calvin Crandall

Center: Equipment in the new milk plant, 1960

Below: Bottled milk in the cooler

a new milk plant to better serve a growing Church. He also met with the Salt Lake Board of Health to receive their suggestions. These people provided much assistance in determining how the proposed plant was to be designed. After two years of study and much prayer and hard work, work on the new plant was ready to move forward.

President Alex F. Dunn of the Tooele Stake, who had been appointed as regional welfare chairman, initiated the preparations for construction. The proposed facility was presented in detail to the fifteen stake presidents of the Pioneer Welfare Region, who approved it and pledged to provide the entire cost. When President Dunn was succeeded as regional welfare chairman by President W. Howard Allen of the Granite Stake, President Allen took the leadership of building the new milk plant. (President Alex Dunn served a total of thirteen years in the leadership of Welfare Square—ten years as vice chairman and three years as regional chairman.)

The firm of Dean L. Gustavson and Associates was selected to do the architectural work. Having recently built a new

Condensed milk to be labeled and shipped

milk-processing plant for Winder Dairy, the firm had gained considerable experience.

President Allen and the manager of Welfare Square contacted Rolf Christiansen, President of Christiansen Brothers Construction Company, who agreed to be the general contractor. Brother Christiansen made many valuable suggestions, which eventually saved the welfare region over $39,000. He was very cooperative, and the region was allowed to donate as much of the labor as possible. All the resources of the contractor were put at the disposal of the Church. Simon Christiansen was assigned to be the superintendent of the construction.

Two Church members, Wilbur Parkinson, head of the Salt Lake City Board of Health, and Ralph Schow, the city's chief sanitation officer, accepted Church assignments in the erection of the plant. They gave great service in helping to plan the building and making sure it complied with all health and safety rules. Like all dairies and other food-processing plants, the Welfare Square milk-processing plant was under the strict supervision of local boards of health and other government agencies. Every effort was made to maintain high standards of sanitation, efficiency, and quality of products.

For the new building, it was necessary to purchase almost all new equipment, including a pasteurizer, clarifier, bottle filler, bottle washer, and homogenizer. One of the most important pieces of new equipment was a milk-drying machine purchased from Minnesota.

The total cost of the plant was more than $384,000 and was paid for entirely by the stakes in the region with no subsidy from the General Welfare Committee. In addition to cash donations, the records show that 932 men donated 31,348 hours.

It was necessary to replace the old heating plant on Welfare Square to take care of the increased load that would

Completed milk plant on Welfare Square

be created by the milk plant and a future new cannery. Christiansen Brothers Construction Company was also the contractor for this facility, which was completed and in operation by January 1960.

The milk-processing plant was completed during March of 1960. An open house was held on May 18, 19, and 20 to allow interested members of the Church and representatives from the dairy industry to inspect the new facility.

William T. Nightingale and George Hamilton were the first managers of the new plant. In the first year of operation, they were assigned to process 287,000 quarts of grade A, pasteurized, bottled milk. In addition, the plant produced 181,389 pounds of powdered skim milk, 617,440 cans of condensed milk, 88,000 pounds of butter, 27,000 pounds of cottage cheese, and 15,820 quarts of buttermilk. Over 695,000 gallons of raw milk (or 5,700,000 pounds) were required to produce these items. All of this milk was provided by Church-owned dairy projects. By 1981 the milk plant was receiving about 12,000,000 pounds of raw milk.

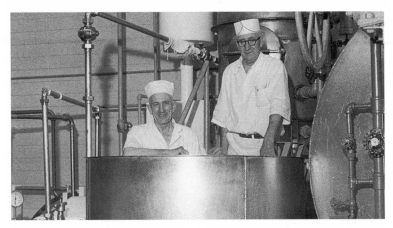

George Hamilton and William T. Nightingale in the old milk plant; they later managed the new processing plant

In 1993, with larger equipment and additional modernization, 20,500,000 pounds were processed. The plant had a
few paid employees and a large number of volunteer workers
who donated nearly 15,000 hours of labor. In 1994, more
stakes were asked to provide volunteers, and more than
34,000 hours of labor were donated to the milk plant.

In 1960 there were eight Church-owned dairies. These
dairies have since been consolidated into two large dairy
projects that furnish all the milk used in the Church welfare
program today.

At first, a small refrigerated tank truck holding 1,500 gallons was purchased to pick up milk at the dairies. Today, the
Church welfare program owns three modern milk-transport-
ing tankers. Their capacity is from 5,600 to 6,400 gallons each.

The milk-processing plant has been upgraded twice, once
in the late 1970s and again in 1993. Today it is as modern as
any plant in the area.

Even though there have always been paid employees at
the plant, until recently most of the processing and packaging was done by welfare recipients who were working for

Right: First
Church-owned
tank truck for
hauling milk,
1960; E. V.
Ronneburg
(left) and
Elwynn S.
Hewlett

Center: The
second milk
tanker, 1973

Below: One of
three milk
tankers, 1994

Above: Inspecting butter
in the cooler that is
ready to be cut and
packaged

Left: The new milk-
processing plant uses
cartons instead of glass
bottles

commodities. However, in order to increase efficiency and to improve the product, much of the work has become automated. Paid employees now operate the plant, assisted by a large number of volunteer workers.

Powdered Milk

In 1960 when powdered milk was first produced by the welfare system, it was shipped to all Church storehouses. But the product was not readily accepted by the patrons. Back then people were unfamiliar with powdered milk and didn't know how to use it. A large surplus of powdered milk resulted, and it was important to find a way to get needy members to use it.

The manager of a large dairy in Utah inquired about the possibility of purchasing the surplus powdered milk. Glen L. Rudd, the manager of Welfare Square, told him that products processed at the square could not be sold commercially. However, because the company very much needed the powdered milk, the dairy manager persisted, asking that permission for the sale be requested from the General Welfare Committee.

Brother Rudd wrote a letter to the committee telling them of the request. He expected a negative reply but hoped for suggestions on how to move the surplus milk. The letter explained that the commercial dairy would pay a premium price because the Welfare Square product was superior to theirs.

A few days later, Bishop John H. Vandenberg reported that he had brought up the matter in the General Welfare Committee meeting, and Elder Harold B. Lee's answer was, "Absolutely not, not one pound is to be sold." When asked if he had any suggestions about what to do with the surplus milk, Elder Lee had said with a smile, "Tell Glen that he created the problem; he can solve the problem."

Chocolate Drink

The leaders at Welfare Square decided to package the powdered milk in smaller quantities with instructions for its use. This approach helped somewhat, but a better solution was still needed. They decided to investigate using the milk for making a chocolate drink. Representatives from Welfare Square met with several dairy processors to see how they made their chocolate drink. Samples of chocolate were ordered from California, and experiments began with preparing a dry mix that could be made into a hot or cold chocolate drink. After several months of trials, an excellent recipe was developed.

Some of the dry mix was sent to the General Welfare Committee. Bishop Vandenberg later called and said they had found the drink to be excellent. He gave authorization for Welfare Square to proceed in manufacturing the new product. Within a few months most of the surplus powdered milk was gone. Over the last thirty years, the dry chocolate milk mix has proven to be a popular product. In addition, many more people are using the regular powdered milk.

It is important to emphasize that not even one pound of processed milk has been sold on the open market since the Church has been in the milk business.

New Cannery

The original cannery on Welfare Square had been in service since November of 1939, and the work accomplished in

Courtesy of *Deseret News*

Beginning construction on the new cannery, 1962. Left to right: Glen L. Rudd; Bishop Rudolph H. Luckau; Wally Christiansen, construction superintendent; President C. Leland Davey, regional chairman

Courtesy of *Deseret News*/J. M. Heslop

**President W. Howard Allen presenting a retirement gift to
Ida Alvord, November 1961**

it was some of the finest in the history of welfare. In the first
ten and one-half months of 1961, more than one million
cans of commodities were produced in the cannery, the most
that had been produced in a one-year period. When the one
millionth can came off the line on 7 November 1961, the
workers held a celebration. Two weeks later Sister Ida Alvord,
the cannery supervisor, was honored for her excellent work.
President W. Howard Allen, the regional priesthood leader,
presented her a beautiful trophy of a silver-plated can
mounted on a base.

But the cannery was becoming outdated and now needed
repairs and modernization to meet the increased demand.
Rather than remodel the old cannery, regional welfare leaders and the Brethren decided to build an entirely new facility. President C. Leland Davey, chairman of the Pioneer

Welfare Region, and those who worked with him made preliminary plans for the new cannery. It was decided that the building would adjoin the milk-processing plant, giving the two buildings a combined length of almost a football field.

Serving as a resource to President Davey, the Welfare Square manager took E. V. Ronneburg, his assistant, and R. Clay Allred and Don Lane to visit an all-purpose cannery located at the Colorado state penitentiary. Most commercial canneries process only one or two products, whereas the Colorado facility processed a variety of products, as the Church cannery did. They then visited canneries in Idaho and throughout Utah to obtain ideas that could be incorporated into the construction of the new cannery. The cannery was to be as modern as possible to serve Church needs well into the future.

The architect for the cannery building was Dean L. Gustavson, who designed the milk plant. The new building was to be similar in design to the milk plant. The same general contractor, Christiansen Brothers Construction Company, was also used. Once again, these people were very easy to work with and allowed the Church to do portions of the work with volunteer labor, saving the region several thousand dollars.

The cost of the new cannery was a little over $350,000. All of the money was donated by the stakes involved with the regional operation at Welfare Square. Once again, no general Church funds were used.

Construction began in 1962. President Henry D. Moyle visited the construction site several times. He was very interested in everything going on. The manager of Welfare Square would call him when something special was to happen, and he would leave his office and come to the square.

On one occasion the construction workers were pouring the concrete floor, and President Moyle was as excited as a young boy. He even got into the concrete to where his shoes were covered, but he wasn't concerned. He was anxious to be part of the growth of this program that was so important to the needy of the Church and to him personally.

Cannery Dedication

The cannery was completed in May 1963, and a dedicatory service was held on the 15th of May. Many members from the stakes of the region were in attendance. There was even a group of people ready to begin the first canning project at the conclusion of the dedicatory service.

President C. Leland Davey welcomed everyone and gave introductory remarks. The invocation was offered by President William B. Martin, a vice chairman of the region. The Welfare Square manager spoke. Then President Henry D. Moyle gave an address and the dedicatory prayer.

In his talk, President Moyle called everyone's attention to conditions in the past. He said: "When I came out a week or so ago and went through this building, and it was practically completed, I thought to myself, 'Little did we dream of such a facility on this square at the time [the land] was purchased from Mr. Hogle.' And, of course, at that time we did not have the grain elevator or any of the facilities on this block as we now have. It was vacant property."

President Moyle had been so involved with the development of the buildings and the production of commodities on Welfare Square that he felt almost like the owner. He had, in fact, watched over it from the very beginning.

In his talk, he reminisced about the construction of the first root cellar. He reminded everyone of President David O. McKay's analogy that those involved in the work of Church welfare were like the engineer of a large locomotive who took his engine out into the dark night. He could see only as far as the light of the engine projected ahead, but when the engine reached the most distant visible point, the light projected yet onward to a new and more distant point. President Moyle testified that Welfare Square leaders had been following the light and that the building of the new cannery was the result of inspiration from the Lord through the local leaders of the Church. (See pages 61–62 for the full analogy given by President McKay.)

He was particularly happy that this cannery could also be used for group or family canning, allowing individuals or families to can products for their food storage programs.

President Moyle said: "There were prophetic utterances made at the time this program was started. It was not uncommon for President Clark to tell us it was divine revelation that this program was instituted; and it was also assured us that, if we did our duty in the directing of the work of the Welfare Program, there would never be a time in the future when we could not take care of all of the membership of the Church who needed assistance."

In the dedicatory prayer President Moyle said: "We dedicate this building unto thee, along with all of the other buildings and structures upon this block, which heretofore have been dedicated, that this facility may take its place with all the others and fall heir, as it were, to thy protecting care and influence and be a place where thy spirit and inspiration may be, as has been promised in the other buildings on this square, that they may all constitute and comprise, in a way, one unit dedicated unto thee for the unselfish devotion of thy people and for the preservation of the lives of those who need assistance."

Because he knew there was a large group waiting to begin canning, President Moyle shortened his remarks so that the first canning project could begin. The congregation sang "We Thank Thee, O God, for a Prophet." President Nicholas

The first group to work in the new cannery at the conclusion of
the dedication ceremony, 15 May 1963

J. Teerlink, a vice chairman of the welfare region, offered the
closing prayer.

The cannery was officially opened at 7:30 P.M., and the
group began processing Mexican sugarloaf pineapple.

During the first twenty-two months of operation,
2,135,000 cans were processed. Eighty-five percent of the
canning was done by Church members for their family food
storage programs. During this time, 869 different groups,
made up of 18,000 people, participated in the canning.

Among the participants during the first year was a group
of sisters from Anaheim, California. They came a day before
the general Relief Society conference so they could use the
cannery. After the conference they took their commodities
home with them.

The most popular commodities during the first years were
apricots and apricot juice. These were followed by applesauce, pineapple, green beans, and potatoes. Thirty-three different products were canned, all with a spirit of thanksgiving.

The cannery proved to be a great blessing to families who wanted to accumulate a year's supply of food for storage. In addition to family storage, the cannery provided fruits and vegetables for the storehouse distribution system.

Many years have passed since the dedication, and the cannery has rarely been idle. The cannery will be completely remodeled in the near future and new equipment installed, making it once again current with the most modern cannery of this type.

COLD-STORAGE FACILITY

In 1967 a large building was built on the east side of Welfare Square to replace the old root cellar. It is a mechanical, all-purpose cold-storage facility, large enough to hold fifty large truckloads of potatoes, as well as large quantities of carrots, cabbages, onions, apples, and other vegetables and fruits. As with the root cellar, the cold-storage facility is large enough for trucks to enter at one end and exit at the other.

The building is modern in every way. It also has space for welfare workers to sort potatoes and prepare other vegetables and fruits for storehouse distribution.

NEW STOREHOUSE ON THE SQUARE

The original storehouse built in 1939 served for a while as the central storehouse for the Church, in addition to being a regional facility. The central storehouse was operated by the General Welfare Committee, and it provided commodities for all the regional storehouses. At the end of World War II, the Church moved the central storehouse from Welfare Square to 40 South 200 West in Salt Lake City. Later the Church purchased part of the small-arms plant on the west side of the city, and the central storehouse was moved to this location. This location is still used as a central storehouse.

These moves gave the operations on Welfare Square much more space, which was greatly needed. The Welfare Square Regional Bishops' Storehouse was serving more people than any other storehouse in the Church. Commodities were coming and going at a very rapid pace, and by 1973 it was evident that the old regional storehouse needed to be replaced. On 11 December 1973, in an area welfare council meeting under the direction of President Philip T. Sonntag, regional chairman, the stake presidents discussed building a new and better facility at Welfare Square.

At the meeting, representatives from Welfare Square displayed a preliminary design of the storehouse facilities they needed, with a rough drawing showing where the new storehouse could be located on the square. The council unanimously approved the ideas. The new storehouse was recommended to the General Welfare Committee, whose members approved the project.

Breaking ground for the new storehouse, 10 June 1975. Left to right: Glen L. Rudd; Lee H. Nelson; President Marion G. Romney; Elder H. Burke Peterson; President Philip T. Sonntag, regional chairman; Bishop Eugene Packer

Courtesy of *Deseret News*/Dave ConLey

New Welfare Square storehouse, 25 March 1976

Glen Ashton Lloyd and Associates was chosen as the architectural firm, and Dean Whiting, of Intermountain Construction Inc., was chosen as the building contractor.

On 10 June 1975, the official ground-breaking ceremony was held. It was conducted by President Marion G. Romney.

The footings for the building were poured in July of 1975. The first concrete blocks were laid on 29 August and by 10 September, the east wall of the storehouse was up to the square. The masonry work was finished in October. A concrete roof was installed by the Otto Buehner Company. It took three and one-half days to lay the giant concrete slabs that formed the roof of the building.

By January the interior and finishing work was begun. The new storehouse building was completed on 29 March 1976.

Dedicatory services were held on 25 May 1976, with President Philip T. Sonntag conducting. The invocation was offered by President Nicholas J. Teerlink, the area welfare chairman when the plans were first made for the erection of the new storehouse. Presiding Bishop Victor L. Brown gave a few remarks, and the Welfare Square manager spoke briefly. President Spencer W. Kimball then spoke and dedicated this modern facility.

Features of the New Storehouse

The storehouse contains more than 46,000 square feet of space, with the front section used as the distribution storehouse. The building contains administrative offices, a meat market, a grocery section, and a clothing and shoe department. In the northwest corner is a visitors' center, which accommodates thousands of visitors each year. The back area of the building is a warehouse for the large supply of commodities constantly being distributed.

At the time the building was built, Welfare Square served seven priesthood regions containing twenty-six stakes in all. Today the bishops and branch presidents of 210 wards and branches write orders on the storehouse, which has the

Inside the new Welfare Square regional storehouse

Above: Produce inside Welfare Square regional storehouse

Left: Dairy products in Welfare Square regional storehouse

Clothing department in Welfare Square regional storehouse

Storage area in Welfare Square regional storehouse

largest distribution of any storehouse in the Church welfare system.

The new storehouse resembles a combination supermarket and department store. It has a clothing department with items for the whole family, such as underwear, socks, pants, dresses, and coats. It also has a good selection of fabric for those who are able to make their own clothing. People are encouraged to sew their own clothing if possible and can be assisted by Relief Society sisters, who have long had the responsibility to assist other sisters in this skill.

For years, this and other storehouses have been filled with clothing items made by welfare recipients and other volunteer sisters who are willing to perform this service. Many beautiful hand-sewn clothes are kept in stock for children and adults.

The storehouse also maintains a supply of bedding items, such as sheets, blankets, and pillows.

There is a shoe department to meet the needs of various family members. Not all storehouses are able to do this, but some of the larger ones keep a good stock of shoes on hand for children and adults.

There has been a barbershop in the Welfare Square storehouse since the mid 1950s. While there has never been a paid barber, there always seems to be a retired barber or someone else with this skill available to manage the barbershop. A bishop prepares a storehouse order form for a family to receive haircuts just as he would for them to receive commodities.

There is a large refrigerated storage area where various commodities are stored for later use. The warehouse is filled with tens of thousands of items on pallets to be distributed at the proper time.

Dairy products are kept in refrigerated display cases. Fruits and vegetables are kept on tables and in bins on the storehouse floor. Canned goods and household items are stocked on shelves. Meat products are frozen and stored in display cases.

All items are listed on a Storehouse Stocklist. Bishops, assisted by their Relief Society presidents, review the stocklist with a family to be helped and prepare a list of items that the family needs during the next week or two.

In the office at the entrance to the storehouse, the bishops' orders are received and processed. Orders are checked and sorted if they are to be delivered.

The Welfare Square storehouse has always had a delivery system with up to four or five trucks. Deliveries are made to those who are unable to come to the storehouse or have others do it for them.

Those patrons who are able to do their own shopping can use the storehouse exactly as they would a modern supermarket. They fill their shopping carts with the items that are on the signed bishop's order. When they have completed their order, they go through a check stand to make certain that the order has been filled properly.

Like a Bank

A bishops' storehouse is similar to a bank. In the commercial world a person deposits money into his account. Later when he needs money to purchase something, he writes a check on his account. In a modern bishops' storehouse, the commodities are produced on welfare projects and in canneries and "deposited" in the bishops' storehouse. A bishop then reviews and signs a bishop's order (a "check"), usually prepared by the Relief Society president, to be "drawn" on the storehouse. The welfare recipient presents the order at the storehouse and is allowed to "withdraw" the prescribed commodities. Thus, the process of withdrawing from the bishops' storehouse is as orderly and dignified as withdrawing from a bank.

This system was developed in the years between 1930 and 1936 in the original stake storehouses and became the system used by the entire Church when the welfare program was announced in 1936.

CONTINUED GROWTH

The Welfare Square multiregional operation continues to grow with the passing years. In the 1960s the services of a storehouse in the northern part of Salt Lake City were absorbed into the Welfare Square storehouse, as were those of a storehouse in the Sugarhouse area of the Salt Lake Valley.

In 1969, four regions, containing fifteen stakes, were divided from the Welfare Square multiregion, and a new Granger welfare area was created. All of the stakes west of Redwood Road in the Salt Lake Valley and the stakes in Tooele County were in this new area.

President William B. Martin of the Magna Stake was chosen as the area welfare chairman. He and the Welfare Square manager designed and supervised the building of the new Granger Regional Bishops' Storehouse. Sidney M. Horman donated a ten-acre piece of property near Magna, just west of Granger, for the storehouse. In addition, he furnished a construction superintendent and draftsman to assist in the construction. These donations made up one of the largest contributions given to the welfare program since its beginning.

The Murray storehouse was discontinued, and a new storehouse was built in Sandy to serve the south end of the Salt Lake Valley. These three storehouses—Welfare Square, Granger, and Sandy—serve the entire Salt Lake Valley.

ADDITIONAL BUILDINGS ON WELFARE SQUARE

In 1981 a modern Deseret Industries facility was built on Welfare Square on the properties that the Church had purchased on Seventh South in the early 1960s.

In 1983 a large multipurpose two-story building was constructed at the rear of the new bishops' storehouse, facing Eighth South. The top floor of the building houses the area welfare offices for finance and employment services. The entire main floor houses those offices of LDS Social Services that assist the same regions as does Welfare Square. This multipurpose facility has been a very valuable addition to the other buildings on the square.

The services provided by Welfare Square have grown steadily over the years, and the square is now filled with modern buildings and adequate parking.

In 1941 a large garage was built on the southeast corner of Welfare Square for the central storehouse trucks. The garage also housed a repair shop for all of the trucks owned by the central storehouse and other welfare operations. When the central storehouse moved from Welfare Square to the small-arms plant, the garage was made available to Welfare Square for use as a maintenance facility. Later a portion of the garage was used as an expansion of the carpenter shop. Since that time it has had a number of uses. Today the building is used as a bakery that supplies bread to bishops' storehouses, and a laundry that serves most of the operations on the square.

GEMS OF PURE RELIGION

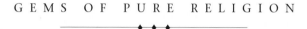

The Barbershop

In about 1955, an elderly gentleman was sent by his bishop to the storehouse to work. He was to receive commodities for his service. When he was interviewed, he said he could no longer do any heavy work. He said he could not lift anything, he did not have any skills, and he was distressed because although he was willing to work, there was nothing he could do. The interviewer asked him what he had done in his early life. (He was from a Scandinavian country and had a strong accent and a great testimony.) He said, "The only thing I have ever done is to play my violin." The interviewer suggested that he could play his violin in the devotionals, but it wouldn't be a part of his everyday work.

The man then mentioned that he had been a barber for many years. The interviewer told him that there would be a barbershop for him to work in when he returned the next day. The man wasn't aware that at that moment there weren't any barber facilities. Within the next few hours, a good brother donated a barber chair. Some clippers, scissors, and other barber tools were purchased for less than twenty-five dollars. In the basement of the storehouse a room was cleaned out and painted. Mirrors were put on the wall. By the time the brother arrived for work the next day, a beautiful new barbershop was waiting for him.

Bishops soon became aware of this shop and began to send people from their wards to receive haircuts as part of their welfare assistance. This brother, who incidentally did play the violin very well, worked for a few years and then was followed by other barbers.

------- ◆ ◆ ◆ -------

Shriners' Hospital

Shortly after the new cannery on Welfare Square opened in 1963, the Welfare Square manager received a call from the people in charge of the Shriners' Hospital in Salt Lake City. They told him that a large truckload of peaches was being given to the hospital by people in Grand Junction, Colorado. The truckload contained more peaches than could possibly be used without spoiling. They asked if the Church would be willing to let them use the cannery facilities to can the peaches. The manager said that the Church would be more than happy to let them come into the cannery with their workers and do the canning. He told them that if they would pay for the cost of the cans, the Church would furnish supervisory help and even supply additional help if needed.

This large group of nonmembers came to the cannery the next night and, under the direction of the supervisors there, canned several thousand cans of peaches. They were delighted to leave with a truckload of canned fruit that would supply them for several months.

This is one of the first instances of a nonmember group using the Church's canning facilities. The policy of the Church is to allow groups from other churches, from civic clubs, and from any other organized group to use the canneries in the same way that Church members use them.

Stewart B. Eccles instructing truck drivers at the
Sugarhouse Deseret Industries, 1941

CHAPTER 5

DESERET INDUSTRIES AND WELFARE ACTIVITIES OUTSIDE SALT LAKE CITY

DESERET INDUSTRIES

In the early years of the Church welfare program, Brother Harold B. Lee and others, under the supervision of the First Presidency, spent considerable time discussing the possibility of establishing a business similar to Goodwill Industries.

One day Brother Stewart Eccles, a thirty-two-year-old businessman, had an impression to visit Brother Lee. When he arrived, the secretary told him that Brother Lee was waiting to see him. This greatly surprised Stewart.

After a brief interview, Brother Lee instructed Stewart to put together some ideas on how the Church might organize to create employment opportunities for handicapped people and to accomplish certain purposes consistent with the original goals of welfare.

Brother Eccles was asked to go to California and spend time studying the Goodwill Industries operation. Ten days later he returned and submitted a three-page proposal to the Brethren. Not long after, he was authorized to begin collecting used items that could be refurbished and sold. The Brethren suggested that he contact Holgar M. Larsen, who lived in Paris, Idaho, and who had recently presided over the Danish Mission. Brother Larsen joined with Brother Eccles in establishing the first Deseret Industries store.

Deseret Industries was originally to be called Welfare Industries, but just before the stationery bearing the name was to be printed, President Heber J. Grant called Brother Harold B. Lee and said that he did not feel good about the name. He felt that the new operation should be called Deseret Industries. Brother Lee and Brother Eccles made the change immediately.

The first Deseret Industries store opened in Salt Lake City on 12 August 1938 in an old post office building that was obtained for minimal rent. It was located at 342 West 200 South. Initially, thirteen people were employed. During the first week of operation, 179 calls were received from persons wanting to donate goods. Brother Eccles began designing a workable system for handling the different kinds of items that were being contributed.

The first organized collection drive was conducted in Ensign Stake, and it wasn't long before the response of Church members caused the Deseret Industries to grow rapidly.

Courtesy of Deseret News

First Deseret Industries store, located in Salt Lake City, 1938

Courtesy of Deseret News

Stewart B. Eccles, manager of Deseret Industries, and Holgar M. Larsen, assistant manager, look over the first Deseret Industries truck, 1938

In the same month of August 1938, the First Presidency and Presiding Bishopric sent a letter to bishops and stake presidents to stimulate support of the new Deseret Industries operation:

"In a further effort to provide opportunities for individuals to become self-sustaining, there has been organized in the Salt Lake Region of the Church Welfare Plan a project to be known as Deseret Industries.

"We see great promise for this project if Stake and Ward workers will cooperate fully in stimulating an interest on the part of every homeowner within each Ward, member and non-members, to such an extent that they will be willing to give liberally of those articles that might have value in the Deseret Industries but [are] of little value to the present owner. We desire that this letter be read in your Sacrament Meeting on August 14, 1938, and that you give opportunity for a representative of your Stake or Ward Welfare Committee, or other designated person, to explain fully this

First Deseret Industries store in Los Angeles, California, 1939

proposed activity and that you do your utmost to give encouragement and enthusiastic support to this meritorious movement" (10 Aug. 1938).

Soon there were stores operating in Murray, Midvale, Tooele, Ogden, Logan, Provo, and Los Angeles.

The original Deseret Industries building on 200 South quickly reached its capacity. In 1940, the Brethren secured another building in the Sugarhouse area of Salt Lake City, at 2234 Highland Drive. This store is still in operation, even though a good portion of the building was destroyed by a fire not many years after it opened. At the time of the fire there were one hundred workers employed at the store. It was a bleak day for many of them, for they desperately needed their employment. Fortunately, most of these employees were absorbed into other welfare facilities or local businesses.

Stewart Eccles

Many feel that Stewart Eccles was the father of Deseret Industries. He became the first general manager of Deseret

Industries, originally asked to serve for six months. However, he held this position for thirty-three and one-half years until his retirement. He also became a member of the General Welfare Committee and traveled throughout the Church with General Authorities for many years.

Purposes of Deseret Industries

Deseret Industries was established to help people help themselves by encouraging independence rather than dependence, work rather than idleness. Deseret Industries is a nonprofit welfare enterprise built on the principles of thrift, work, giving, and sharing.

In keeping with these purposes, work opportunities are given to individuals who have found it almost impossible to find work on the open market because of physical, mental, and other disabilities, such as those associated with age, personality deficiencies, illness, and language differences. Many need to be rehabilitated and learn to take care of themselves. Employment policies were established at the outset so that able-bodied people would not eventually take over all of the work opportunities.

In the early days, the workers were paid a fixed wage, usually one-half in cash and the other half in commodities through the bishops' storehouse.

The bishops of the Church were notified that they could write bishop's orders on Deseret Industries stores in the same way they could on bishops' storehouses. Bishops have first claim on the items in Deseret Industries. They also have an obligation to teach members of the Church to contribute items that can be renovated and made usable for resale.

From the very beginning workers were urged to improve their working skills so that they could move into regular commercial employment and become self-sustaining. This would make room for others to develop skills. Some workers

Above: Women's
sewing depart-
ment, Deseret
Industries, 1939

Left: Deseret
Industries
upholstering
department, 1939

Below: Rug
making, Deseret
Industries, 1939

Lucas Venema, 82 years old, employed at Deseret Industries, 1939

have greater needs than their employment with Deseret Industries can meet. Bishops are then authorized to provide additional storehouse commodities to these people.

There has been constant pressure to employ more and more people at each of the Deseret Industries stores. One of the factors that limits the number of workers who can be hired is the volume of items contributed by Church members. As donations have increased, more Deseret Industries facilities have been built and an increasing number of needy members have been hired and blessed.

Deseret Industries Silver Anniversary

Few programs in Church welfare have affected the lives of people more than Deseret Industries. Twenty-five years after Deseret Industries was established, a silver anniversary celebration was held. On that occasion, President David O. McKay said:

"The Prophet Joseph Smith has repeatedly given us the assurance that the idler has no place in this Church. This meant all members of the Church, and we had those who

Deseret Industries shoe repair shop, 1939

were handicapped. These faithful people were praying for their golden opportunity to earn their bread by the sweat of their brow, their chance to hold their heads high as they made their own living.

"The inception of Deseret Industries, twenty-five years ago, filled their need. These industries also have brought something to do for many of our people whom private industry has called too old for gainful employment.

"In Deseret Industries, the individual's labors are fitted to his capacity for labor. Here, I am sure, are found some of the most happy people on the face of the earth. They are working, they are producing, and not accepting something for nothing in return."

ACTIVITIES IN SOUTHERN CALIFORNIA

It wasn't only in Salt Lake City that the Church welfare program was being used to care for the Saints. Things were happening in many other areas of the country, especially in the West where larger numbers of Church members lived.

For example, welfare help was greatly needed in southern California. Many members of the Church had moved there in the early part of the Depression to look for better work opportunities. Jobs were more available than in Utah, but many Latter-day Saints were unemployed.

In 1932, the Los Angeles Stake established a relief and employment office under the direction of the Adams Ward. This ward was in one of the areas hardest hit by the Depression. Every ward in the stake was asked to assist in finding employment for members. Work directors were appointed, and priesthood quorums and Relief Societies were involved in welfare activities. Some conducted clothing and furniture drives so that these items could be distributed to the needy.

From a history of the Los Angeles Stake comes the following:

"Initially, each ward provided the means for distributing clothing and furniture, but for better efficiency and service a bishops' storehouse was created in the old mission home. A

Long Beach California Bishops' Storehouse, 1940

storehouse was also created for food items, which initially were distributed at ward houses or from the homes of local leaders. At first anyone could come and select items from the storehouses, but as time progressed and abuses were noted it was decided that materials could be obtained only with an order from a bishop or a Relief Society president" (Chad M. Orton, *More Faith Than Fear: The Los Angeles Stake Story* [Salt Lake City: Bookcraft, 1987], p. 118; most of the following information about southern California comes from this book).

After the First Presidency announced the Church Security Plan in 1936, the Church leaders in southern California carried on as they had done for the previous three or four years. They had already implemented the mechanics of the welfare plan. They even had a Deseret Industries program in operation very soon:

"In March 1938, the Hollywood and Pasadena stakes opened a cooperative self-help salvage program in Glendale, which, by the end of the year, proved so successful that it was taken over as part of the Church's southern California welfare efforts and its scope expanded to include all the

Compton Ward, Long Beach Stake, canning pears, 1940

Hay in Chino Valley, California, 1938

Saints in Los Angeles. In October 1939, this effort of helping people to help themselves became the Deseret Industries of Southern California" (Orton, *More Faith Than Fear*, p. 118).

Various Relief Society groups organized canning projects as well as projects to grow fruits and vegetables. Many LDS physicians and dentists donated their services. The welfare work continued to grow through these efforts.

Food production and processing proved to be difficult in the urban setting, so in 1948 a stake sewing center was established in the former California mission home located next to the Adams Ward meetinghouse. This sewing center was soon called the "shirt factory" and became generally known throughout the welfare program. For many years it supplied men's and boys' shirts for distribution through bishops' storehouses. A woodworking shop was also established in the same area.

Soon after John M. Russon became president of the Los Angeles Stake, he and the presidents of the South Los Angeles and Inglewood Stakes felt that rather than have individual stake storehouses and other individual welfare

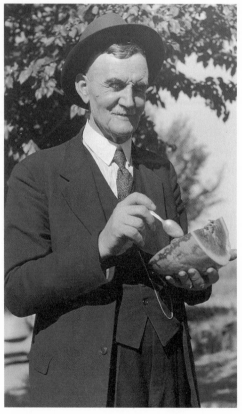

Above: Cannery
at Chino Valley,
California, built from
adobe bricks made on
the stake welfare
project, 1938

Left: Mark Austin,
member of General
Welfare Committee,
enjoying watermelon
in Chino Valley,
California, 1938

operations, they should have one central place to serve the needs of the entire Los Angeles area. They succeeded in finding an excellent piece of ground in east Los Angeles on Soto Street between Eleventh and Twelfth Streets. The priesthood leaders immediately began to develop one of the leading welfare centers in the Church. Within a year or so, Deseret Industries and all of the other welfare activities moved to the Soto Street property.

About this time, the ten stakes in southern California were organized into the Southern California Welfare Region. President Howard W. Hunter of the Pasadena Stake was appointed as regional chairman, with Presidents John M. Russon, Los Angeles Stake, and Noble B. Waite, South Los Angeles Stake, as vice chairmen.

The Perris Farm

With this strong leadership and a substantial welfare center on the Soto Street property, the priesthood leaders were very interested in purchasing either a regional welfare farm or individual stake welfare projects. At this time the leaders were asked to demonstrate their faith and commitment, as recorded in Howard W. Hunter's biography:

"With Church membership in Southern California growing rapidly, members were frequently asked to contribute to ward and stake building programs—and some regional ones as well. The first such request during Howard Hunter's administration came on Saturday, June 10, 1950, less than four months after he became a stake president. Presidents of the ten Southern California stakes were invited by telegram to meet with Elder Henry D. Moyle of the Quorum of the Twelve at a special meeting in Los Angeles.

" 'We wondered what could cause such an emergency,' Howard recalled, 'but when we got to the meeting, he explained that the Church had purchased the 503-acre horse ranch of Louis B. Mayer at Perris, California, from the estate of Ellsworth Statler for the sum of $450,000.' Elder Moyle said that the Church would sell the ranch to the stakes at cost if they could raise $100,000 as a down payment and pay the remainder over the next five years.

"The stake presidents discussed the proposal during a brief recess, then reported that they could raise the down payment in six months. That did not satisfy Elder Moyle. 'In his opinion, if we could not

Howard W. Hunter, president of Pasadena Stake and regional welfare chairman

raise it in a month, it was a lost cause,' Howard said. 'We talked it over again and decided to show him we could do it.'

"What happened next set the pattern for an even greater financial commitment to come. The stake presidents decided they would each write a check for what they considered to be their own individual fair share of the money to be raised. Then each of them called his counselors and high council members that night and asked them to do the same. At six o'clock the next morning the stake presidents met with bishops, who responded with their fair share, and the bishops in turn met with their own counselors, ward leaders, and priesthood members. By mid-afternoon that Sunday, representatives of the ten stakes had collected the money and wired the $100,000 to Elder Moyle. It arrived in Salt Lake City before he did" (Eleanor Knowles, *Howard W. Hunter* [Salt Lake City: Deseret Book Co., 1994], pp. 125–26).

This unity and faith demonstrated to everyone concerned that there were strong priesthood leaders and faithful Latter-day Saints in the greater southern California area.

The Perris property contained several guest cottages and a lovely ranch house. There were eleven barns containing horse stalls, a race track, a garage, a blacksmith shop, a paint shop, a machine shop, chicken coops, feed sheds, farmland, and all the equipment needed to operate the farm. It also had an extensive underground irrigation system, five wells, and thirty-five miles of fencing that had been installed at a cost of $10,444 per mile.

The Perris Farm was operated by the Saints for a number of years. It was felt after some years that it would be better for stakes to obtain individual projects closer to home, so this large property was sold at a fair profit. The money was then used to purchase a citrus grove and other welfare production projects. This project proved to the Brethren that, in this part of the Church, nothing was impossible.

The Perris Farm experience had far-reaching effects on many people. Many had faith-promoting, spiritual experiences in working on this huge project. President John

General Authorities at the dedication of Riverside, California, welfare farm, January 1952; left to right: Elder Henry D. Moyle, Elder Harold B. Lee, Elder Marion G. Romney, Bishop LeGrand Richards

Above: Women's
work center,
Wilshire Ward,
Los Angeles
Stake, 1940

Left: San Diego
California
Bishops'
Storehouse

Courtesy of R. H. Stone Studio

Russon felt that the project's importance extended far
beyond welfare work. He said that raising the $100,000 "was
the Lord's way of preparing the hearts of the people of
Southern California to respond to the request to help build
the kingdom. . . . I believe that that was the seed that
enabled us to have fertile ground in the hearts of the people
to gain their sustaining vote and have the overwhelming
success that we did when it came to raising the funds for the
temple . . . and had it not been for that and the faith of the
people demonstrating that they would respond and could
raise those sums of money, I don't think we would have had

the temple nearly as early as we did in the Los Angeles area" (quoted in Orton, *More Faith Than Fear,* p. 146).

Members of the General Welfare Committee and other Church leaders also expressed the opinion that through welfare activities, the members in southern California prepared themselves to receive the Los Angeles Temple.

Soto Street Cannery

In August of 1957, Elder Harold B. Lee was assigned to a conference in southern California. He took Glen L. Rudd with him, who had had considerable cannery experience. When they arrived they were met by President Howard W. Hunter who, with his associates, had spent much time discussing the need for another cannery in southern California. There were several small canneries in the area, but there was a great need for an all-purpose cannery with more capacity. President Hunter took the visitors to see a large, vacant building that could be purchased for about one-fourth of its real value.

Canning in San Diego, 1940

139

When they had toured the building, Brother Lee asked for their comments. Brother Rudd pointed out that the building was a fine financial purchase, but a tremendous amount of money would be required to convert it to a cannery. The floors would have to be changed. Electrical work would have to be redone. The existing ventilation would cause condensation on the rafters. A cannery had very specific requirements, and there were serious problems with considering this building for one. President Hunter, though he had his heart set on the building, said, "This is not the right building for our cannery."

The brethren discussed what could be done. After visiting the storehouse property on Soto Street, they decided that there was enough room there to build a large cannery and design it to meet all requirements and specifications of a modern cannery.

The cannery was built in 1958 under the direction of President Hunter and the other stake presidents in the welfare region. It was built primarily to can orange juice, although it was designed to handle many other products.

The character of President Howard W. Hunter surfaced those many years ago when he realized that the building he had located could not be put to practical use as a cannery. He changed his mind and sustained those who counseled him. He later led the welfare workers in southern California as they erected one of the finest canneries in the Church.

ACTIVITIES IN ARIZONA

Many welfare projects and storehouses were established in the western states, bringing blessings to the lives of thousands of people. The efforts of priesthood leaders in Arizona are typical of what was happening in many other places.

Almost immediately after the Church welfare program was announced by the First Presidency, the presidents of the stakes in Arizona and other priesthood leaders began to establish welfare production projects.

In the northern part of the state, they established cattle ranches and a hog project that for many years furnished beef and pork to the storehouses. Oranges and grapefruit were produced in large quantities in the Mesa and Yuma areas. Yuma still produces grapefruit for the storehouse system. A large dairy project was brought into the Church program in Chandler, Arizona, and it produced milk for the welfare program for a number of years. Wheat was also produced on several projects.

A cotton farm of approximately one-hundred acres was purchased by the Mesa, Maricopa, and Phoenix stakes. This farm required a great amount of work, and the people of the wards and stakes were very faithful in filling assignments. Sometimes as many as one-hundred workers were out in the fields doing the tedious and difficult work. The cotton that was produced was sold, and the cash was used to buy cotton commodities for the storehouses.

Donated labor and equipment on the St. Joseph, Arizona,
stake welfare farm, 1940s

Left: Oldest cotton picker on the job, Maricopa Arizona Stake, 1940

Below: Weighing cotton picked by elders quorum, Maricopa Arizona Stake, 1940

Along with the production projects, the stakes established many small storehouses during the first years of the welfare program. In the early 1940s, when a larger regional storehouse was needed, the members in the Mesa area built a beautiful new storehouse, complete with all facilities.

There was a unique sister involved in the welfare work in Mesa. Sister Clara Emmett, dressed in her overalls, worked side by side with the brethren in the construction of the new regional welfare center. She became the manager of all the storehouse facilities under the direction of the priesthood

Maricopa stake welfare council, 1940

leaders. Sister Emmett was busy in community and political activities, but her real love was the welfare program. For twenty-five years, she managed the welfare facilities in Mesa. Many General Welfare Committee members had the privilege of visiting in that storehouse and knew from personal experience that Sister Emmett was one of the finest storehouse managers in the welfare program.

Brother Harold Wright, president of the Maricopa Arizona Stake for twenty-two and one-half years, was the regional welfare chairman during those early years of welfare.

G E M S   O F   P U R E   R E L I G I O N

♦ ♦ ♦

Concern about Helping Nonmembers

Bishop Rudy Luckau, of the Fifth Ward of the Temple View Stake, came to visit me on one occasion. He seemed distressed over something he had done as a bishop concerning the storehouse. He said that one night he answered a knock at the door of his home to find a gentleman who was a minister of a local congregation. The man said that he and his family were desperately in need of food. Bishop Luckau invited him in and gave him some of his own food and some money and said he would meet him in the morning. The next morning, after interviewing him, Bishop Luckau gave the man a bishop's order to get enough food for his family for a week or so. In his usual manner Bishop Luckau counseled the man and sent him on his way.

A few days later Bishop Luckau got nervous about distributing welfare commodities to a nonmember. That is when he came to see me. I suggested to him that if he felt okay about it when he wrote the order, he should not second guess his decision, but be at ease.

I discussed this matter with Elder Harold B. Lee the next day. Elder Lee said, "Tell Bishop Luckau to look to the scriptures." He turned to 2 Nephi 26:33 and read the verse, "He inviteth them all to come unto him and partake of his goodness; and he denieth none that come unto him, black and white, bond and free, male and female." Elder Lee felt very comfortable about what had happened and said that more of our bishops ought to reach out and help those who come to them.

The Sacred Cow

A young family moved into the San Jose area. They had a small amount of land and decided to get their children a calf so they could learn to care for it. However, as the calf grew, she started eating more, including the flowers, and the family decided that the calf should have a bigger home. But the children didn't want anything bad to happen to their cow. The father decided to donate it to Deseret Industries with the stipulation that it be taken to a good home. Someone said that he could take the cow to Sacramento in a truck, and a veterinarian in the Sacramento area said he would check her over. He found that she was just "ready to go into season."

In the meantime, Brother Turley, the Deseret Industries unit manager, started calling the regional agents in the area to see if they had any use for a cow. Within a few hours, one of the agents called back with an exciting story. One of the bishops he had contacted had been visited the week before by a concerned father. He had three young sons and very much wanted these boys to go on missions, but there was no way he could raise the money to do this unless he could get a cow, sell the milk, raise and sell the calves, and save the money he earned. He had about ten acres of land and could feed the animals. The bishop couldn't believe that a cow had been donated, the father was very pleased, and the cow not only found a loving home but helped to send three boys on missions.

Blue Creek Grain Project in northern Utah, early 1950s. President J. Reuben Clark, Jr. (seated at wheel of grain combine); left to right: Elder Harold B. Lee, Elder Henry D. Moyle, Bishop Joseph L. Wirthlin, Elder Marion G. Romney

CHAPTER 6
PRODUCTION PROJECTS

ANNUAL PRODUCTION BUDGETS

During each of the first five years of the welfare program, Brother Harold B. Lee, managing director of the Church welfare program, Brother Roscoe Eardley, supervisor of all storehouses, and other general committee members visited in each welfare region to discuss with regional leaders their ability to produce certain storehouse items. Stakes at that time were urged to have some kind of a welfare project to produce storehouse goods.

Bishops throughout the Church were requested to estimate the welfare needs of their ward members for the coming year. These estimates, based on past experience and present conditions, were compiled by each stake and submitted to the General Welfare Committee. Using this information, the committee, assisted by the General Relief Society Presidency and Presiding Bishopric, compiled the total welfare needs for the Church for the coming year. This was known as the annual production budget. A certain portion of the budget was to be supplied by each welfare region.

The general committee usually did not tell a stake what its project should be. Rather, each year each region was given an assignment to produce a certain quantity of food, clothing, or other items of value during the following year for the storehouses of the Church. The executive committee of the regional council would receive this assignment and would then make specific assignments to each stake according to ability. A meeting in each stake was held annually with all priesthood and Relief Society members, at which time they formally received their assignment for the coming year.

After receiving its annual production budget, each stake had the responsibility to fulfill its assignment as close to 100 percent as possible. If stakes failed to produce enough of a commodity, stake presidents would raise funds and give the money to the storehouse system so that items could be purchased.

In the early days of the welfare program, the annual assignments were almost always enthusiastically received because priesthood leaders felt strongly about the purposes of the welfare program. They wanted to know what they could do to help, and they gladly accepted their labor and commodity assignments.

The following are sample production assignments given to some of the stakes of the Salt Lake Region in 1941:

Stake	Commodity
Highland	30,000 pounds of cereal and $1,000 in cash
Liberty	200 cases of bar soap
	200 cases of Sopo (powdered soap)
North Davis	12 acres of sugar beets
	10 acres of tomatoes
	2 acres of onions
	Surplus fruits and vegetables
	1 beef or 4 veal
Oquirrh	5 tons of baled hay
	10 acres of wheat and straw
	5 acres of peas
	100 bushels of apples
	20 mutton
	12 hogs
	4 beef or 16 veal

Pioneer	20 acres of beets
	5 acres of garden produce
	500 rabbits
	Poultry project management
Riverside	100 hogs
Salt Lake	100 hogs
South Davis	5 acres of garden produce
	Surplus fruits and berries
	50 hogs
	1 beef or four veal
Tooele	30 sacks of beans
	500 bushels of wheat
	5 acres of potatoes
	50 mutton
	50 hogs
	5 beef or 20 veal
	1,000 chickens (to raise)
Wells	$2,000 in processed building materials

Hardy, healthy, happy hogs having a hearty, hopeful holiday before heading for hog harvest, 1940; Salt Lake Stake hog project

West Jordan   1,000 bushels of wheat
21 acres of barley
90 tons of straw
25 tons of hay
150 tons of beets
5 acres of peas
10 hogs

For many years Elder Marion G. Romney went to regions throughout the Church to give production assignments to priesthood leaders. He was accompanied by Brother Irvin Nydegger, a staff member, who worked full time supervising the rather complicated system of the annual production budgets.

The Brethren did not want to give cash assignments. However, once in a while this was necessary because stakes were unable to produce some items needed in bishops' store-

Rockville Ward of Zion Park Stake, southern Utah, clearing and planting sixty acres of grain, 27 September 1940

Above:
Juab-Nebo Sawmill,
Santaquin Canyon,
central Utah, 1938

Right: Santaquin-
Tintic Welfare
Sewing and
Canning Center

Portland Oregon Cannery; salmon fresh and in cans, 1940; left to right: Elmer Stoddard, Terrill I. Deck, Dr. Paul B. Firth, George L. Scott, president of Portland Oregon Stake

Clothing department, Provo Utah Regional Bishops' Storehouse, 1940

Hurricane Utah Cannery, 1940; 35,000 cans of fruit
were canned in three weeks

houses. Cash could be obtained from a crop that was produced and sold; then items could be purchased and submitted to fulfill an assignment in lieu of a production
commodity. The Brethren wanted to eliminate any welfare
assignment that resulted in cash coming into the storehouse. It was more important to get usable commodities for
storehouse distribution and canning.

The year 1941 marked the first time that every stake in
the Salt Lake Region was able to fulfill its annual production
budget. This represented substantial progress over the previous four or five years when many stakes could contribute
only cash because they did not have production projects.

For many years the General Welfare Committee published an annual report which, among other things, listed
the assigned production items for the entire Church. The
1946 report contained the assignments for the following
year. Assignments included 84 different food items, 9 household supply items, 13 types of drugs and sundries, 6 furni-

Above:
Welfare Square
Cannery, 1938
or 1939

Left: Early
sewing center

ture and wood items, 2 types of fuel (coal and wood), and 36 clothing items. Among the drugs and sundries were castor oil and vitamin C pills. Miscellaneous items assigned included hides for shoes, rendered tallow, and some concrete and cinder blocks. A most interesting assignment was to produce 282 caskets. Some of these caskets were in storehouses for many years. It appears that no other assignments for caskets were ever made.

Picking beans, Seattle Washington Stake, 1959

Opening of Mt. Timpanogos Regional Storehouse in 1957.
Left to right: Mark B. Garff, Elder Clifford E. Young,
Elder Harold B. Lee, President J. Reuben Clark, Jr.,
President Phil Jensen

WELFARE PRODUCTION PROJECTS

In order to fill the shelves of the many bishops' storehouses, over the years the Brethren have urged stakes and wards to produce as many items as possible. In this spirit of self-reliance, many welfare production projects have been developed. Stake and ward leaders have generally been anxious to be involved in these projects, providing the strong leadership that is needed for the projects to be successful.

Today stake leaders usually give production assignments to bishops, and then bishops make assignments to priesthood quorum and group leaders and Relief Society leaders. Most production projects require careful organization and the faithful service of many willing Church members.

The welfare program has many production projects, of which the following are representative examples.

Potatoes

Through the years there have been many potato projects assigned. Before potatoes can be put on the tables of the needy, much work has to be accomplished. First, proper farmland must be made available. It is then leveled and pre-

Potato cellar, Ogden, Utah

Visiting a potato cellar, 1940. Left to right: Mark Austin;
President Heber J. Grant; President J. Reuben Clark, Jr.;
Sister Luacine Clark; Elder Reed Smoot, Elder Albert E. Bowen

pared for planting. After planting, the potatoes are culti-
vated and watered and otherwise cared for until harvest
time. Then large numbers of faithful Latter-day Saint youth
and adults go into the fields to bag and load the potatoes
and transport them to the storehouse root cellar. Next, the
potatoes are graded and packaged and put in the storehouse
for distribution. Then the bishop, assisted by the Relief
Society president, writes an order for a few pounds of potatoes for a needy family. Finally, the storehouse has to restock
its potato supply. After this long process of faith, organization, encouragement, and hard work, the potatoes become
part of the meals of grateful families.

Texas Peanut Butter

Since 1955 the welfare program has had a peanut
butter project in Texas. Like all agriculture, growing and
harvesting peanuts requires much effort by the Saints.

The original peanut but-
ter cannery in Texas was
housed in an old theater in
Bay Town. The building had
been given to the Church
by Brother Howard E.
Brunson, the owner. After
the building was cleaned
and remodeled and equip-
ment was installed, mem-
bers used it to produce
peanut butter for the storehouses of the Church.

For years this cannery
was kept busy processing
many thousands of cans of
peanut butter. In the earlier
years, about one-quarter of

**Hopper and grinders at peanut
butter cannery in Houston, Texas**

the cans were processed by individuals and families for their
family food storage programs and the rest went to the welfare system. In later years, the family canning has increased
to include half of all the cans produced.

In the late 1980s, a modern new cannery was built in
Houston. It is now in full operation under the direction of a
stake president assigned to the project. The members in all
of the stakes in the region are given the opportunity to work
in the cannery. Using new equipment and modern tech-
niques, the cannery produces about 200,000 jars of peanut
butter annually for the welfare system.

Brother Fred Turk helped to establish the peanut butter
project. He worked with it for twenty-four years as a high
councilor, as a member of the stake presidency, and again as
a high councilor. He continued to serve faithfully for some
time afterward in this important project.

Liberty Stake Soap Project

One of the longest run-
ning production projects in
the Church is the soap
factory that was originally
operated by members of
Liberty Stake in Salt Lake
City.

In 1935 Brother Max O.
Stange, a member of the
Liberty Stake who later
became the bishop of the
Second Ward, purchased a

Products of Liberty Stake soap factory, 1940

small soap manufacturing business and operated it for about
four years. This was during the depths of the Depression,
and he barely managed to make a living from his efforts.

Faithful to instructions from the Brethren, the presidency of Liberty Stake wanted to develop some type of welfare project to help supply the bishops' storehouse. They
discussed this desire with Brother Stange, who expressed his
willingness to give his business to the welfare program and
stay on as the manager, working under the direction of the
stake welfare committee.

On 16 May 1939 this business officially became the soap
production project of the welfare plan and was known as the
Liberty Products Company. Bishop Stange continued as
manager for the next thirty-three years until he retired.
During that time he traveled to Europe to purchase modern
equipment. Today much of the operation is computerized.

As the needs of the Church grew, the General Welfare
Committee felt that other stakes should be involved in the
Liberty Products Company. Therefore, Park, Sugarhouse, and
Wells Stakes, and later the Central Stake, were combined

Packaging soap products, 1940

with Liberty Stake to expand the project into a regional effort. The name was changed to the Deseret Soap Company. This successful welfare project has been an opportunity for many welfare recipients and volunteers to make a worthwhile contribution.

During the first years of its operation, the project produced hand soap, laundry bar soap, hand cleaner, and laundry flakes. As the ability to make the products increased, additional items were added, such as bleach, bowl cleaner, cleanser, hair shampoo, hand bar soap, laundry detergent, and liquid dish detergent. At one time liquid bubble bath, water softener, powdered hand cleaner, and liquid hand soap were also produced.

For many years the region made assignments to the various stakes and wards for the workers needed. However, for the last several years the region has made few work assignments because the work is done adequately by many needy individuals and families being assisted by their bishops.

Some of the people who take care of the sophisticated equipment are paid employees, but the great bulk of the work is done by welfare recipients and other volunteers.

On 11 October 1972, an open house was held to honor Bishop Max O. Stange for his many years of service. Hundreds of people attended, including Elder Mark E. Petersen, who at one time was a member of the Liberty Stake presidency.

In 1972 Max L. Bramall was a young man working in the bishops' storehouse at Welfare Square as an accountant in the office. His leaders felt that he needed a challenge and that he might be able to learn quickly how to manage the soap factory. He accepted the assignment and worked closely with Max Stange for a while before taking over the management. Brother Bramall supervised and improved the work of the factory over the next several decades. It is interesting to

Bishop Max O. Stange retires as manager of Deseret Soap Company, October 1972. Center: Sister Stange, Bishop Stange; rear, left to right: President Don R. Earl; Max Bramall, project manager; President Nicholas J. Teerlink; President Louis Roos; President Henry H. Andersen

note that for over sixty years, there were only two managers of this project—both named Max.

Many other individuals have contributed to the success of the soap factory. Brother Alfred Lieber, a chemist and a convert, arrived from Switzerland in 1949 and was invited to become the chemist for the project. He served in that capacity until he passed away. His son, who is also a chemist, continued to make suggestions and to assist in the production of soap products.

Over the years the project has provided the poor and needy with adequate quantities and varieties of much needed cleaning products.

Deseret Coal Mine

In the early 1940s, most homes in Utah were heated by coal stoves or furnaces. The Orangeville Stake in Emery County, Utah, led by President J. Frank Killian, began a small coal mine project to provide coal for needy stake members. As the project grew, it began shipping a few truckloads of coal to the bishops' storehouse in Salt Lake City for the new welfare program. This humble effort was the beginning of a necessary and successful Church welfare production project.

The First Presidency, assisted by Elders Harold B. Lee, Henry D. Moyle, and Marion G. Romney, were most anxious to provide coal to the needy in the Church through the new welfare system. Leonard Adams, president of the Spring Canyon Coal Company, was called to be a member of the General Welfare Committee, and in 1942, he spearheaded the inclusion of the Orangeville Stake coal project in the Church welfare program. The project was renamed the Deseret Coal Mine.

Brother Shirl C. McArthur was appointed as the manager of the coal mine and served for approximately thirty years. He had the support and respect of the General Authorities

General Authorities and General Welfare Committee members at
Deseret Coal Mine, Emery County, Utah, 1940

and members of the General Welfare Committee. He made an outstanding contribution to the welfare program, not only because of his skill and leadership in running the coal mine, but because of his great spirituality. His employees were all faithful Church members and regular temple patrons.

Stewart B. Eccles and Roscoe W. Eardley coordinated the delivery of the coal to bishops' storehouses throughout the western states. Later, Arben O. Clark, of the general Welfare Office, was given these responsibilities. Charles Knighton was responsible for the movement of coal trucks to and from various storehouses.

The Brethren assigned three stake presidents the responsibility of furnishing the labor at the coal mine and helping in its operation. They were President Cecil Broadbent of the North Carbon Stake, President Elton Taylor of the Carbon Stake, and President Eldon G. Luke of the Emery Stake.

Many bishops' storehouses had sizable amounts of coal storage and were able to provide coal to members in need. Sometimes individuals would take a bishop's order to the

Coal at stake storehouse, 1940

storehouse and pick up the needed coal. Occasionally, store-houses were able to deliver coal directly to homes.

For many years the mine served large numbers of families and meetinghouses throughout Utah, Idaho, Nevada, and northern Arizona. The hospitals owned by the Church, Brigham Young University, some temples, and several other facilities also used the coal.

In the early 1970s, because the use of coal for heating homes and facilities had diminished, the Church sold the Deseret Coal Mine to Utah Power and Light Company with the provision that the Church would have access to all the coal it needed in the welfare program in the future.

Deseret Bakery

In 1945, while Carl W. Beuhner was serving as president of Granite Stake in Salt Lake City, someone donated to the stake some equipment from a bakery that was no longer in use. President Beuhner and his counselors felt that they should establish a welfare production project to furnish the bishops' storehouses with bread.

They rented a building on south State Street in Salt Lake City, and the Granite Stake Bakery was born. It was one of the few projects in the Church that processed farm commodities rather than producing them. Flour was received from the Church flour mill, and bread assignments were filled. One man was employed full-time as a baker, and several other people from the stake worked as volunteers.

The bread was very much needed in some of the storehouses in the Salt Lake Valley. At one time, there was some debate about whether bread should even be in the storehouses. Some people felt that families should bake their own. However, the General Welfare Committee recognized that there were widows, older men, and other individuals who could not possibly do their own baking. Therefore, the bakery became a welfare production project.

Courtesy of *Deseret News*/J. M. Heslop

Glen L. Rudd, Elder Harold B. Lee, and Elder Marion G. Romney
present a birthday cake to Elder Henry D. Moyle on his 70th birthday,
April 1959; cake made by Deseret Bakery

When W. Howard Allen served as president of Granite Stake, the bakery was moved to the center of the stake, into a building on Seventh East. Spencer H. Osborn was closely associated with the bakery during the years he served as a counselor in the stake presidency and then as stake president. To date, there have been at least nine stake presidents involved in this project.

Part of the bakery was eventually made into a commercial operation, but the major portion was retained to produce the increasing quantities of bread needed for the storehouses. New and upgraded equipment was added, and the bakery was enlarged, making it very modern. The commercial portion of the bakery was discontinued in 1983.

In 1986 the bakery was moved to Welfare Square and renamed Deseret Bakery. It can now produce 3,000 loaves of bread daily for the storehouse system. The project has a limited number of paid employees and requires volunteer labor.

Approximately 7,000 hours of labor are donated yearly by members of the Salt Lake Riverside Stake, which now supervises the bakery. The bakery produces approximately 387,000 loaves of white and whole wheat bread each year.

Sugar Beets

In April of 1936 President Heber J. Grant sent a letter to stake presidencies and bishoprics requesting that each ward in the Church begin to produce sugar beets if able to do so. He gave detailed instructions about how to proceed. Part of the purpose of this request was to furnish employment for the unemployed. (See appendix D for a copy of this letter.)

Many stakes and wards responded and began to produce sugar beets on local farms. Sugar beets were successfully raised in Utah, Salt Lake, Davis, Weber, Box Elder, and Cache counties. Many faith-promoting stories came from the Saints' united efforts. The following story is one example.

Above: Workers on a sugar beet project, Wellsville Ward, Hyrum Stake, Cache Valley, Utah

Right: Harvesting sugar beets, Wellsville Ward, 1940

President Paul C. Child wrote a short history of the beginning of the welfare program in Pioneer Stake and recorded that as a result of President Grant's letter, the stake presidency felt they should grow some sugar beets on the farm they had near Thirteenth South. They wanted to sell the beets for cash to use in the welfare program. The city agreed to give them free water.

The stake president, Harold B. Lee, sent some soil samples to Utah State Agricultural College in Logan, Utah. The college reported that the soil was not suitable for the produc-

Stake and ward authorities inspecting welfare crop in Cache Valley,
Utah; President Alma Sonne on the right

tion of sugar beets. However, the brethren felt that if President Grant wanted sugar beets they should go ahead and plant them. This they did. They plowed the property, prepared the soil, and worked long, hard hours. Then President Lee invited the high council to a meeting at the farm. President Lee made a few remarks. Then, President Child reported, "we prayed unto the Lord that He would bless our efforts and bless the soil that it would yield abundantly. Following this we set about to further prepare the soil for seeding, etc. We cared for our crops as well as we knew how and when the harvest time came, imagine our joy as we harvested these beautiful beets, many weighing from 20 to 25 pounds!" (Paul C. Child, "Physical Beginning of the Church Welfare Program," *BYU Studies,* Spring 1974, p. 384).

Wells Stake Tannery and Leather Factory

In 1946 the presidency of Wells Stake in Salt Lake City were invited to a meeting with Elder Harold B. Lee. Elder Lee asked them if they would be willing to build a tannery to produce leather for the welfare program. Another stake had tried the project and failed. Wells Stake accepted the assignment, and in 1946 President Fred W. Schwendiman and his counselors, Nicholas J. Teerlink and Clarence E. Schank, helped to establish a welfare project to tan hides and prepare fine leather.

About this time, Brother J. Lowell Fox, who had studied the process of tanning leather hoping to make it his business, needed financial backing to get started. Elder Lee asked Brother Fox if he would consider tanning leather for the Church and working under the direction of the Wells Stake. Brother Fox accepted, and the tannery project began its operation.

Sometime later, Brother Fox wrote about what he called a miracle:

"We have experienced many blessings at our welfare tannery. Let me tell you of a miracle which happens there every

Wells Stake Leather Factory, Salt Lake City; members of the stake presidency and stake welfare committee

weekend. It was brought to our attention the day following our first holiday. (At this time it was not recognized as a miracle.)

"Upon returning to the tannery after the holiday the hides being processed were spoiled, and we wondered what caused it. A careful check was made to see if these hides had been handled in a different way. They had been washed, cleaned, cut, and placed into large vats filled with lime water where they were to stay for four days. At the end of this time the hair would come loose from the skins.

"On regular work days the hides were removed from the vats every twelve hours, the solution strengthened with fresh lime, stirred thoroughly, and the hides returned to the lime solution. This had not been done over the holiday. However, the change was never made on Sundays, and we had never found spoiled hides on Monday morning. That could not be the trouble! There seemed to be no reason for the spoiled hides.

"All went well at the tannery until the next holiday when the incident repeated itself. Once more the hides spoiled. Not understanding why, we wrote the Technical Institution of New York to help us solve our problem. They verified the fact that while hides are soaking in the lime solution they must be stirred several times each day in order to keep them from spoiling during the time the hair is being loosened; they must be taken from the vats every twelve hours, while fresh lime is added to the solution.

"This brought a strange fact to our minds: holidays are determined by man, and on these days just as on every week day, the hides need to have special care every twelve hours. Sunday is the day set aside by the Lord as a day of rest, and He makes it possible for us to rest from our labors as He has commanded. The hides at the tannery never spoil on Sundays. This is a modern-day miracle, a miracle that hap-

Courtesy of *Church News*

Leaders of Wells Stake examine samples of shoes produced in
the new factory; left to right: Clarence E. Schank, President Fred W.
Schwendiman, Nicholas J. Teerlink, J. Lowell Fox, Ingerman H.
Bendtsen, Joseph W. Anderson, Frank O. Green

pens every weekend!" (*Handbook for Guide Patrol Leaders*
[Primary manual, 1964], p. 37).

The tannery had the ability to produce leather of excellent grade and texture according to specifications. The
chrome method of tanning was used. The process of producing finished leather took thirty days and required thirty-
two steps.

The tannery primarily processed deer and cow hides from
Utah and four surrounding states. After a period of time
there was a large stockpile of fine leather waiting to be used
in the welfare program.

In July of 1955 the Wells Stake also created a small factory, located at 3057 South State Street in Salt Lake City, to
produce leather goods, primarily shoes. They made shoes of
excellent quality and style for men, women, and children.
These were distributed through the bishops' storehouses.
The factory also produced gloves, brick pads, work aprons,
and other leather items.

171

The leather factory was under the management of Brother Ingerman H. Bendtsen, a convert to the Church from Denmark. His crew consisted of four men and five women who operated the machines and produced the needed leather articles.

The stake sent Brother Bendtsen back to Denmark to purchase new sewing machines and other needed equipment. The Lord blessed him in his assignment, and the equipment came into the United States duty free.

The factory had a daily capacity of 150 pairs of shoes. The workers were able to make a very good quality white shoe that could be used by temple workers. The shoe production prospered for a time but was eventually discontinued. Church leaders felt that the welfare program could purchase shoes and thereby get more variety in style and size than could be produced in the factory.

This factory operated for only a few years. When the Church was no longer in need of leather and leather goods in the storehouse system, Elder Henry D. Moyle went to the Wells Stake conference and released the stake from its assignment with the tannery and leather factory. The project was sold to the employees as a commercial venture.

Deseret Pasta Plant

Since 1963 the Church has maintained a plant to produce pasta products. The plant has generally been known as the "noodle factory." One of the stakes in Kearns, Utah, purchased a small macaroni factory located near the Denver and Rio Grande Railroad depot on the west side of Salt Lake City. The pasta plant had one paid employee and several volunteers until the storehouse demands began to outgrow the capacities of the equipment and space.

In 1977 a piece of property and a building at 5405 West 4700 South were purchased. The building was enlarged to enable it to house a modern pasta operation. Brother Artie J. Henderson, a volunteer in the original plant, became a full-time employee in 1977 and worked for many years in that capacity.

The pasta plant uses products from other welfare projects. For example, durum hard wheat is raised on a welfare production project in Montana. For the last twenty-five years this wheat has been sent to the Church's mill in Kaysville, Utah, to be made into semolina flour. The flour is then delivered to the pasta plant to be made into pasta products.

At the present time spaghetti, macaroni, lasagna, noodles, and the alphabet letters for a dry soup mix are produced at the pasta plant. The rest of the ingredients in the soup mix are purchased and mixed with the alphabet letters. The pasta products and soup mix are distributed to Church canneries to be packaged for the storehouse system and to be used in family dry-pack canning.

In 1980 the old machinery was replaced by modern equipment. The plant is large enough to meet all the Church

Drying ovens at Deseret Pasta Plant

welfare needs. It has the capability to expand to meet future production needs.

This plant provides work opportunities for many welfare recipients and other volunteers. There are five full-time employees and one part-time employee. The plant operates three shifts a day, between 8:00 A.M. and 10:00 P.M. Eleven volunteers work on each shift. They come from two regions that have a total of 17 stakes and 104 wards. One of the stake presidents is the agent stake president. The project is in the Kearns East Stake and currently operates under the overall direction of the Kearns East Stake presidency. The pasta products are an important addition to the storehouses throughout the entire Church.

INTERNATIONAL WELFARE PROJECTS

Initially, welfare projects were developed primarily in areas of the western United States where large numbers of Latter-day Saints lived. However, it was not long before many local leaders, both inside and outside the United States, established small welfare production projects to meet the needs of their members. These leaders felt that they should put their people to work to produce their own welfare commodities. The General Welfare Committee was not involved in these projects, and no official record was made of them, so we do not know how much was produced and distributed. Undoubtedly, thousands of dollars worth of commodities were distributed to needy members through these kinds of projects.

In the late 1970s the General Welfare Committee sent representatives to visit some of the international welfare projects in areas such as Mexico, England, and the Pacific. The representatives were instructed to answer members' questions and to assist them in the production projects they had or those they desired to establish and operate.

Above:
Welfare farm
in Melbourne,
Australia,
1978

Right: Orange
grove, Sydney
Australia Stake
project, 1978

In Australia the Church acquired six welfare projects. One was in the Melbourne area, where a fifty-acre farm, operated by one stake, was used for year-round intensive gardening. Another was a fifty-acre project near Melbourne operated by another stake. Another project was in Brisbane, where a concerted effort was made to find a good farm. As a result, a 2.6-acre plot of fertile ground was obtained right in the middle of one of the stakes. People could walk to this farm, and it became a very productive vegetable garden, producing crops throughout the year. Even though it was small, this farm was considered a very successful welfare project.

Harvesting prawns grown on a welfare project in Laie, Hawaii

The Sydney Stake had a grove of about sixty acres of producing orange trees. Some vegetables were grown, but the main emphasis was oranges for use in the greater Sydney area. This project had plenty of water and expert help and was successful for many years. In the south part of Sydney, another large parcel of land was purchased, the land was cleared, and more than twenty-five acres were put into good production.

Priesthood leaders all over Australia were enthusiastic about these welfare production projects.

In New Zealand, the Church acquired seven production projects and put them into operation. The one that proved to be the most successful was a ten-acre fruit orchard near the city of Hastings, the best fruit-growing area in the country. This project is still active and receives good care.

In Hawaii the Church managed an eighty-acre farm of corn and other vegetables as a welfare project. Even though it required a considerable amount of labor, it was very successful. Much of the produce was distributed through the bishops' storehouse in Honolulu. The Saints were delighted with the opportunity to produce in behalf of others. They also had seven large ponds in which they grew prawns. The prawns were harvested and sold commercially, and the money was used to help further welfare work. Since sales of welfare-produced commodities on the open market has been discontinued, the prawn project is no longer operated.

The Church also operated two or three projects in Samoa that grew coconuts and other crops.

In Tonga, three welfare production farms produced commodities. On the island of Eua, about four hours by boat from the main island of Tonga, the Church owned a large welfare farm. On Monday mornings, a large group of men and boys would leave their homes in Nuku'alofa and travel

**Elder Harold B. Lee visiting welfare project in
Hawaii, 1945**

Above: Welfare project in Eua, Tonga, 1977

Left: Preparing coconuts on welfare project, Tonga, 1977

by boat to Eua, where they would work until Friday afternoon. They would then take home boat loads of produce for the Saints on the main island. Because the produce was harvested year round, there was no need for the type of bishops' storehouse used in the United States. The fresh commodities were regularly distributed to the needy and other members of the Church. This was one of the most productive welfare projects that the Church has had.

In England, the Church had a three-hundred-acre dairy and sheep farm. One-hundred dairy cows produced milk, which was processed by a local dairy. The bishops' storehouse then distributed milk products to those in need.

Church members thoughout the world want to be an active part of the welfare work of the Church in order to serve their needy brothers and sisters. Over the next years, many more welfare projects will undoubtedly be developed for the benefit and blessing of Church members in all parts of the world.

JOSEPH L. WIRTHLIN

For many years, the leaders of Church welfare felt that every stake should be involved in some way in producing items used in bishops' storehouses. Sometimes two or three stakes would combine efforts on a project. Brother Henry D. Moyle in particular worked hard to get everyone involved. Members of the General Welfare Committee traveled throughout the Church urging participation in welfare projects.

Joseph L. Wirthlin,
Presiding Bishop

Bishop Joseph L. Wirthlin, a Counselor to Bishop LeGrand Richards and then the Presiding Bishop himself, was a most valiant and active worker in assisting stakes with their projects. He was interested in all projects, but particularly in those that produced cattle and other animal products. Bishop Wirthlin was energetic and willing to travel and help the local people with their problems. In a quiet, unassuming way, he gave willingly of his expertise and time.

Even after he was released as the Presiding Bishop, he supervised and assisted cattle ranches and other projects as a special assignment from the Brethren.

GEMS OF PURE RELIGION

✦ ✦ ✦

A Scrawny Calf

"A member of the Thirty-second Ward [in Salt Lake City] turned in a calf to the Storehouse which was underfed. It was in very poor condition and the Storehouse, not wanting to refuse the contribution, accepted it gratefully, still wondering what to do with it.

"Bishop Tingey of the Centerville First Ward happened to be in the Storehouse and told us that he would be willing to give us twenty dollars worth of produce in kind for the calf although the calf was not worth a fourth of that amount.

"We gladly accepted his offer and he took the calf to his farm and cared for it. However, the calf grew into a first-class milk cow and became one of the best cows on his farm. Bishop Tingey claimed that this was a blessing which came to him because he was willing to take the calf off our hands and turn it into real value of produce for us."

Jesse M. Drury, *For These My Brethren* (reprint, 1991), p. 50

✦ ✦ ✦

Who Will Wear the Work of My Hands?

Who will wear the work of my hands, I say
As I sew on our welfare assignment today.
Lord, help me to make it plain and neat,
And think of thy children precious and sweet
Who will come in need and ask for clothes,
And will wear the work of my hands.
In humility I ask of Thee—
Guide my heart, my hands and see
That I never find fault or complain
Because of the work that may yet remain

For the less fortunate souls
Who will wear the work of my hands.
Perhaps tomorrow I'll be one to receive,
Then I will know and truly believe
That by the welfare plan are we blessed,
And I'll want to know I have done my best
In my sewing assignments—
I now wear the work of my hands.

Anonymous Relief Society Sister

Top: Inside Dallas Texas Bishops' Storehouse
Bottom: Storehouse, cannery, and employment office in Dallas, Texas

CHAPTER 7

EXPANSION OF WELFARE
FACILITIES

In 1976 the First Presidency (Presidents Spencer W. Kimball, N. Eldon Tanner, and Marion G. Romney) and the Presiding Bishopric (Bishops Victor L. Brown, H. Burke Peterson, and Vaughn J. Featherstone) decided that it was time to expand the physical facilities of the welfare program throughout the United States and into parts of Canada. The welfare program at that time was forty years old and was well established in the western part of the United States. There was a storehouse in El Paso, Texas, and one in Denver, Colorado, but there was nothing farther east.

President Ezra Taft Benson said at the April 1977 welfare session of general conference: "A bishops' storehouse should be made available to every bishop. At the present time, the General Welfare Committee is initiating an expansion program to establish more production and processing projects and to build more storehouses" (*Ensign,* May 1977, p. 83).

There were many welfare production projects scattered across the eastern United States, but there were no welfare buildings of any kind. The managing director of the Welfare Department, R. Quinn Gardner, assisted by Keith B. McMullin, Lowell D. Wood, and other staff members, developed a plan of expansion that was to guide the welfare program during the next few years.

At the beginning of 1977, the Church had one bishops' central storehouse, 39 regional bishops' storehouses, 18 canneries, 3 grain-storage facilities, and 677 production pro- jects. There were also 47 cash storehouses in various parts of the United States. These were not physical storehouses, but bishops were able to write orders on local grocery stores and pay for the items with funds received from Church head- quarters. These funds were derived from welfare production projects. The bishops also used fast offerings to aid their people.

It was determined that the Church would build an addi- tional 45 regional bishops' storehouses in the next five years.

CONTACTING PRIESTHOOD LEADERS

Before anything was built, however, the First Presidency felt that someone should visit all of the priesthood leaders involved to make certain they wanted to have the full facili- ties of welfare and were willing to pay their local share. The local share in each case was 30 percent, with the Church paying 70 percent from the general fast-offering funds.

The Presiding Bishopric assigned R. Quinn Gardner, man- aging director of the Welfare Department, and three other brethren to spearhead this work. These men were Keith B. McMullin, Lowell D. Wood, and Glen L. Rudd.

During the next few years they made sixty trips into the eastern part of the United States to visit with stake presidents in the cities selected for storehouses and canneries. They were well received, and the responses to their proposals were positive in every instance.

REPORTING TO PRESIDENT KIMBALL

On 20 May 1977 President Kimball and his Counselors invited the Presiding Bishopric and Brothers Gardner, McMullin, and Rudd to meet with them to report on their success in meeting with priesthood leaders. President Kimball was particularly anxious that no pressure be put on

Top: Welfare complex in Mesa, Arizona
Middle: Storehouse and cannery in Missoula, Montana
Bottom: Storehouse and cannery in Lethbridge, Alberta, Canada

185

Top: Storehouse and cannery in Greensboro, North Carolina
Bottom: Welfare complex in Atlanta, Georgia: storehouse, cannery,
employment and social services offices, and grain-storage facilities

anyone and that no welfare facility be built unless the local priesthood leaders were unanimously in favor of it.

The brethren told President Kimball that in every case the stake presidents had responded positively. Some even wanted to write a check at that moment for their portion. President Kimball was pleased to hear about the response.

President Kimball then asked, "What are you brethren doing about grain storage?" The room was silent for a moment. They had not thought of granaries as part of the expansion program. President Kimball then said that the Church could not build storehouses and canneries without granaries. As soon as the meeting was over, Brother Lowell Wood, manager of production, and his associates began to organize a grain-storage program to go along with the storehouses and canneries.

STATISTICAL GROWTH

The expansion of welfare facilities moved forward carefully and effectively. By 1980 there were 9 bishops' central storehouses instead of one, and 63 regional bishops' storehouses where there had been 39. The Church had 32 canneries where there had been 18, and 17 grain-storage facilities instead of 3. The Church also had 863 production projects.

In 1976 welfare projects processed 4.2 million cans of food, but by 1980 the quantity exceeded 10.5 million cans. The number of bishops' orders rose from 167,000 to over 250,000.

In the first several years of expansion, regional storehouses were built in Nashville, Tennessee; Columbia, South Carolina; Jacksonville, Florida; Tampa, Florida; Atlanta, Georgia; Greensboro, North Carolina; Washington, D.C.; Indianapolis, Indiana; Dallas, Texas; and Denver, Colorado. New facilities were also built in the Northwest and in California.

The number of employment centers and Deseret Industries facilities also increased. Every phase of welfare work has grown in the years since President Kimball and the Brethren gave instructions to expand welfare in the United States and Canada.

GEMS OF PURE RELIGION
♦ ♦ ♦

Out of the Depths of Despair

"One Saturday morning after a heavy rain storm, a young woman came into my office asking to see me. Having an order for food and clothing, she still seemed somewhat depressed. I sent out to the Clothing Department for the Supervisor, feeling that the woman needed an extra bit of help. She was thrilled with some of the articles of clothing— among them, a nice coat. She came back into the office to again ask if she might have it. I could not help but notice the neatness of her appearance and the well-cultured tone of her voice. She appeared to have been a person of means and her present condition of destitution was very new to her. Going into some detail, I explained about the articles of food and clothing which her Bishop had ordered for her. She seemed well pleased with what she selected.

"I watched her as she left, following her out on the loading platform. She was aware of my presence and turned to me. There were tears streaming down her face, but her countenance was one of radiant happiness. For the first time in many days, she could see the beauties of the world. I could see by her expression that a great burden had been lifted from her shoulders. Life was more than a mere struggle: It was worth living! She smiled as she said: 'It is a beautiful day; isn't it good to be alive?'

"I don't believe I ever felt a deeper appreciation of life than I did in that moment I listened to her. She smiled again as she left and I went back to my office.

"A few minutes later the Bishop phoned me to see if she had come. When I told him she had already been here and related my contact with her, he seemed very pleased and then told me about her.

"Only last night the girl had contemplated suicide. Then she knelt down by her bedside and prayed to the Lord. She was so impressed to go to the Bishop that she went to his home immediately. He received her kindly and during the course of the conversation, she opened up her heart to him and told him of her misfortune. The Bishop told her that the Church had a Welfare Plan that took care of the needs of its people. No one need go without the necessities of life.

"After this little talk with the Bishop, she felt somewhat lifted from this mood of depression and began to plan about her immediate future. She had a job to go to next week and felt that if she could get aid to care for her until then, she would be able to make out all right.

"It is strange how little acts of kindness which we some-times unknowingly render in the course of our duties have such far reaching results and touch someone's soul which is craving for a kind deed or sympathetic word."

Jesse M. Drury, *For These My Brethren* (reprint, 1991), pp. 54–55

**President Ronald Reagan and President Gordon B. Hinckley with Charles Manley
at the Ogden Utah Bishops' Storehouse**

CHAPTER 8

THE EYES OF THE WORLD ARE UPON US

VISITORS TO WELFARE SQUARE

At the October 1936 general conference, President J. Reuben Clark, Jr., said that in connection with the welfare program of the Church, "the eyes of the world are upon us" (in Conference Report, Oct. 1936, p. 114). This has proven to be true in many different ways over the years.

Since the first visitor to Welfare Square in 1940, the square has seen a constant flow of visitors. During the October 1940 general conference, the First Presidency invited all members and visitors to see Welfare Square. Bus transportation to the square was provided. At the dedication of the grain elevator on Welfare Square in 1940, President David O. McKay is reported to have said that next to Temple Square, Welfare Square will become the next best known place in the city.

The number of visitors to Welfare Square has increased each year, especially since the facilities were upgraded in the 1960s. In 1953, in order to better handle the visitors, 18 persons were called by their stake presidents to act as part-time guides at Welfare Square. In that year there were 1,829 visitors. In 1955, with 41 guides, there were 10,532 visitors, and by 1956, 70 guides were needed to handle the many thousands of visitors. In 1965 more than 27,000 people went out of their way to see the Church's welfare plan in action. To

Visitors arrive at Welfare Square on chartered bus, 1966

Courtesy of *Deseret News*/ Wallace Kasteler

date, well over one-half million tourists have visited the square.

In the early 1950s, President J. Reuben Clark, Jr., Elder Henry D. Moyle, and Elder Harold B. Lee were anxious that all visitors who came to Church headquarters be allowed to visit Welfare Square. They authorized funds to provide round-trip bus service between Temple Square and Welfare Square. For a number of years the bus left Temple Square each morning at 10:00 A.M. and returned before 12:00 noon. The cycle was repeated beginning at 2:00 P.M.

On 12 August 1941, Elder Harold B. Lee said: "There have come to this Welfare Square some of the greatest minds in this and other nations. They have come here sometimes to criticize; often to satisfy curiosity; but almost unanimously and, so far as I know, in every instance, they have gone away greatly impressed at the revelations of what they have seen here" ("Defense against Idleness and Depression," address to regional welfare committee meeting, 12 Aug. 1941).

For a number of years the Brethren desired that all missionaries going through the missionary training program,

Courtesy of *Church News*

Above: Union
Pacific Railroad
Board of Directors
visit Welfare
Square, May 1963;
Elder Harold B.
Lee facing camera

Right:
Missionaries tour
Welfare Square,
1960s

conducted at that time in Salt Lake City, be taken through Welfare Square so their questions could be answered about the Church welfare program.

At the general welfare meeting held 8 January 1963, Elder Marion G. Romney told of his visit to Welfare Square the previous day with an official from Mexico. The man's name was Licenciado Antonio Martinez Baez. The gentleman expressed his appreciation for the courtesy shown to him by the Church. He said the thing that most impressed him was his visit to Welfare Square to see the work being done there. He said that he would be reporting his visit to the president of Mexico as soon as he returned. In his further remarks,

Brother Romney was very complimentary toward Welfare Square and said that all those present at the meeting ought to visit Welfare Square occasionally.

There has never been an organized attempt to proselyte among the visitors. Several have asked to hear more about the Church, and referrals have been given to the missionaries for these people.

When the new bishops' storehouse was built on Welfare Square in 1975, a visitors' center was included as a part of the building. A film telling the story of Church welfare is shown to those who are interested, and guided tours are offered throughout each day.

Visitors' Comments

In April of 1975, Norman Vincent Peale and his wife spent more than two hours at Welfare Square, including a personal visit with the manager, where many of their questions were answered. At the conclusion of the visit, Mr. Peale expressed his feelings about what he had seen and wrote on his referral card: "Here is one of the greatest demonstrations of practical Christianity I have ever seen."

Many of the visitors have come from foreign countries. They represent leaders of nations, members of parliaments, presidents of universities, and other important leaders—but mostly they are the ordinary good people of the world.

Following is a sample of comments made by visitors to Welfare Square:

Jewish from Israel: "Never before have I felt the spirit of the Bible so alive as within the Mormon Church."

Congregationalist from Colorado: "This is the most unforgettable experience we have had in a long time. Only divine guidance could have formed such an organization."

Methodist from Texas: "This morning was one of the most profitable of my life. I saw religion at work—really."

Union Pacific Railroad Board of Directors tour grocery
department at Welfare Square storehouse, May 1963

Danish Folk Church from Denmark: "I want to say that of
all that I have experienced during my journey through the
USA, nothing has impressed me more than the welfare program of the Church of LDS."

Methodist from Oregon: "Fantastic what the Church is
doing. I'm wondering if I'm on the right boat."

Catholic: "As anyone can see, God has his eyes on this
organization. May the people continue to live this way. It's
uplifting to anyone's morale to see that people can still work
together."

"A little of all religions" from California: "The only
Church I know of that takes care of its people in true brotherly love fashion, and the way God meant it to be."

Christian from California: "This is the most humane and
complete program for sharing and giving I have ever heard
of, or about. It makes one feel you are the only people who
really live the Bible teachings."

Reorganized LDS from Michigan: "This is the most remarkable system I have ever seen. God bless you in your wonderful endeavor."

Methodist from Indiana: "Inspiring—Christianity in action."

No church listed, from Canada: "Wonderful. Think I would like to become a member."

Presbyterian from New Jersey: "The work done here should be universal, and until we have it there will be no hope for peace."

Baptist from Texas: "Very interesting. A true picture of pure Christianity."

Baptist from Louisiana: "I have found no other faith who loves and cares for the Church membership as does the LDS. I truly enjoyed the tour through your welfare program building."

Christian from Missouri: "The most wonderful place I have ever been."

Protestant from Switzerland: "I am amazed that such a thing exists in today's world."

OBSERVATIONS BY PRESIDENT RONALD REAGAN

On 16 September 1981, Elder Thomas S. Monson received a call from the White House inviting him to attend a special breakfast with President Ronald Reagan and other leaders to discuss the subject of welfare initiatives in the private sector. Five days after receiving the call, Elder Monson had the privilege of visiting the White House and having breakfast with the President of the United States.

President Reagan pointed out the necessity of moving from the government sector to the private sector in welfare matters. He said, "Seated at the table is Elder Monson, who represents an organization which truly knows how to care for its own." President Reagan then described aspects of the welfare program of the Church. (Elder Monson later stated: "This was the finest compliment that a person in high office could possibly pay the Church. I think we have never had a president who has been more laudatory in his comments or praiseworthy to the Church than President Reagan.")

As the breakfast progressed, President Reagan told all who were present of his visit to the LDS Church welfare cannery in Sacramento, California, during the time he served as governor of California. He said that the genius of the Church program is that neighbors help one another and all are involved for the good of others.

Elder Monson was appointed as a member of the President's Task Force on Private Sector Initiatives. He went to Washington, D.C., and in December of 1981, was sworn in by Vice President George Bush. Elder Monson was well qualified to represent the Church in this capacity, having had many years of personal experience with welfare matters. At the age of twenty-two, he was called to be the bishop of a

Official Photograph, The White House, Washington

President Ronald Reagan visiting welfare cannery in
Ogden, Utah, 10 September 1982, with President Gordon B. Hinckley

Official Photograph, The White House, Washington

**Bishop Kenneth Dallinga shakes hands with President Ronald Reagan
at Ogden cannery; President Gordon B. Hinckley looks on**

Salt Lake City ward that had 1060 members and one of the
largest welfare loads in the Church. Few bishops have helped
as many needy people as he did, and many inactive members of the Church were strengthened by his kindness and
generosity. Since his call to the Council of the Twelve
Apostles, he has spoken out vigorously on many aspects of
the welfare program.

In Washington, D.C., Elder Monson, with other task force
members, had lunch with President Reagan. The President
explained to the committee the importance of their assignment. Their objective was to "rekindle the ingenuity of
American business and philanthropy as to a better way of
caring for the social problems which confront us, as an alternative to placing the entire responsibility at the door of the
federal government."

At the luncheon, President Reagan again made complimentary remarks about the Church. He went out of his way
to praise the Church in his personal conversation with Elder
Monson.

As a member of the task force, Elder Monson had numerous opportunities to explain the doctrines of the Church, particularly the work of the welfare program. He showed the film *Welfare: Another Perspective* to the members of the Contributions Strategy Committee of the task force, who were delighted with the presentation and showed their appreciation by applauding at the end of the film. A member of the committee was His Eminence Terence Cardinal Cooke of the Catholic Church of New York City. Later, Cardinal Cooke said to Elder Monson, "I like the way you made a clear statement on abortion and worked it in so nicely." He was so impressed that he sent a Catholic official from Chicago to visit the Church welfare program in Salt Lake City to learn more about how the Church takes care of its own.

The subject of tithing came up in the committee, and a member said that the Mormon church continues to prosper because of the faith of its members in living the law of

Courtesy of Deseret News

President Ronald Reagan, President Gordon B. Hinckley, and Elder
Thomas S. Monson in Ogden Utah Bishops' Storehouse

tithing. This gave Elder Monson an opportunity to bear his testimony about this important principle.

President J. Reuben Clark's statement, "The eyes of the world are upon us," proved to be true with Elder Monson's experiences on the president's task force.

On 10 September 1982, President Ronald Reagan visited the welfare facilities in Ogden, Utah. He was accompanied by a number of White House aides, Secret Service agents, and media personnel. President Gordon B. Hinckley, Elder Thomas S. Monson, and Bishop Victor L. Brown greeted the President. Arthur Haycock, secretary to the First Presidency, and Larry Whiting, welfare area director, were also part of the group hosting President Reagan.

A large group of people were canning tomatoes at the cannery that day. As President Reagan moved from place to place through the cannery, he stopped and shook hands and visited with these faithful workers. He was very pleased and courteous and interested in the things he saw that day.

A luncheon was served during the day. It consisted of Deseret brand food from the bishops' storehouse.

Elder Thomas S. Monson wrote a short letter to Brother Larry Whiting commenting on the visit:

"I with you so much enjoyed the recent visit of President Ronald Reagan as he toured the cannery in Ogden.

"I mentioned to President Hinckley and others that this was a signal honor to think that the President of our country would visit a welfare facility and single our program out for commendation before the national press.

"I expressed the same sentiments in our meeting in the temple last Thursday. I stated to the First Presidency the feeling that our Heavenly Father would permit the pioneers in the welfare program such as Presidents J. Reuben Clark, Jr., Harold B. Lee, and Henry D. Moyle to be made aware of this honor" (letter written on 23 Sept. 1982).

GEMS OF PURE RELIGION
◆ ◆ ◆

A Feeling of Security

One day a very lovely young mother came into the bishops' storehouse. She was a widow with six little children. As she walked through the storehouse pushing a shopping cart, she put into it meat, milk, potatoes, rice, soup, canned fruit, vegetables, soap, and a few other necessary items.

In talking with her, I asked her how she was getting along and how she could face the future alone with all her dependent children. She replied, "I am not afraid. I have a good bishop and the Church to help me as I do the best I can for myself and my children."

◆ ◆ ◆

Good Deeds

He builds our faith through kindly deeds
We scatter through our days,
And blesses those who share this joy
With others on their ways.

God our Father, God of love
Will bless us for good deeds,
For those we give a helping hand
In their times of need.

And as we seek to do God's will
To do what good we can,
We'll find that we'll be serving God
Through serving fellowman.

Nona Hansen, welfare worker

Elder David E. Sorensen meeting with people who received commodities
in Vladivostok, Russia

CHAPTER 9

CHURCH WELFARE OPERATIONS TODAY

BISHOPS' CENTRAL STOREHOUSES

Since the beginning of the welfare program, food, clothing, and other necessities have been distributed through the storehouses of the Church. In the first years small storehouses served members' needs throughout many communities. With the improvement of transportation and roads, these storehouses were combined to become multistake or regional storehouses. Later, bishops' central storehouses were developed.

Bishops' central storehouses are strategically located in the United States and Canada. These facilities are warehouses for regional bishops' storehouses and cannery operations. An inventory of a bishops' central storehouse consists of raw commodities to be distributed to canneries for processing, and finished products that have been received back from canneries, processing plants, and commercial institutions. These and other items are later distributed to regional storehouses. The products are moved into and out of bishops' central storehouses at the rate of about 350 semi-truck loads per month.

Bishops' central storehouses also house disaster relief materials. The Salt Lake Bishops' Central Storehouse also contains the Church's primary emergency short-wave radio system.

Granger Utah Bishops' Storehouse

REGIONAL BISHOPS' STOREHOUSES

At the present time (1995), the Church has 100 regional bishops' storehouses in operation. Over 325,000 bishop's orders were written during a recent year. Storehouses have been established in most major cities in America, and additional storehouses will be established as conditions require.

The bishops of the Church assist about 1.5 percent of the total member families in any given month. In 1993 a typical recipient family earned $8,800 annually. Sixty-three percent of the recipients also received assistance from their extended families. (There is an upward trend in the amount of extended family assistance given.) The average duration of assistance is approximately four months.

It should be noted that there are members of the Church who are needy but who, for one reason or another, will not go to their bishop and ask for help. In many instances the bishop is not aware of their need. They seek assistance elsewhere.

To help the welfare program become more successful and complete, the bishops of the Church are urged to—

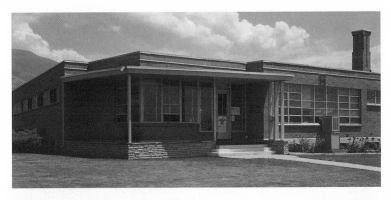

Top: Kaysville Utah Bishops' Storehouse
Middle: Honolulu Hawaii Bishops' Storehouse
Bottom: Local delivery van at regional bishops' storehouse
in Birmingham, England

Mobile storehouse serving each stake in England, 1990

1. Seek out and care for the poor and needy of the Church.
2. Assist with commodities rather than cash as much as possible.
3. Assign work for assistance rendered to those who can and should work.
4. Encourage proper contribution of fast offerings.

CANNERIES

When the Church builds storehouses, almost immediately there is a need for canneries. Welfare canneries have always played a vital role in stocking the storehouse shelves.

The Church now has eighty-four canneries of various capacities processing approximately thirteen million cans of food a year. Seventy-five percent of these cans go into the storehouse system. The balance are canned by Church members for their own home food storage programs. Fifty of these canneries do wet-pack canning, and all of them do dry-pack canning.

Dry-pack canning is the canning of basic dry food products such as beans, wheat, dry milk, lentils, rice, and other foods that can be stored for long periods of time. This service has been added to the cannery program in recent years. The primary purpose of dry-pack canning is to help members accomplish what they have been counseled to do for nearly sixty years—store a year's supply of basic foods. More and more Church members are using dry-pack canning facilities. Member use may turn out to be one of the primary reasons for having Church canneries.

The Brethren have repeatedly taught that the effectiveness of Church preparedness depends on the preparedness of each family in the Church. In a major emergency, the Church storehouse system would be able to provide suste-

A variety of Deseret brand products produced at canneries throughout the Church

nance for only a small percentage of needy members. Elder James E. Faust taught:

"The Church cannot be expected to provide for every one of its millions of members in case of public or personal disaster. It is therefore necessary that each home and family do what they can to assume the responsibility for their own hour of need. If we do not have the resources to acquire a year's supply, then we can strive to begin with having one month's supply. I believe if we are provident and wise in the management of our personal and family affairs and are faithful, God will sustain us through our trials" (in Conference Report, Apr. 1986, p. 26; or *Ensign,* May 1986, p. 22).

President Thomas S. Monson taught, "We should remember that the best storehouse system would be for every family to have a year's supply of needed food, clothing, and, where possible, the other necessities of life" (in Conference Report, Oct. 1988, p. 57; or *Ensign,* Nov. 1988, p. 47).

President Ezra Taft Benson said: "Our bishops' storehouses are not intended to stock enough commodities to care for all the members of the Church. Storehouses are only established to care for the poor and the needy. For this reason, members of the Church have been instructed to personally store a year's supply of food, clothing, and where possible, fuel. By following this counsel, most members will be prepared and able to care for themselves and their family members, and be able to share with others as may be needed" (*Ensign,* May 1977, p. 82).

The challenge for all Church members is to have a personal storehouse in their own homes. Dry-pack canning has greatly helped members to do this.

DESERET INDUSTRIES

Deseret Industries is an important part of Church welfare. There are now forty-seven Deseret Industries stores. Many of these stores manufacture items as well as distributing products. On any given day there are about 2,200 individuals who are earning their living by working at Deseret Industries.

One of the purposes of Deseret Industries is to prepare its workers to move into the commercial market and hold responsible jobs, thus becoming self-supporting. More than half of the workers have mental or physical challenges. The other half have language barriers or lack of job skills. In a recent year, over 1,300 people received training, obtained job skills, and moved from Deseret Industries into employment in their local communities. In the five-year period from 1990 through 1994, a total of 4,809 Deseret Industries workers were placed in outside employment.

Deseret Industries is a nonprofit organization with a gross income of several million dollars annually. This income is used to pay the salaries of the disadvantaged workers and to pay the overhead costs of this huge business. In the past few

Display of furniture made by Deseret Industries Manufacturing

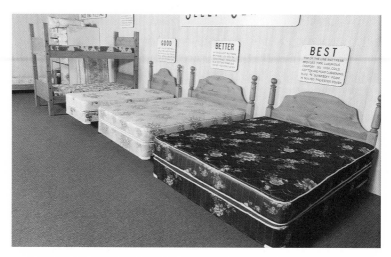

Mattresses and beds made by Deseret Industries Manufacturing

years, Deseret Industries has been able to financially sustain itself, generating enough revenue to pay operating expenses.

Some of the fast offerings contributed by members are used to build new Deseret Industries buildings, which in turn create more work opportunities for needy members and provide good, usable products for sale to the public.

Those who patronize Deseret Industries stores can be assured that everything necessary is done to assist them; for example, all donated clothing that is not brand new is laundered or cleaned before being placed on the floor for sale to the public.

Deseret Industries Manufacturing

Deseret Industries Manufacturing is located in a large facility on the west side of Salt Lake City. It produces a variety of new items that are sold in all of the Deseret Industries stores. The enthusiastic and knowledgeable manager of Deseret Industries Manufacturing best tells the story of this welfare operation:

"Our facility is a federally certified sheltered workshop. Our purpose is similar to the other Deseret Industries facilities in that we provide training, work experience, and job placement assistance to individuals referred here by their bishops.

"Our work areas are divided into three major categories: a sign shop, where we produce signs for Church meetinghouses; a mattress operation, where we produce bedding and sleep products; and a woodshop, where we produce a wide range of wood products for Deseret Industries and for meetinghouses. Each year we produce 60,000 mattresses and 50,000 wood items such as bedroom sets and tables—and we are growing. There are many people in the Church who need the furniture and the mattresses that we make.

"At Deseret Manufacturing, our primary purpose is to train and place a wide variety of individuals—those who are learning disabled, mentally and physically limited, prison parolees, and immigrants. Among the immigrants are political refugees from a Tibetan relocation program and Russians

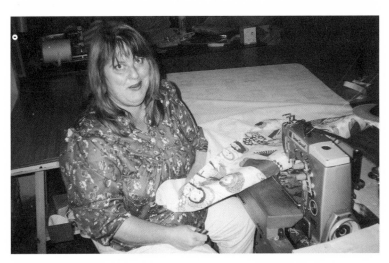

Sheila, being trained to earn her way in private industry

Paul, a legally blind Native American, being taught a trade at Deseret Industries Manufacturing

from the Tolstoy Foundation. Some people are referred here because they have low self-esteem, problems with substance abuse, or other problems that have made them unqualified for employment. We work with almost anyone who is unable to qualify for or keep a job.

"We teach people real skills, and they are able to sustain their families because this facility exists. We find that there really is a way to place previously unemployable individuals in commercial jobs. After their experience here, we are able to place approximately two-thirds of our entire enrollment every year into career positions.

"We give people job experience, a wonderful environment in which to work, and experience in getting along with people. We help the Lord's children move in a positive direction" (conversation between Homer Cook and the author, Dec. 1993).

DESERET INDUSTRIES SORT CENTER

In recent years the First Presidency has established the Deseret Industries Sort Center. All surplus clothing items that cannot be sold through Deseret Industries stores are shipped to this center. Fifty-one percent of these items are good, usable clothing that can be distributed.

The sort center is located on two floors of a large building on the west side of Salt Lake City. It employs 130 workers

Above: Donated clothing at the Deseret Industries Sort Center ready to be sorted

Right: Baled clothing at the sort center ready to be shipped

who have been referred by their bishops. These people have various disadvantages in finding regular work in the labor market, such as poor job skills or inability to speak English. They labor five days a week and receive above the minimum wage. As their skills improve, their salaries increase because salaries are based on piece work. Approximately ten supervisors work with these people.

The volume of clothing handled at the sort center is exceptionally large. Each day over 45 tons of clothing are

sorted and bound into 120- to 130-pound bales for shipment. At the present time, approximately 225 tons of usable
clothing are prepared to be shipped each week.

Aid to Russia

In August 1993, more than sixteen tons of clothing and
shoes arrived in St. Petersburg, Russia, where local Church
members spent several weeks distributing the goods to the
needy. These goods came primarily from the Deseret
Industries Sort Center.

The large bales of clothing were labeled in the Russian
language. Each bale contained sweaters, hats, jackets, coats,
gloves, and other items of clothing of various sizes for winter wear. The heavy bales were carried up two flights of stairs
to an apartment where they could be stored in preparation
for distribution. During periods of rest, the workers sang
Church hymns, including "I Am a Child of God."

The district president, Vyacheslav I. Efimov, was in
charge of distributing the clothes to members living in ten

Courtesy of Church News

Russian priesthood holders unload bales sent from
Deseret Industries Sort Center, 1993

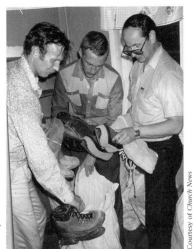

Tatiana Akmova, Relief Society
worker, sorts through clothing,
1993

Russian priesthood
holders sort shoes for
distribution, 1993

branches in St. Petersburg and two branches in Vyborg. He worked to see that the members received the goods based on their needs. This follows good welfare procedures.

President Efimov said: "In addition, our members will contact government authorities to locate individuals and families in need. . . . This will include the elderly, those with illness, and families with several children. Our members will take clothing and shoes directly to their homes.

"We will try to involve every member of the Church in these efforts. The missionaries will also participate."

The district Relief Society president, Sister Irene Maximova, said:

District president,
Vyacheslav I. Efimov

215

"These goods are greatly appreciated. Our people spend most of their income on food, which is becoming increasingly expensive. They cannot afford to buy warm clothing.

"Both members and non-members of the Church will be very pleased to have these. Our women can sew, and, if needed, will be able to remodel and tailor the clothing."

When these commodities arrived, conditions had reached a point where the people just did not have enough to live on. The members expressed appreciation to the members of the Church in America who had made all of this possible. This was the third shipment of commodities that had been sent to them by the Church. (See *Church News*, 4 Sept. 1993, p. 3.)

Photograph from India

In 1992 the manager of the Deseret Industries Sort Center received a photograph of a large group of people in the northern part of India near Nepal. It shows dozens of chil-

People in northern India wearing clothing from the
Deseret Industries Sort Center, 1992

dren and adults wearing the American clothing sent to them from Church members through the sort center.

Similar photographs could be taken in many parts of the world. Wherever these goods are sent, they are received with grateful appreciation.

Other Projects in the Sort Center Facility

In addition to clothing, the sort center manages other important projects. Illiteracy is a major problem in developing countries, where sometimes more than 50 percent of the people cannot read. The sort center has been able to ship over 100 tons of textbooks and educational materials into many developing countries to support local literacy efforts.

The sort center also handles donated medical equipment, gowns, beds, books and journals, and other hospital-related

Courtesy of *Church News*

President Thomas S. Monson, President Elaine L. Jack, Elder James E.
Faust, Elder Rex D. Pinegar, and Bishop Robert D. Hales
at the Deseret Industries Sort Center; infant incubators are sent
to various countries in humanitarian relief efforts

items contributed by medical facilities around the country. If necessary, the items are repaired or rebuilt. However, much of the medical equipment is brand new, some of it government surplus that is still packaged for emergency use.

As reported in the 25 May 1994 *Deseret News*, the Church sent a large shipment of medical supplies and equipment to the Hanoi Plastic Surgery Center in Hanoi, North Vietnam. This shipment, weighing approximately eight tons, included such items as surgical equipment, hospital gowns, and bedpans. Dr. Nguyen Huy Phan, Vietnam's surgeon general and director of the center, received these commodities gratefully. This was the third shipment of supplies the Church had sent to them. One of the former shipments included a number of schoolbooks and up-to-date medical texts.

Dr. Ngoc Dung, a plastic surgeon from the Hanoi center, spent six months in Virginia receiving special training in plastic surgery in order to improve her ability and technique. The Church assisted with her travel expenses. She was also assisted by Operation Smile, a group of American doctors and medical staff that is actively involved in giving medical care to children in a dozen third-world countries.

This small hospital in Vietnam is growing and accomplishing wonderful things with the assistance of the Church and others.

Sort Center Service Projects

Several thousand volunteers, working in their own homes or in groups throughout the Wasatch Front area, participate in service projects supervised by the sort center. The volunteers produce a variety of new items such as bootie socks, children's clothes, flat crib sheets, maternity clothing, cloth diapers, receiving blankets, undershirts, children's hospital nightshirts and pajamas, washcloths, hand towels, layettes, hospital gowns, and wall hangings. Volunteers also

Items at the Deseret Industries Sort Center made by volunteers

make crocheted and knitted items such as baby booties, leprosy and tropical-sore bandages, balls, toys, mittens, scarves, stocking caps, and slippers. Other new items made by these compassionate people are quilts, cloth toys (stuffed animals, hand puppets, sock dolls), wooden toys (blocks, games, puppets, puzzles, cars, and trucks), and special kits for school, first aid, hygiene, and newborn infants. All these items are shipped throughout the world for distribution to distressed families and individuals.

HUMANITARIAN SERVICES

When the Church welfare program was started in the 1930s, small welfare production projects struggled to produce what was needed, but as time went by the ability to produce increased. Now Church welfare projects can produce commodities not only for the poor and needy within the Church, but for worldwide humanitarian purposes also.

219

The Prophet Joseph Smith declared that it was the duty of a person to "feed the hungry, to clothe the naked, to provide for the widow, to dry up the tear of the orphan, to comfort the afflicted, whether in this church, or in any other, or in no church at all, wherever he finds them" (*Times and Seasons*, 15 Mar. 1842, p. 732).

Today the First Presidency, Quorum of the Twelve, and other Church leaders are vitally interested in what is happening to Heavenly Father's children in every part of the world. Through the Humanitarian Services of the Church, they sponsor activities to (1) help relieve suffering and meet people's basic needs by providing life-sustaining assistance and (2) foster long-term self-reliance.

Major short-term projects provide help in times of natural disaster. Long-term projects use the skills of willing Latter-day Saints to provide health care, literacy training, and other service in refugee camps like the Phanat Nikhom

Children from Africa before and after receiving clothes from the Deseret Industries Sort Center

Refugee Center near Bangkok. Large volumes of food, clothing, medical supplies, blankets, and other essential items, as
well as cash, are distributed to needy nonmembers through
established and reputable relief agencies. The Church also
administers a fund that supports research projects concerned
with children's health throughout the world.

In the April 1993 general conference, President Thomas S.
Monson reported that during the previous year, the Church
had participated in more than 350 hunger relief, community
development, and in-kind projects in Asia, eastern Europe,
Africa, Latin America, the Caribbean, Canada, and the
United States.

For example, the Church's Humanitarian Services sent
7.6 million pounds of sorted, used clothing from the Deseret
Industries Sort Center to overseas and domestic destinations
for distribution to refugees, displaced families, and others in
need. In Africa, the Church provided food for famine relief
as well as clothing and blankets. The Church also donated a
half-million pounds of food to food banks and feeding programs for the homeless in the United States and abroad.

President Monson also reported that couples are now
serving full-time humanitarian service missions in Europe,
Africa, Asia, Mongolia, and Latin America. Others, including
doctors, nurses, and educators, also serve on short-term con-
sulting assignments in many countries. (See Conference
Report, Apr. 1993, p. 63; or *Ensign,* May 1993, pp. 48–49.)

In July and August of 1994, over $1,000,000 in com-
modities and cash were sent to Rwanda for the relief of a
very destitute people.

In the October 1994 general conference, President
Monson said that the humanitarian efforts of the Church
"have reached into every corner of the globe. Millions of the
earth's needy have been blessed as members of the Church
have consecrated their means to provide life-sustaining food

Above: Clothing from the Deseret Industries Sort Center being worn in Zimbabwe, 1992

Left: Isaac Ferguson fitting child in Bombay, India, for clothing from the sort center, 1992

and clothing, establish immunization and infant feeding programs, teach basic literacy, dig freshwater wells, foster village banks, create new jobs, sustain hospitals and orphanages, teach basic self-reliance, and act in many other ways to help Heavenly Father's children improve their lives both spiritually and temporally.

"The scope of humanitarian aid given is dramatic:
- Total humanitarian cash donations $23,750,000
- Total value of assistance $72,480,000
- Countries served 109
- Food distributed 3,615 tons
- Medical equipment distributed 243 tons

"All of the foregoing is in addition to the conventional welfare program of the Church fundamentally financed through regular fast-offering contributions" (in Conference Report, Oct. 1994, pp. 58–59; or *Ensign,* Nov. 1994, pp. 43–44).

In the United States, thousands of homeless and low-income families receive substantial donations of food from the Church, distributed through food banks, pantries, soup kitchens, and other charitable organizations. Great quantities of food are steadily being contributed and distributed.

Because of the generosity of Church members through voluntary contributions, primarily fast offerings, the Church is able to maintain its efforts to help many needy people.

Family Relief Boxes

In the late summer and fall of 1994, the Welfare Department began preparing family-size boxes of commodities and shipping them to areas in need.

In October, 1,350 boxes were shipped to Haiti in response to the request of the North America Southeast Area Presidency. The approximately 5,000 Church members in Haiti were suffering because of political unrest and a deteri-

A family relief box being prepared in a bishops' storehouse for shipment to areas of need

orating economy. The Atlanta Bishops' Storehouse was given the assignment to prepare boxes of commodities. Included in each thirty-pound box were dry beans, rice, turkey chunks, peas, powdered milk, cooking oil, and hand soap. Each box could sustain a family of four or five for about a week. Twenty cases of salt were also included in the shipment.

Volunteers assembled and prepared the boxes in one day. The boxes were transported by truck to Miami, sent by boat to Haiti, and distributed by the mission president, Fitzner Joseph. Additional commodities will be shipped to the general populous and distributed by the Feed the Children organization.

In November 1994, 5,280 boxes were shipped to Vladivostok, Russia, in response to requests by Elder Neal A. Maxwell and Elder David E. Sorensen, President of the Asia North Area. Many people in the area were suffering because

Family relief boxes being taken home in Vladivostok, Russia

of heavy rains, an earthquake, and subsequent tidal waves. The Welfare Department immediately made assignments to the Welfare Square, Sandy, and Granger storehouses in the Salt Lake Valley. Relief Society sisters and young men and women assembled 5,280 boxes in five days. Each box contained ten pounds of flour, oil, beans, rice, dried milk, beef chunks, and beef stew. Eighty boxes of hand soap were prepared separately.

As boxes were assembled, photographs were taken, and the young people wrote letters expressing appreciation for the opportunity to assist others. A photograph and letter were included in each box.

The boxes were distributed in Russia, primarily to nonmembers, by the Catholic Relief Services Agency. Erick Anthony Jones, a Church member and the second in charge at the American Consulate in Vladivostok, helped to oversee the process.

Unique Use of Church Canneries

The many canneries throughout the Church not only produce commodities for the Church welfare system, but they now provide a unique humanitarian service. Each cannery receives an assignment to can a large amount of varied food products for distribution to the nonmember poor. Invitations are extended to all churches and community organizations in the cannery area to join with the Latter-day Saints in canning commodities for the homeless and other poor and needy. The commodities are used not only in the communities, but in other areas of the world.

Members of the Church throughout the world should rejoice that their fast offerings, tithing, and contributed labor are building up the Church and enabling the Church to bless the entire world.

Surgery in the Philippines

In recent years, doctors working with the Deseret International Foundation have provided medical services in the Philippines that have blessed the lives of hundreds of people. The work of these doctors has been financially supported by the Church. The doctors have provided an average of one-hundred surgeries per month during each of the last six years. Many of these surgeries have been to correct cleft lips.

DESERET TRANSPORTATION

Deseret Transportation is the private transport fleet of the Church. It has twenty-five tractors and approximately seventy-five trailers. The majority of the trailers are dry van and refrigerated types. The fleet also has bulk-hauling capabilities, including the ability to haul coal. It has a tanker that carries fuel, a lowboy trailer for heavy equipment, and a

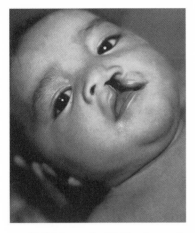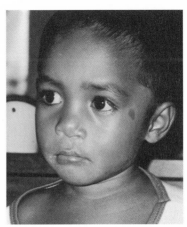

Child from the Philippines whose cleft lip has been corrected by
doctors partially supported by Church funds

trailer chassis for hauling containers to and from the rail-
head and to seaports for ocean transport to foreign countries.

The most common transport service of Deseret Transportation vehicles is moving commodities between various
bishops' central storehouses, and hauling commodities to
the regional bishops' storehouses in the United States and
Canada.

A fully equipped shop and five full-time mechanics and
other helpers maintain this fleet of diesel- and gasoline-
powered trucks, which travel two million miles annually.
This shop also provides maintenance and other services for
motor vehicles owned by Deseret Industries, regional bishops' storehouses, and other Church entities.

A year's supply of fuel for all these trucks is stored in Salt
Lake City and throughout the country at welfare facilities. A
year's supply of tires and maintenance parts is also kept on
hand. These reserves enable the Church to properly respond
in nearly every emergency. The Church practices what it

teaches its members to do—be prepared to remain independent for at least a year in case of an emergency.

DESERET MEAT-PROCESSING PLANT

In 1980 the Church purchased a small meat-processing plant in Spanish Fork, Utah, which was remodeled and enlarged for use in the welfare program. It began operation in March 1981 and now supplies packaged meat for most of the storehouses and canneries in the Church welfare system. Roasts, chops, steaks, and ground beef are produced, as well as boneless ham, bologna, and franks.

Between 5,000 and 6,000 beef cattle and 2,000 hogs are processed each year. The number of hogs can be increased to about 4,000 head. The beef is produced on sixteen welfare production projects, which involve a number of stakes. Two projects in Utah, one in Willard and one in Lehi, produce the hogs.

The plant is operated by thirty-five paid employees and a number of volunteers who come each day to help clean up.

Dennis Lifferth, Elder Joseph B. Wirthlin, President Thomas S. Monson, and others in one of the large coolers at the Deseret Meat Processing Plant

A federal inspector is at the plant during each work day. The inspectors have said that this is one of the finest plants for quality and safety in this area of the United States.

EMPLOYMENT PROGRAM

The employment program of the Church is the oldest of all the facets of the modern welfare system. It was unemployment that caused the greatest difficulty during the early days of the Great Depression. When serious unemployment became prevalent, the Presiding Bishopric had the responsibility of helping members find employment. One of the Counselors spent a large part of each day interviewing applicants and helping them find work. This approach became too time consuming and was discontinued. Six stakes in the Salt Lake Valley then organized their own employment office.

Eventually, nearly every stake and region had an organized employment program. Stake presidents and bishops each designated one of their counselors as the employment counselor. Priesthood quorums and Relief Societies also had employment counselors. Unemployed members were quickly identified, and an entire ward would be able to assist a person who needed employment.

In those days, there was a "green card" made up for every Latter-day Saint that listed the member's skills and talents. These were kept on file by those in charge of employment at the ward level. Each ward cared for its own members if they could. To increase effectiveness, the ward employment leaders would contact the stake employment leader, who notified all wards so that the whole stake was involved in the process of finding work for unemployed members.

Over the years there has been little change in this process, and it has continued to work well. Each bishop now appoints a ward employment specialist, and each stake president appoints a stake employment specialist. These specialists serve on ward and stake welfare committees and help members to prepare for and find employment.

In addition to ward and stake employment programs, the Church has 103 employment centers established throughout the United States and Canada. These centers are professional resources for ward and stake employment specialists. Thirty-nine are managed by paid employees, and sixty-four are completely managed and staffed by Church-service missionaries and other volunteers. At the present time, there are approximately 250 Church-service missionaries assisting in the employment program. In recent years, these centers have been able to find employment for approximately 35,000 individuals each year. Several thousand more people found employment through their local ward and stake employment specialists.

In addition to employment centers in the United States and Canada, the Church has centers in England, the Philippines, Australia, New Zealand, South Africa, Mexico, Guatemala, and five South American countries—Brazil, Uruguay, Paraguay, Argentina, and Chile.

Many unemployed and physically disadvantaged individuals feel discouraged and defeated when they are hunting for a job. As a result, they do not always present themselves as well as they should. Volunteer workers help them learn how to fill out an application and how to dress and speak when they are interviewing for a job. Sometimes they actually accompany the person seeking employment.

For example, a few years ago a sister in her thirties was suffering from depression and spent time in a mental hospital. When she was well and able to leave, she began to look for employment. It wasn't long before she became discouraged and went to her bishop asking him to let her go back into the mental hospital.

The bishop was naturally distressed and spoke with the stake president. They decided to assign this sister some clerical work suitable to her skills at Welfare Square. She worked at this position until she had regained her confidence. During this time, she was looking for long-term work without success. She reported her job hunting disappointments to her supervisor at Welfare Square, who discovered that she had gone to the doors of business establishments but had never had the courage to go inside. The supervisor decided to have a welfare volunteer go with her to introduce her to the personnel officers of businesses that were hiring someone with her skills. This proved to be a solution to the problem, and the sister was able to find worthwhile employment.

The successes of employment centers more than compensate for the effort needed to help unemployed individuals find jobs. The joy of seeing people able to support their families with dignity and self-respect is worth any effort.

GRAIN STORAGE

After the grain elevator on Welfare Square was built, other grain-storage facilities in different cities were soon constructed, usually in association with storehouses and canneries. At the present time the Church has sixty-four different locations where large quantities of wheat and other grains are stored. At least 50 percent of the grain is produced on the Church's production projects. The balance is purchased commercially because of the cost of transporting grain to areas of the United States and Canada that are a great distance from grain-producing projects.

Twenty-five percent of the grain is rotated out of storage every year. The grain is therefore no more than four years old at any time.

Emergency Communications

To assist in fulfilling its responsibility of assisting the poor and needy during emergency conditions, the welfare program has established a communications system called the Emergency Response Radio System (ERRS). It consists of shortwave radio stations throughout the world, with a central system located in the Church Office Building in Salt Lake City. The system is under the supervision of the Welfare Department.

This system helps provide necessary communications when normal communications systems are disrupted. Using a computer program, the central radio operates twenty-four hours a day. When an emergency message is received, the computer immediately relays the message to designated individuals. An operator receives the incoming message and takes immediate action.

ERRS helps priesthood leaders to report on the status of members and property in a disaster area, to request relief supplies and assistance as needed, and to communicate with Area Presidencies and other priesthood leaders. Stations that are part of ERRS have weekly contact with the central radio to ensure that the system is in a state of readiness.

The Mercury Amateur Radio Association (MARA) is a group completely independent of the Church that provides a valuable resource in emergency communications. Through MARA, many Church members receive training and develop their skills. The association is a resource for providing amateur radio operators who can be called as station operators for ERRS.

MARA also assists the Church in helping members determine the health and welfare of family members in disaster areas. It provides assistance to other relief organizations such as the American Red Cross. The president of MARA attends

ERRS management meetings to provide a bridge between these two entities.

Wherever circumstances warrant, local Church leaders call emergency communications specialists. These persons work through stake communications specialists to report emergency status and request assistance if necessary.

SPEARHEAD UNITS

The Church welfare program has twelve large tractor-trailer rigs known as spearhead units. A spearhead unit is a single forty-foot trailer, underslung with a 2,000-gallon water tank. Within the trailer are tents (including large tents for latrines, food preparation, first-aid stations, and child-care centers), sleeping bags, food (including high-energy items like granola bars and cookies), personal hygiene kits, flashlights, first-aid supplies, cook stoves, food preparation equipment, cups, plates, utensils, napkins, lanterns, a power generator, work tools (including a chain saw), a television, an AM/FM radio and other radios for communication purposes. In addition, supplementary materials are available from the Salt Lake Bishops' Central Storehouse that could provide for cold weather and other difficult circumstances.

One spearhead unit is designed to support 1,000 people for forty-eight hours.

These units have been deployed in the last few years to assist in emergencies caused by flooding, hurricanes, tornadoes, and earthquakes in the Midwest, Arizona, Texas, Florida, California, and several other areas. The units are strategically located throughout the United States and Canada and can leave on short notice to go to an area affected by a disaster.

When Hurricane Andrew struck southern Florida, the spearhead unit in Atlanta, Georgia, moved into the northern part of Florida well before the storm reached land. After the

A spearhead unit

storm, working in cooperation with the Red Cross and government agencies, the unit moved into the Miami area and was stationed at an LDS meetinghouse. Large diesel generators were placed in two different meetinghouses to supply power when it was needed. The food, water, and other necessities were immediately available to both members and nonmembers. The radio in the spearhead unit was in contact with Atlanta and Salt Lake City immediately after the storm subsided and throughout the emergency rescue period.

The Church learned from the Florida experience that chain saws, generators, rolls of plastic, signs, and hard hats are most helpful, though they were not in the original spearhead units. Modifications have been made to the units to make them more efficient.

The earthquake that struck the Northridge, California, area on 17 January 1994 caused extensive damage and displaced thousands of families, many of them Latter-day Saints. The effectiveness of the Church welfare program and the spearhead units is reflected in this excerpt from a newspaper article:

"Local LDS leaders in California had not asked for assistance from church headquarters in Salt Lake City. The large concentration of church members in the area and the presence of bishops' storehouses have made such assistance from Salt Lake City unnecessary at this time, church officials said.

"A semitrailer truck [spearhead unit] from the LDS Bishops' Central Storehouse in Colton, Calif., arrived at a stake center in Van Nuys at 3 A.M. Tuesday, loaded with food, generators, toilet tissue, propane and 2,000 gallons of water" (*Deseret News,* 19 Jan. 1994, p. A3).

LDS SOCIAL SERVICES

LDS Social Services is a private, nonprofit corporation that provides services to Church members in accordance with gospel principles. Bishops are able to refer members to LDS Social Services for such things as adoption, services to unwed parents, foster care, Indian student placement, and counseling. Priesthood and Relief Society leaders can consult with LDS Social Services practitioners to receive assistance in counseling individuals with special needs.

The Church now has over forty LDS Social Services agencies, staffed by approximately 200 professional, highly skilled personnel who give valuable service to those needing assistance. Agencies are located from coast to coast in the United States and Canada. LDS Social Services has also served in Japan and Korea, and presently there are two agencies in Australia and one each in New Zealand and England.

There is an interesting history behind the present LDS Social Services. In 1917 a Utah license was issued to the LDS Relief Society Social Service and Child Welfare organization. Relief Society workers provided social services to Church members for many years. Amy Brown Lyman, General Relief

Society President, was probably the Church's first professional social worker and could be called the "mother" of LDS Social Services. Sister Belle S. Spafford, who succeeded Sister Lyman as the Relief Society General President, was also professionally trained. She had a direct hand in the administration, policy making, and ongoing work of child welfare agencies in the Church for nearly thirty-five years. She never ceased to be interested in this work.

For a period of time the Church had three different programs, all with trained personnel, to assist those in need. These were the Relief Society Social Services (for adoptions), the Indian Student Placement Program (begun in 1949), and the Youth Guidance Program. During the summer of 1969, several of the Brethren met to discuss the possibility of uniting the three programs. Elder Harold B. Lee felt that the work could be much more efficient if these services were unified. Elder Lee gave Elder Thomas S. Monson the charge to oversee the proposed changes. Elder Monson met with President Alvin R. Dyer and later with Elders Spencer W. Kimball and Marion G. Romney and others to work out the details of this challenge.

These brethren recommended to the First Presidency that the three programs be combined into one operation to create greater economy, efficiency, and correlation of the work. Elder Monson suggested that the new combined program be called Unified Social Services. These recommendations were approved, and Marvin J. Ashton was called to serve as the managing director. Shortly thereafter, Brother Ashton was sustained as an Assistant to the Council of the Twelve. He continued to serve faithfully and effectively as the managing director under the direction of a priesthood committee chaired by Elder Marion G. Romney. Elder Ashton was succeeded by Elder Robert L. Simpson. Unified Social Services became more formally affiliated with the

Church welfare program when Victor L. Brown became the Presiding Bishop.

In 1973, the Church created a new corporation called LDS Social Services. President Harold B. Lee authorized the formation of this corporation and gave it its name. Over the years this important part of the welfare program has given service to thousands of members.

CHURCH-SERVICE MISSIONARIES AND VOLUNTEERS

In all aspects of Church welfare, there are people serving who have received formal mission calls as Church-service missionaries. There are also volunteers who contribute a portion of their time each week in welfare activities. In recent years there have been nearly 700 missionaries and more than 300 volunteers working together in welfare programs. They have contributed more than 1,220,000 hours of work each year. This is equivalent to approximately 610 full-time employees.

PRODUCTION PROJECTS

In 1982 an extensive study was conducted of the many production projects of the Church. The study found that the projects were producing far more commodities than were needed in the storehouse system, necessitating the sale of welfare-produced commodities on the open market. Even though the funds received from these sales went back into the welfare program, the Church was inadvertently in the position of competing with farmers and others in their normal business affairs.

After careful consideration of this situation, the First Presidency announced in the April 1983 general conference that modifications were being made in the welfare program and that the numbers of projects would be greatly reduced. Some projects would be combined or traded among stakes in order to increase the efficiency of the projects and better meet the abilities of stakes to maintain them. Several less-productive or poorly located projects would be sold. The majority of the rest of the projects to be removed out of the production program would be leased to farmers, ranchers, and others. The leases would be designed to enable the Church to bring some projects back into welfare production if the need ever arose. Today, the Church can operate the welfare program and fill the storehouses with less than 200 projects.

Some of the surplus welfare farms would not be managed by stakes, but by the Farm Management Company, which is a tax-paying operation of the Church. The farms would still belong to the welfare program, but they would be operated to produce commercial income.

Many stakes would no longer have a welfare production project. The Brethren emphasized that they were not doing away with production projects, but they were changing the emphasis to family preparedness and self-reliance.

Deseret Soap Company, 1994

Besides the changes in production projects, the Brethren announced that the annual storehouse commodity budget assessment would be discontinued and all unpaid assessments would be cancelled. Fast-offering funds would be used for all cash needs.

Cash participation in the construction of storehouse facilities was also eliminated. All construction of welfare facilities would be funded by general Church funds. All welfare funds that were in the possession of stakes and regions would be turned in to the general fund.

The Brethren emphasized that with all these changes there would be no departure from the foundation principles of Church welfare.

Some have wondered if the Church has decreased its ability to take care of the Saints in need. The truth is that the Church is now in a far better condition than it was before the modifications of 1983. The Church has more storehouses and other welfare facilities with which to bless the members. The welfare program continues to increase in its ability to achieve its original goals and follow the principles that have been so well established.

Current Welfare Projects

Currently the Church has production projects that provide dry beans, citrus fruits, milk, various grains, honey, fruits, various vegetables, grapes, beef, turkeys, pork, peanut butter, and other products. It also has seven processing projects:

Deseret Soap Company
Deseret Pasta Plant
Deseret Dairy Products
Independence Gelatin Plant
Deseret Bakery

Centerville Cereal Plant

Houston Peanut Butter Plant

These production and processing projects enable the Church to keep the storehouses well supplied with the commodities necessary to meet the needs of the members.

A New Concept of Welfare Projects

Many stakes in the Church do not have a welfare production project, but the members in these stakes should not feel that they are no longer involved in the welfare program. The responsibility of all Latter-day Saints is to first,

**Some of the many items produced at current
Church welfare projects**

Small dry-pack cannery in Centerville, Utah

pay a full tithing and contribute a generous fast offering, and second, volunteer their services in canneries, store-houses, Deseret Industries, and other Church welfare activities, such as caring for the aged, widows, single mothers, and neighbors in need.

All Latter-day Saints should realize that there is a tremendous amount of welfare work to be done. There are needs in every ward and priesthood quorum. There are older members who need help in keeping up their yards and homes. There are single mothers struggling to maintain their families, who do not have the time or energy to keep up their homes as they desire. There are widows whose homes and yards are in need of attention. Any bishop or quorum leader or Relief Society president who takes the time to study the needs of the members will discover that there are dozens of wonderful service opportunities that are really welfare production projects.

Many of these projects can be accomplished by Aaronic Priesthood young men or young women of the same age. Many can be handled by Relief Society sisters. Most of the work can be done by members of priesthood quorums.

The emphasis on serving one another has been shifted from the welfare farm, which was sometimes miles away, to within the members' ward and branch boundaries. When priesthood leaders succeed in putting the membership of the Church to work in assisting each other at the local level, the Saints will become the kind of brothers and sisters that the Lord intended them to be. The time should come when the Church has thousands of "welfare projects" being filled to bless the lives of those in need.

When every yard is neat and clean, when all homes and garages are repaired and painted, when each person in need feels that other people care about him or her, and when all able people are busy helping each other as true and faithful Latter-day Saints, then the welfare program will be enjoying its finest moment.

GEMS OF PURE RELIGION

◆ ◆ ◆

Mongolian Visitors to the Sort Center

"In February of 1995, the Church hosted two gentlemen from Mongolia who were visiting in Salt Lake City. They were Dr. R. Gonchigdor and Dr. D. Sukhbaatar, members of the Mongolian parliament. They visited Temple Square, the Church Administration Building, and some of the family history facilities of the Church. But the highlight of the day was their visit to the Deseret Industries Sort Center.

"When they arrived, they found that by coincidence, a shipment was just being completed for Mongolia. The shipment included educational supplies, which were badly needed in their country, and medical supplies. The eyes of the two men glistened as they opened some of the boxes and looked through the materials. They held the books in their hands and turned the pages in order to better comprehend this great treasure.

"They both expressed their deepest appreciation for the Church and the volunteers who made this shipment to their country possible."

Mary Ellen Smoot, Church Hosting

——————————— ♦ ♦ ♦ ———————————

The Teddy Bears

The Church members in western Europe helped with the shipment of commodities to nonmembers suffering from the conflict in Croatia and Bosnia. They boxed the commodities and then, remembering the children, included a bag of teddy bears with the load. When a member couple unloaded the shipment in Croatia to begin distributing the food, they found that there were fifty-nine teddy bears included.

When the food distribution began at a local refugee center, the member couple counted sixty-one children present. Since they did not want to disappoint any of the children, the sister said she would go into town and try to buy two more teddy bears. Her husband discouraged her, feeling that they should move ahead. As they handed out the boxes of food and teddy bears, they found that there were sixty-one teddy bears!

President George Albert Smith; Harry S. Truman, president of the United States; and Herbert B. Maw, governor of Utah, 1945

CHAPTER 10

RESPONSES TO
WORLDWIDE DISASTERS

Over the years, the welfare program has helped many people suffering from the effects of disasters. When disaster strikes and there are no members of the Church in the area, the First Presidency generally makes a respectable cash donation and at times gives food and clothing to aid the victims. When a disaster strikes an area where large numbers of Latter-day Saints live in organized stakes, leaders at Church headquarters generally wait until the local priesthood leaders request assistance from them. In these areas, stake leaders rarely need much assistance from headquarters because members have understood and practiced the principles of welfare and are able to help themselves. Local leaders are generally able to assist their own people with their own resources. Storehouses located in the disaster area can also be of service.

There are times when a severe disaster creates needs that far exceed the resources of the local members. When this occurs, the rest of the Church comes to their aid. The following are a few examples of what the members of the Church, through the welfare system, can accomplish.

WELFARE ASSISTANCE TO EUROPEAN SAINTS

When the Church welfare program was not yet ten years old, it was called upon to assist the Saints in Europe. President George Albert Smith explained that the Church's involvement began with a visit he made in 1945 to Harry S. Truman, president of the United States.

"When the war was over, I went representing the Church, to see the president of the United States. When I called on him, he received me very graciously—I had met him before—and I said: 'I have just come to ascertain from you, Mr. President, what your attitude will be if the Latter-day Saints are prepared to ship food and clothing and bedding to Europe.'

"He smiled and looked at me, and said: 'Well, what do you want to ship it over there for? Their money isn't any good.'

"I said, 'We don't want their money.' He looked at me and asked: 'You don't mean you are going to give it to them?'

"I said: 'Of course, we would give it to them. They are our brothers and sisters and are in distress. God has blessed us with a surplus, and we will be glad to send it if we can have the co-operation of the government.'

"He said: 'You are on the right track,' and added, 'we will be glad to help you in any way we can.'

"I have thought of that a good many times. After we had sat there a moment or two, he said again: 'How long will it take you to get this ready?'

"I said: 'It's all ready.'. . .

" 'Mr. President while the administration at Washington were advising the destroying of food, we were building elevators and filling them with grain, and increasing our flocks and our herds, and now what we need is the cars and the ships in order to send considerable food, clothing and bedding to the people of Europe who are in distress. We have an organization in the Church that has over two thousand homemade quilts ready.'. . .

"Now, we couldn't have done that a hundred years ago. We were seeking food ourselves. Our people in this valley then were digging thistle and sego roots for food, and they were utilizing every means possible to get food to keep the soul and body together. In a hundred years the desert has been made to blossom as the rose" (in Conference Report, Oct. 1947, pp. 5–6; or *Improvement Era,* Dec. 1947, p. 703).

When the Church was permitted to send clothing and commodities to the Saints in Europe, the Brethren announced a special Churchwide drive to collect clothing, shoes, coats, and other items for these destitute members.

The members of the Church in America responded by donating large amounts of new and used clothing and other goods. These were received at Welfare Square in the cannery building, where they were sorted and prepared for shipping. The cannery was not being used during the winter that year. The amount that came in almost filled the building. Many people volunteered to help in this effort.

The items were all packaged in cardboard boxes. About twenty volunteer sisters typed the shipping labels. Government regulations limited the weight of parcel post packages to no more than eleven pounds each. There were also certain restrictions right after the war on the quantity of packages that could be sent.

The Church elected to ship the packages to central locations in Europe so that they could be properly distributed when they arrived. Local branch presidents and other Church leaders were able to divide the goods according to the needs of each family.

The first shipments were sent to Denmark, France, Belgium, Netherlands, Norway, Sweden, and Finland. Later shipments were received in Germany, Austria, and Czechoslovakia. Great Britain also received help.

The first packages contained bedding, clothing, and food. By late December 1945 word was received at Church headquarters that welfare packages were being received in

Holland in good condition and were being distributed as quickly as possible to the Saints. It was not long before many letters of appreciation began to be received from these Saints. Approximately 7,000 packages were sent to Europe by the end of 1945.

President Smith told the Saints in a conference talk that he had received word from Europe that there were still many cases where the people were having most difficult times, but that in general they had been faithful to God and to the Church. He told of receiving expressions of gratitude for the food, clothing, and bedding sent to them in their time of need.

A Generous and Kind Prophet

When the donations were being sorted and packaged, Elder Harold B. Lee and Elder Marion G. Romney took President George Albert Smith to Welfare Square. They observed the generous response of the membership of the Church to the clothing drive and the preparations for sending the goods overseas. Brother Stewart Eccles, who was with the Brethren, reported that tears ran down President Smith's face as he watched the workers package this great volume of donated clothing, shoes, and other goods. After a few moments he removed a new overcoat that he had on and said, "Please ship this." The Brethren said to him, "No, President, don't send that; it's cold and you need your coat." But President Smith would not take it back. Brother Eccles went into an office and had a secretary type a note to put in the pocket of the overcoat so that the person eventually receiving it would know that it came from the President of the Church. President Smith insisted that he didn't need his coat to go back to the Church Office Building. The brethren helped him get into the warm car and returned him to his office.

Elder Marion G. Romney, President George Albert Smith, and Elder
Harold B. Lee inspecting boxed goods to be sent to Europe, 1946

This incident was never forgotten by those who saw
President Smith make a contribution on that occasion.

Summary of Shipments

Following is a brief summary of what the Church sent to
Europe:

2,342,000 pounds of wheat products
1,114,000 pounds of clothing, including shoes and coats
2,600,000 pounds of fruit, vegetables, and milk
400,000 pounds of meat products
200,000 pounds of dry beans

This is the equivalent of 133 boxcar loads. In addition,
the Church sent by parcel post the equivalent of another
seven boxcar loads of clothing, bedding, and food. The value
of all of these commodities was $1,232,391—in 1940 dollars!
Add to this the shipping costs of $503,867.93, and the total

amounts to $1,736,258.93 worth of goods sent to Europe between October 1945 and the end of 1949.

Elder Ezra Taft Benson's Mission to Europe

Immediately following World War II, the Presidency of the Church and the general Church membership turned their thoughts toward doing whatever possible to alleviate the suffering of the people of Europe. The First Presidency appointed Elder John A. Widtsoe, of the Quorum of the Twelve, and Elder Thomas E. McKay, an Assistant to the Quorum of the Twelve, to go to Europe to supervise the work there, particularly the distribution of welfare commodities.

Before Brother Widtsoe and Brother McKay were able to leave, President Smith made a change and gave this important assignment to Elder Ezra Taft Benson, one of the younger members of the Quorum of the Twelve. President Smith realized that the task would be physically difficult and therefore made the change. Elder Benson was to serve as the president of the European Mission. Elder Benson invited Frederick W. Babbel, a recently returned German-speaking missionary, to go with him and be his aide and secretary.

Elder Benson and Brother Babbel left the United States in January of 1946. They were accompanied at times by Chaplain Howard C. Badger and various mission presidents, some who had presided during the war years and some who had recently arrived from America. Everywhere Elder Benson and Brother Babbel went, they met with difficulties that seemed to block their path. But the hand of the Lord opened their way time after time. The events of the following ten months contain some of the most touching stories of faith, unity, and service in the history of the Church.

Elder Benson's main responsibilities were to set the Church in order, to reorganize missions, and to help the struggling leaders. He was also to fulfill the giant task of making preparations for welfare supplies to be distributed to the needy. They met people everywhere who were hungry— both to see leaders of the Church from America and to receive food, clothing, and household goods.

Many of the European Saints needed good soap. Because the Church had a very productive soap project, there was plenty to send them. The diets of the people were lacking in vitamins and fats. These were provided to them as quickly as possible. Shoes and clothing for children were greatly needed. These needs were also met. Those who received the assistance reported that the Christmas of 1945 was their best Christmas of the previous six years.

By February of 1946, at least four boxcar loads of food and clothing had been sent to New York to be shipped to Norway and Holland. Soon other carloads followed.

When reading the reports of this strenuous and difficult mission, it is easy to sense the love that members of the Church in America and Europe had for each other, although separated by thousands of miles. The commandment of the Lord that the Saints were to care for the poor was tested to the limit by the experiences in Europe. The Church welfare program proved its capacity, even just ten years after being established. (See Frederick W. Babbel, *On Wings of Faith* [Salt Lake City: Bookcraft, 1972]; and *Labor of Love: The European Mission of Ezra Taft Benson* [Salt Lake City: Deseret Book Co., 1989].)

In 1963 Elder Benson related some of his experiences in Europe. He said that people were discouraged and down-trodden. The countries were in distress, and there was some starvation. "It was terrible to see a great industrial city idle. But most terrible is to see people without food. The Brethren prayed to be able to get welfare supplies to the people to help them. . . . They used potato peelings for sacrament in some places." Elder Benson told of one man who was going

251

blind because he needed some fat in his diet. Brother Benson took some from London into Europe and gave it to this man. Gradually his sight came back. (Address given at Great Falls Montana Stake welfare meeting, 2 Feb. 1963.)

In June of 1946 the first shipments of welfare supplies for the Saints in Germany and Austria arrived in Geneva, Switzerland. Elder Benson later said, "One of the happiest days of my life was that day when the first supplies arrived in Berlin" (address given at Great Falls Montana Stake welfare meeting, 2 Feb. 1963). Precautions were taken to ensure the security of the supplies and to arrange for distribution in an efficient way. Elder Benson was assisted in this work by Max Zimmer.

An interesting account is shared in *Ezra Taft Benson: A Biography*:

"When the first shipment of welfare supplies arrived in Berlin, Elder Benson took acting mission president Richard Ranglack to the battered warehouse that, under armed guard, housed the precious goods stacked nearly to the ceiling. 'Do you mean to tell me those boxes are full of food?' President Ranglack asked. 'Yes,' Ezra replied, 'food, clothing, bedding, and a few medical supplies.' To prove his point, he pulled down a box of dried beans. As Ranglack ran his fingers through the contents, he broke down and cried. Ezra opened another box, this one filled with cracked wheat. Ranglack touched a pinch of it to his mouth. When he could finally speak, he said, 'Brother Benson, it is hard for me to believe that people who have never seen us could do so much for us' " (Sheri L. Dew, *Ezra Taft Benson: A Biography* [Salt Lake City: Deseret Book Co., 1987], p. 219).

Elder Benson was notified that he would be succeeded as president of the European Mission by Elder Alma Sonne near the end of 1946. Elder Benson had thought he might remain longer and when the time came, it was difficult for him to

Elder Ezra Taft Benson and President Cornelius Zappey inspecting
welfare shipments received in Holland, 1946

return home. Elder Sonne arrived in November of 1946, and
he and Brother Benson left immediately on a strenuous tour
of the countries of Europe. Brother Benson departed for
London on 11 December 1946. During a ten-month period,
he had traveled over 61,000 miles by airplane, train, ship,
bus, jeep, and automobile. The mission presidents were now
established in most of the European missions, and large supplies of welfare commodities had reached their destinations
to the blessing of thousands of Latter-day Saints and many
other people.

Under the direction of Elder Sonne, for three more years
the Church continued to provide and distribute continuous
shipments of food, clothing, and other necessities—until the
European Saints could sustain themselves.

Six years later, in the October 1952 general conference,
Elder Benson explained how the experience in Europe had
changed him and how he appreciated even more deeply his
testimony, the priesthood, and the gospel. And he reflected

on memories, many of which were beyond his power to describe:

"I presume you have never had the great and trying experience of looking into the faces of people who are starving when you are unable to give them even a crust of bread. We faced that as we first met with the Saints in parts of Europe.

"But when the welfare supplies came, it was a time never to be forgotten by these faithful Saints. I can see them now in tears, weeping like children" (in Conference Report, Oct. 1952, p. 118; or *Improvement Era*, Dec. 1952, p. 941).

Dutch Potatoes for Germany

After the war, the Saints in Holland used the welfare program to bless the German Saints in a most inspiring way. This story shows the application of the Lord's command to "love your enemies, bless them that curse you, do good to them that hate you" (Matthew 5:44). The following account is taken from the *Church News* of 6 December 1947.

"In the first week of November [1947] ten huge trucks moved across Holland. They headed towards the east and contained a costly cargo—seventy-five tons of potatoes, a gift from the Dutch Church members to the Saints in Germany.

"Here is the story of these potatoes:

"In 1945 when Holland was liberated from five years of German occupation, it was completely exhausted of nearly all of its resources. What a joy it was when the mission's first welfare goods were received. No words can describe the thankfulness of the members when they were supplied with food and clothing from Zion.

"For eighteen months a group of missionaries and local members worked day after day in the central welfare house in The Hague to supply the members with necessary clothing and to distribute cans of vegetables and fruit to them regularly.

"Special meetings were called for this purpose in order to convey to the members the depth and beauty of the Welfare Plan.

"In the spring of 1947, the members within the Dutch mission were asked to begin a Welfare Project of their own. The proposal was welcomed with enthusiasm. There was nothing the Saints would rather do than show their willingness to give as well as receive. The priesthood went to work and within a short time every quorum had found a suitable piece of land for the project. It was recommended that potatoes and green vegetables such as beans, peas and cabbage be grown. Potatoes are the basic food of Holland since they yield an abundant harvest. The women as well as the men worked the entire summer on the land.

"In many branches the planting of potatoes was made a special occasion, and the branch members turned out en masse. There was singing, speaking and praying at the end of which the potatoes were entrusted to the soil. Soon there

Dutch Saints loading potatoes for German Saints, 1947

came news of good prospects for the harvest and cautious estimates were made as to how large the yield would be."

During the time the potatoes were growing, Walter Stover, president of the East German Mission, visited the Dutch Mission in Holland. During his visit, with tears in his eyes, he told of the hunger of the Church members in Germany. They were in a very bad condition because supplies had not reached them as quickly as the Saints in Holland.

The Dutch Mission president was Cornelius Zappey. He felt compassion for the German Saints, knowing how greatly they had suffered. A thought came to President Zappey:

" 'If we—if we could only give our potatoes to the members of our Church in Germany. What a beautiful lesson could be learned from this; but what would they say if we should ask them for the food for which they had worked so hard to give to the people who had caused them such suffering and depredation—the people who had ruthlessly confiscated the last bit of their food and exposed their little children to starvation. And if they should approve of the idea, how would we be able to export the potatoes, for the exportation of food to Germany is strictly forbidden by the Dutch government, because the Dutch people don't possess sufficient food for their own use.' "

The thought did not leave President Zappey's mind. He was nervous about approaching the Dutch people to see what they would do. However, he began to inquire a bit.

"The result was startling. The Saints thought it a wonderful plan. The word 'enemy' was not heard. The progress of the potato project was now watched with double interest and proudly came the reports, 'We have so many potatoes for Germany,' and 'We have so much.' "

When potatoes on the various welfare projects were harvested, trucks began hauling them to The Hague, where they were put in a warehouse in preparation for shipping. These

President Cornelius Zappey and missionaries handling potatoes
for Germany, 1947

trucks came at all hours of the day and night, and the Saints in The Hague were willing to unload the precious potatoes so they could be moved into Germany on time.

The branch presidents were told that they could keep a portion of the food in the warehouse to distribute to the widows and the needy in their own branches. One older Dutch widow received a sack of potatoes and then heard that the potatoes were to be given to the members in Germany. She said, "My potatoes must be with them," and returned the sack of potatoes.

President Zappey had a most difficult time trying to gain permission to ship the potatoes from the Netherlands into Germany. It was simply impossible. He was turned down time and time again, but the Lord intervened. Elder Alma Sonne visited in Holland and quite by accident met an old friend of his from Logan, Utah, Dr. P. Vincent Cardon of the United States Department of Agriculture. Dr. Cardon had been attending an agricultural conference in Geneva,

Switzerland, and had been asked to go to The Hague to a conference on animal feed. Elder Sonne asked Dr. Cardon to write a letter of introduction for the Church to Holland's Minister of Food Supply. This letter helped to open the doors that allowed for an exception to be made. Every other church and relief organization that had presented similar requests had been refused, but President Zappey's request was approved. President Stover and President Wunderlich of the West German Mission were informed that seventy-five tons of potatoes would soon be on their way. Originally, it was estimated that fifteen tons of potatoes would be sent, but the fifteen had grown to seventy-five!

The permits that had to be obtained from various transportation companies were all difficult to get. However, with the blessings of the Lord, one problem after another was solved. There was great joy when the potatoes were finally loaded into a number of large trucks.

"During the night of November 6 and 7, the trucks began their eastward trek, heavily laden with precious potatoes—a symbol of a practical application of a living religion" (*Church News,* 6 Dec. 1947, pp. 1, 6–7).

The following four statements typify the great appreciation people felt for the contribution of the Dutch Saints:

"This is one of the greatest acts of true Christian conduct ever brought to my attention. The Dutch Saints are to be congratulated that they can perform this act of welfare service to members of the Church who live in a country which has caused them so much suffering and hardship during recent years" (President David O. McKay of the First Presidency).

"This is an achievement which is little short of miraculous. I am sure the Saints in the Netherlands Mission will experience a sense of great satisfaction in this overture of good will to the German Saints. Back of it is the unselfishness engendered by the Gospel of Jesus Christ. This will go

**Potatoes from Dutch Saints at the German border awaiting entry
into Germany, 1948**

down in the history of the welfare program as an outstanding achievement and as an example of the true love which characterizes the work of the Lord" (President Alma Sonne of the European Mission).

"It is one of the most wonderful events in its moral aspects, to transpire in the Church in Europe since the war. It will no doubt have a tremendous moral effect upon the discouraged spirits of the Saints in Germany!" (President J. Wunderlich of the West German Mission).

"It is the most beautiful and inspiring thing that has ever been my privilege to witness during my entire membership in the Church" (President Walter Stover of the East German Mission). (*Church News,* 6 Dec. 1947, p. 1.)

One Year Later—Potatoes and Herring Sent to Germany

The Dutch Saints showed their generosity on another occasion as well:

"Today we tell another story . . . of a still greater gesture of unselfishness and love on the part of these same Dutch Saints. This year [1948] the welfare harvest of potatoes in this land yielded over 90 tons, all of which were shipped in seven carloads across the border to be received by the German Saints.

"Then to add to their generous gesture, the Dutch members contributed enough money from their own funds with which to purchase one full carload of herring, consisting of nine tons of the finest fish that money could buy.

"Herring was chosen for purchase because of its high protein value and fat content, so badly needed to supplement the meager diet of the German Saints, and the Dutch government's willingness to issue an export permit for them.

"The herring was packed in barrels and trucked to the railroad from the docks. Each barrel contained the big stamp of government inspection, indicating they met highest stan-

President Cornelius Zappey with herring sent to German Saints
by Saints in Holland, 1948

dards of weight and quality. Only the finest fish can stand the rigid inspection for export.

"According to President Cornelius Zappey of the Netherlands Mission, whose energy and enthusiasm directed this year's welfare accomplishment as well as last year's, the Lord certainly blessed their efforts in the potato crop. When the men were loading the last car, they found they had many more sacks than they had figured on. As they had only six cars, they put all possible in the last car.

"The weight broke the springs of the car, but luckily it broke in Dutch territory and that one car was taken out, repaired and the contents put into two cars, following the rest into Germany by a few days" (*Church News,* 15 Dec. 1948, pp. 12–13).

TETON DAM DISASTER

While Elder Thomas S. Monson was a member of the President's Task Force on Private Sector Initiatives (under President Ronald Reagan), he attended a meeting in April of 1982 in the old Executive Office Building adjacent to the White House. Many religious leaders in America were assembled. Elder Monson had an opportunity to make a presentation about the Church welfare program. He chose the experiences of the Teton Dam disaster to illustrate that when a church has a welfare program and the membership understand it, that church can become a partner with civil and other authorities when disaster strikes an area.

He presented to the assembled group a written summary of the Teton Dam disaster, which included the following:

"Let me share with you one example which arose out of a natural disaster.

"At 11:57 A.M. on Saturday, June 5, 1976, the 307-foot-high earth-filled Teton Dam in southeastern Idaho collapsed, unleashing 80 billion gallons of water on homes and

Broken Teton Dam

farmland below it. In a matter of minutes a wall of water 50 feet high slammed into the farming communities of Sugar City, Salem, Hibbard, and Wilford, virtually wiping them off the map. By 2:30 P.M. the rampaging waters, still nearly 15 feet high, reached the city of Rexburg, 15 miles to the south, sweeping away nearly everything in its path. By the time the water was finally contained three days later in the American Falls Dam about 100 miles further down the Snake River, 11 lives had been lost, over 4,000 people were injured, and some 2,000 were left homeless. The flood covered over 300 square miles, ruined 30,000 acres of valuable farmland, destroyed 700 miles of improved roads, and resulted in over $1 billion worth of damage to public and private property."

Well-organized priesthood leaders began immediately to assist the people. What they had learned about welfare service was invaluable in helping them meet their emergency needs. The Church was prepared, and large numbers of volunteers were anxious to aid those in need. Elder Monson's article further stated:

**Idaho Falls residents filling potato sacks with sand; sandbags were
used to protect against water damage**

"An immediate need was to provide temporary accommodations for those left homeless. Through Church leaders
in the area, a call was made at 2:35 P.M. to Church headquarters in Salt Lake City, Utah, some 150 miles away. From
its storehouse resource system, the Church was able to
assemble tents, blankets, mattresses, and bed sheets. By 5
P.M. a tractor-trailer rig was loaded and on its way north to
Rexburg. The truck arrived before nightfall and sleeping
accommodations were prepared for many of the homeless.

"Another aspect of the Church also proved helpful. In
Rexburg the Church operates a junior College known as
Ricks College. The campus is located on a hill which escaped
the flood waters. Less than an hour after the flood hit
Rexburg, school administrators were contacted by the local
Civil Defense director and the college was designated as the
official disaster response center. Student dormitories were
used to house 1,400 victims that first night. Thereafter, for
many days, the dormitories were filled beyond their capacity
of 2,000.

"Fortunately, the water supply of the college was declared by National Guard experts as uncontaminated, and the cafeteria in the student center was used to feed flood victims. Supplies at the cafeteria were supplemented on Saturday night by two trucks sent from Church headquarters in Salt Lake carrying 5,000 pounds of food from the storehouse system. On Monday a larger rig carrying 55,000 pounds of food was sent from Salt Lake and subsequent shipments were made as needed. Red Cross volunteers assisted college personnel in feeding flood victims at the campus cafeteria. On Saturday evening, 1,982 meals were served and nearly 10,000 more were provided the next day. For several days thereafter the Church and the Red Cross worked together in providing food for those in need. . . .

"Medical services were vital during the hours after the flood, and the student health center at Ricks College became the focal point for treatment. First aid and other medical help was provided by the Red Cross, the National Guard, and student health officials at the college. . . .

Damage caused by the breaking of the Teton Dam

"Social Services volunteers of the Church also hastened to Rexburg to assist in the social and emotional needs that arose from the impact of this major disaster. Personal assistance in relieving the trauma surrounding the flood was given to hundreds.

"As the waters finally subsided and the awesome damage could be more clearly assessed, it became obvious that the greatest challenge would be in cleaning up and restoring the damaged communities. Here again the role of the Church as a partner with other agencies was important.

"The first job seemed to be clearing away the mud and debris from the streets, homes, and other buildings which were left standing. A request was made through the Church for five or six tractors and front-end loaders. Soon thereafter the Church welfare services leader in Soda Springs, Idaho, 165 miles away, called and indicated that he had arranged for 150 pieces of such equipment, with operators, to be sent in. Later, there was a need to restore power to homes which had lost this service. A request was made through Church channels for 150 electricians. More than 450 licensed electricians and helpers responded. Most impressive, though, were the volunteers who came with shovels, buckets, crowbars, or whatever they had available to use. A system was set up whereby Church units in southern Idaho and northern Utah would send busloads of volunteers to assist in the cleanup. Without concern for whether those being assisted were members of the Church or not, some 14,000 Church volunteers came during the first week after the flood, and more than 17,000 came during the second week. They continued for several months to work at the request of and under the direction of local Church and civic leaders. An estimate of the time donated by volunteer members of the Church exceeded one million manhours.

Courtesy of *Deseret News*/ Claudell Johnson

Cleanup and repair that continued for months

"The Teton Dam disaster was a real test of the ability of the Church to respond in time of emergency as a partner with both private and governmental relief organizations. The Church met the test. Its help was available immediately. Organizational lines were clear and emergency preparedness planning proved adequate. The volunteer spirit of the people was overwhelming and represented a true outpouring of brotherly love and kindness" (*"Mormon" Church Welfare Services: An Account of the Teton Dam Disaster*, pp. 2–4).

President Spencer W. Kimball spoke at the dedicatory services of the Deseret Mills and Elevator in Kaysville, Utah, on 10 June 1976. He was going to Rexburg, Idaho, later in the week to speak to the Saints and to view the destruction of the flood. He said:

"You have been reading the newspapers these past five days, which have been full of pictures and explanations of the terrible disaster that came to many of your brothers and sisters in Idaho and the Snake River Valley. It's pathetic; it's sad indeed, but we have found many of the people up there doing just as you are doing, we hope, with their year's supply. And when everything else was gone, in many of the cases they were able to go back to their year's supply.

"I hope, and this is my brief message to you today, that no one ever reads one word about that terrible flood and the sadness that it has brought—the loss of life, the loss of live-stock, the destruction of farms, the suffering that has come to those good people—I say again, I hope no one here will ever read another word about that disaster without saying quietly to himself, 'No moment will ever pass when I will not be prepared as the Brethren tell me to do.' One year's supply of commodities, well cared for, well selected, is a minimum. It's the minimum [President Kimball hit the podium for emphasis], and every family, if they have only been married a day or week, should begin to have their year's supply. Now that's basic, and we mean it! [He hit the podium again.] There should be no family under the sound of my voice who isn't already prepared for whatever eventuality may come. We can't anticipate it, of course. We don't know where another dam is going out, or where a river is going to flood, or whether an earthquake is going to come, or what's going to happen. We just are always prepared because the Lord said, 'If ye are prepared ye shall not fear' (D&C 38:30). And the only way to have peace and security is to be prepared.

"May the Lord bless us that not one family of us will go from this room without a determination from this moment forward that there will never be a time when we will not be prepared to meet the hazards that could come."

WATER PROJECTS IN AFRICA

In the mid 1980s, severe drought caused great suffering to millions of people in Africa. In 1985 the Church held two special fast days, one on 27 January and one on 24 November, and encouraged members to contribute generously to its humanitarian effort. Nearly eleven million dollars were freely given. A large amount of this money has been used to bless the people of Kenya.

The executive secretary to the Church Humanitarian Service Committee, after visiting Ngorika, Kenya, stated that one of the greatest needs the people have in that part of the world is clean water. The Church donated $300,000 and, in cooperation with other agencies, helped Kenyans build the Ngorika water system, which carries potable water from rivers and mountain springs to homes.

One woman spoke to the people gathered in her yard for a ceremony to celebrate bringing the first clean running water into the village. She said, "For the past 40 years, I have walked eight miles one way every day to get water for my family." Pointing to the water flowing from the spigot, she said, "This is like a dream" (*Church News,* 18 Mar. 1989, p. 8).

Latter-day Saints had the major role in bringing water into that woman's household and to some 1,100 other dwellings in the area. More than 90 families and 150 institutions, including churches, schools, and businesses in fifteen Kenyan villages are now receiving clean water. This is an area of about forty-five square miles about one-hundred miles north of Nairobi. All of this was made possible by the funds raised through the special fast in November of 1985.

In many other parts of the world, clean water is in short supply and people have to carry it great distances to their homes. The Church is currently helping to provide self-sustaining, potable water systems in many countries.

OFA AND VAL

Within a two-year period, two violent hurricanes, Ofa and Val, hit the islands of Samoa and part of Tonga. On the

Damage to Church property in Samoa caused by Hurricane Ofa, 1990

first four days of February in 1990, Ofa struck the islands of Western Samoa, American Samoa, Niue, and several of the outlying islands of the Tonga chain. The storm caused extensive damage, particularly in Western Samoa. Houses collapsed, roofs were blown off, and water damage was extensive. Approximately 2,200 homes were destroyed on the islands of Upolu and Savaii. Trees were snapped off close to the ground. Winds were sometimes in excess of 200 miles an hour, and much damage was caused by the ocean waves. There was one report of waves as high as ninety feet smashing into the islands.

Two persons were killed and a few were seriously injured. Also, because many crops were destroyed, the major sources of employment and food were eliminated. In Samoa, people primarily earn their livelihood by working with the copra (coconut) crops and growing taro, breadfruit, and bananas.

There was extensive damage to Church property. The structures remained, but windows were broken, carpeting

Damage to chapel in Samoa caused by Hurricane Ofa, 1990

and furnishings were ruined, and in some instances roofs, or parts of roofs, were blown off.

An amateur radio operator named Percy Rivers, a former stake president, used a car battery and his radio equipment to notify the Church of the disaster. The Area Presidency in Sydney, Australia, directed the shipment of goods from Australia, New Zealand, Hawaii, and the United States. (The author of this book was the Area President at the time.) Approval for these shipments was given by the General Welfare Committee.

Within a week of the beginning of the storm, food, basic tools, and tarpaulins were sent from the local Presiding Bishopric storage facility in Apia on the island of Upolu. Members of the Church unloaded the airplanes as they came in. These goods were distributed through stake presidents and bishops to local members in need.

A missionary couple serving in Samoa were assigned to manage the Presiding Bishopric storehouse. The brother was formerly a bishop in Idaho and had had some welfare experience. President Douglas J. Martin, First Counselor in the Area Presidency, was sent from Sydney, Australia, to Samoa to assist the priesthood leaders in the gigantic work before them.

The Prime Minister of Western Samoa made a request to purchase 100,000 pounds of flour from the Church. Within a short time the Deseret Mill in Kaysville, Utah, was grinding wheat. After three or four days the 100,000 pounds of flour, packaged in twenty-five-pound bags, were ready to be shipped to Samoa. There was no charge. The flour was sent as a direct donation, in addition to nearly one-million dollars worth of other food, clothing, and supplies that were necessary until the coconut, taro, breadfruit, and banana crops were back in production.

It was almost one year before conditions on the Samoan Islands were close to normal.

Two small islands many miles north of Tonga were badly damaged, and the stake president in Neiafu, Vava'u, Tonga, immediately sent a small planeload of food and other items to the few Saints in that disaster area.

Twenty months after Ofa struck Samoa, another hurricane named Val hit Upolu and Savaii. This time Pago Pago on the island of Tutuila in American Samoa was also devastated. Val was even more severe than Ofa. Nearly all of the homes in the disaster area were damaged, and the majority were destroyed. Several months of welfare work were again needed to help the Samoan people. This time, however, the bishops were better prepared. President Douglas Martin, who was then serving as the Area President, and other welfare workers were very helpful. Brother Edward J. Bishop, a skilled welfare worker, was serving as the regional director of temporal affairs at this time and was also present to assist. The radio system worked better than before.

The Church leaders had learned a lot from their experiences with Ofa and so handled the extensive restoration work much better. Food and other necessary items were delivered by trucks from the Presiding Bishopric facilities to each village. The bishops and stake presidents received the goods, and the bishops distributed them to their people.

Once again food, clothing, building materials, and other items were shipped to these island countries. For the second time in less than two years, well over a million dollars worth of assistance was given to the people of the Samoan Islands.

HURRICANE ANDREW

In the early morning hours of 24 August 1992, Hurricane Andrew struck the extreme southern part of Florida, becoming, in terms of property damage, the worst natural disaster in the history of the United States of America. Damage estimates were placed at $30 billion.

Before Andrew reached the coast, the Church spearhead unit was moved from Atlanta, Georgia, to Orlando, Florida,

Homestead, Florida, chapel damaged by Hurricane Andrew, 1992; used as an LDS emergency-control center

to wait until it was definitely known where the storm would strike.

The storm blew ashore with a terrible fury. It made neighborhoods look like they had been hit by a bomb. Homes were either totally destroyed or their roofs and other parts were severely damaged. Vehicles were tossed about as if they were toys.

One hundred and sixty square miles of suburban Miami were devastated, an area larger than Rhode Island. Eighty-five thousand houses were destroyed or severely damaged, leaving more than 225,000 people homeless. More than 60,000 jobs were lost. More than 1,000 members of the South Miami Florida Stake were left homeless.

There was neither electricity nor water and, most frightening to the people, the telephones were not operational. This made the people feel that they were cut off from the world and very much alone.

Under the leadership of the stake president and bishops, the members began to carry out their disaster recovery plans. All the members were checked on to determine deaths, injuries, and personal property losses. Remarkably, no members had lost their lives. Three meetinghouses and a home were set up as temporary bishops' storehouses. All of the classrooms in the Church buildings were used to store and distribute food, fuel, medical supplies, and other supplies.

When a person entered a meetinghouse, he or she was directed to meet with an English-, Spanish- or Portuguese-speaking bishop to determine needs. If the person had more than a five-day supply of food for his family, he was told to come back in four days. If the family had very little food, the bishop issued an order according to the number of members of the family. Each family received food for four days.

About a week after the storm, representatives from LDS Social Services arrived to help organize interviews with victims needing counseling. A couple was also sent from Salt Lake City to work as LDS employment specialists.

The beneficiaries of the Church's preparedness efforts were not only Church members. On the day after the storm, volunteer Church members began to arrive to assist anyone needing help. They came from stakes in Florida as well as stakes throughout the southeastern United States. Eighteen hundred Church volunteers came to help on the first weekend after the storm, 5,100 arrived on the Labor Day weekend, and 500 arrived the next weekend. They made temporary repairs to roofs and windows of members' homes, then approached nonmembers and offered their services. When they reached the home of one member, the wife noticed that her nonmember neighbors had workers repairing their roof. The neighbor said that they were paying $400 an hour for this service. When the member wife said that the Church work crews would do the same repairs, including the materials, at no charge, the hired workers were quickly dismissed.

The president of the South Miami Florida Stake had several thousand yellow T-shirts printed with "Mormon Helping Hands" and "LDS Emergency Relief Services." The nonmember friend of a stake president was the helicopter pilot responsible for escorting dignitaries during surveys of the area. At one point he escorted President George Bush and the two other presidential candidates, Bill Clinton and Ross Perot, over the destruction area. They asked, "What are all those yellow T-shirts down there?" The pilot responded, "Those are my friends, Mormon volunteer rescue workers who have come here to help." The responses from the three dignitaries included "Wonderful," "Marvelous," and "God bless the Mormons."

The following is a summary of what the Church volunteers accomplished: Temporary roofs were put on 3,000

Above: LDS
Volunteers
unloading
supplies after
Hurricane
Andrew, 1992

Right: LDS
volunteers in
action after
Hurricane
Andrew

homes. Temporary roofs were put on a Jewish synagogue and three Christian chapels. Tons of debris were removed and dozens of roads were cleared for traffic. Ten trailer loads of food, water, emergency medical, and other supplies were distributed. (Taken from information provided by the president of the South Miami Florida Stake.)

When a disaster occurs and members have prepared themselves as they have been counseled, they are in a position not only to help each other but to give aid to their non-member neighbors. With each disaster this truth is demonstrated.

EARTHQUAKE IN NORTHRIDGE, CALIFORNIA

On 17 January 1994, southern California suffered a devastating earthquake that registered 6.6 on the Richter scale. Fifty-four people were killed, and an estimated $15 billion in damages occurred. At least five to six hundred Church members were displaced. Local Church leaders were well organized, and both leaders and members reached out to meet the physical and emotional needs of members and nonmembers alike.

A new emergency system had recently been implemented by Church leaders in southern California. After the 1991 Los Angeles riots, it was apparent to the Area Presidency that one Regional Representative needed to be responsible for the Los Angeles Basin, one for Orange County, and one for the San Diego area. This arrangement worked very well in this new crisis. Spearhead units moved into place providing food, sleeping bags, and relief supplies to set up several tent cities. Up to 400 people were in one tent city alone.

Members in the Los Angeles area collected funds to purchase additional food and medical, hygiene, and baby supplies. Members donated time to package the supplies in individual kits. Surrounding stakes collected blankets and coats. Young Women and Young Men groups brought candy and balloons for children and organized games for them.

Stake leaders asked members to provide food for a Catholic relief agency to distribute. In just one day's time, members brought in enough food to fill the kitchens in three meetinghouses. Members outside the Los Angeles Basin collected fifteen tons of food and supplies, which were delivered to a Methodist church that was being used as a distribution center. The Church provided relief supplies to the Salvation Army for meals in a Los Angeles park. About 90 percent of those who received these meals were nonmembers.

Every day, the Church sent volunteers to Red Cross centers. Members in local neighborhoods organized their own relief efforts to get supplies to areas of greatest need. Youth from one stake went door to door in their neighborhoods and collected 450 blankets, 540 coats, and 600 sweaters and sweatshirts for distribution to quake victims.

One family was out of town when the earthquake struck. They had extensive emergency supplies in their home, such as food, water, alternative heat, and radios. After hearing of the quake, they called their neighbors and said, "Go into our home and use anything you need." Their neighbors were sustained by this preparation.

Bishops, stake presidencies, and high councilors mingled with the people, held babies, and generally offered encouragement. Missionaries provided translation services for many Spanish-speaking victims.

The process of being displaced is an emotional shock. LDS Social Services helped members deal with the emotional trauma of the disaster.

This relief effort showed true Christlike love in action. Members' lives were enriched by the opportunity they had to serve their fellowmen and by the love they received in return. (See *Church News,* 29 Jan. 1994, pp. 6, 8; and *Church News,* 5 Feb. 1994, p. 3.)

SOUTHERN GEORGIA FLOODS

On 6 July 1994 a severe tropical storm named Alberto hit central and southern Georgia, bringing high winds and heavy rains. For four or five days, the area was inundated with rain, including twenty-three inches of continuous rain during a twenty-four-hour period in Americus, Georgia. Water from the northern part of Georgia began to flow south, feeding into the Flint River. As the Flint River rose, it created a path of devastation along its southward journey.

Above: Ritchie Marbury, president of Columbus Georgia Stake, and others unloading a truckload of Clorox used to sanitize polluted wells in Georgia flood area, 1994

Left: Wheelbarrows sent from the bishops' central storehouse in Salt Lake City to the Georgia flood area

Thirty-five thousand families were evacuated from their homes because of the flooding. Fifty homes of Latter-day Saints were damaged, nine of them severely. More than five thousand people were forced to live in shelters during the height of the crisis. Thirty-four people died as a result of the flooding, and the damage was estimated to be $500 million.

Two Latter-day Saint chapels were used by the American Red Cross to house those who had been evacuated. And within five hours of a request for help, spearhead units dispatched from the Atlanta welfare complex had arrived with the first supplies to reach Albany and surrounding communities, including fresh water, food, work equipment, and medical supplies. Shovels, wheelbarrows, axes, saws, generators, water coolers, extension cords, bleach, ladders, and many other items were immediately ready for use. The Church provided a total of nine, eighteen-wheel truckloads of food and supplies.

As quickly as possible, members of the Church from all over the South prepared to assist. During the first weekend after the flooding, more than 500 Latter-day Saints arrived at the scene of devastation to volunteer aid. During the second weekend, 5,500 Latter-day Saints arrived, and 750 helped during the third weekend.

The regional welfare committee chairman, who lived in the area, coordinated efforts to help both members and nonmembers of the Church.

GEMS OF PURE RELIGION

No Time for Self-Pity

A bishop of a ward with extensive welfare needs called a young mother with a four-year-old son to be the Relief Society president. She had been deserted by her husband and left in destitute circumstances. She accepted the calling, knowing that it would involve large amounts of her time.

She soon realized that she would need to spend some time each day out visiting in the homes of the people in need. She and her son went from home to home helping to prepare bishop's orders for the bishop's signature and otherwise helping in any way they could.

Within a short time she had forgotten many of her own problems and her loneliness because of her constant service. She served faithfully for five years. Her visits and kindnesses brought blessings into the homes of many members, and she was better able to deal with her own problems.

◆ ◆ ◆

A Needy Artist

Just before Thanksgiving in 1994, a transient arrived at the bishops' storehouse on Welfare Square seeking work for assistance. He had come from Las Vegas, where he had been promised a good job as a commercial artist painting holiday themes on windows. When he arrived there, the promise fell through and there was no work waiting for him.

After three frustrating days of looking for work and spending his last few dollars, he climbed aboard a freight train headed for Salt Lake City. He offered his artistic services at downtown stores, but no one would hire him.

A discouraged man ended up at Welfare Square, where he asked for work that could help him get back home to his wife and children. An agreement was made that the man would paint the four large front windows of the storehouse with holiday scenes and do other things as needed. The bishop who was assigned to transients agreed to purchase a bus ticket for the man that would get him home.

An immediate transformation came over the man. He began to smile and act more confident. People stood out in the cold to watch him work and congratulated him for the beautiful job. One of the window paintings contained the words found in Alma 1:30: "They did not send away any who were naked, or that were hungry, or that were athirst, or that were sick, or that had not been nourished; . . . therefore they were liberal to all." When he finished the project, he received a bus ticket and money for meals on the way home. He expressed gratitude to the Church for the opportunity to work and for the help he received.

"Inasmuch as ye have done it unto one of the least of these my brethren, ye have done it unto me" (Matthew 25:40).

CHAPTER 11

WELFARE PRINCIPLES

This chapter presents statements and discussions about welfare principles from General Authorities and other Church leaders. Reading and pondering these statements can help Church leaders and members to more effectively "succor the weak, lift up the hands which hang down, and strengthen the feeble knees" (D&C 81:5).

BLESSINGS OF THE WELFARE PROGRAM

The welfare program has been and continues to be a defense and a refuge from the storms of life. There has come into the lives of Church members a sense of security because they know that they have a bishop standing by ready to help them. This feeling helps people to gather inner strength to fight the battles of life. This is where the real achievement of Church welfare is evident.

The welfare program has given some of its most visible help during times of economic depression, but many of the most serious "depressions" occur to needy individuals or families when others around them are prospering. Often other people are not aware of their circumstances and they suffer alone. Some have gone directly to their bishops. But most of the time, home teachers or Relief Society visiting teachers have brought the problems to the attention of their leaders. The bishop then has been able to reach out and bless lives. There is no way to put on paper the many ways in which bishops have blessed the lives of the needy. They have written millions of bishop's orders and checks drawing on fast-offering funds to help individuals and families. Many families have been lifted and helped in their journeys through life. In turn, the people receiving help have blessed the lives of bishops, Relief Society presidents, and other Church members.

Through genuine welfare service, people take hold of their lives and begin to solve their problems. The finest part of many members' Church service has been to see the welfare program renew people and help them to ascend, to make of their lives what they ought to be. No one bishop or storehouse keeper or welfare worker can tell the whole story. In branches and wards throughout the Church, leaders have the privilege of seeing strength, courage, and physical and spiritual growth come into the lives of their people.

In welfare service, both givers and receivers are blessed. The poor and the needy are a blessing to the Church, for they give members a chance to serve. Those who have participated in the welfare program in any way have been strengthened in righteous living.

THE BISHOP
Responsibility for the Poor

President J. Reuben Clark, Jr., First Counselor in the First Presidency, summarized the bishop's role in welfare services:

The bishop is "to administer all temporal things. . . . In his calling he is to . . . 'administer to the . . . poor and needy'; he is to search 'after the poor to administer to their wants.'. . .

"To the bishop is given all the powers and responsibilities which the Lord has specifically prescribed in the Doctrine and Covenants for the caring of the poor. . . . No one else is charged with this duty and responsibility, no one else is endowed with the power and functions necessary for this work.

"Thus by the word of the Lord the sole mandate to care for and the sole discretion in caring for, the poor of the Church is lodged in the bishop. . . . It is his duty and his only to determine to whom, when, how, and how much shall be given to any member of his ward from Church funds and as ward help.

"This is his high and solemn obligation, imposed by the Lord Himself. The bishop cannot escape this duty; he cannot shirk it; he can-

President J. Reuben Clark, Jr.

not pass it on to someone else, and so relieve himself. Whatever help he calls in, he is still responsible" ("Bishops and Relief Society," 9 July 1941; quoted by Marion G. Romney, *Ensign,* Nov. 1977, p. 79).

Bishop Jesse M. Drury, in a talk given to bishops on 17 April 1962 at Welfare Square, told an interesting story about the early days of the welfare program in Pioneer Stake:

"Brother Lee, when he was a stake president, had a bishop who had no welfare cases.

"He said to this bishop, 'How is it you have no welfare cases in your ward?'

"The bishop said, 'But I don't have any.'

"Brother Lee said, 'How is it this ward next to yours has over 55 cases?'

"He took his lead pencil and marked the boundary line, then he said, 'You go through your ward. I know at least twenty families who need you to extend to them the hand of fellowship.' "

As Elder Lee traveled around the Church he would some-times refer to "inactive" bishops. When Brother Lee saw a look of surprise on the faces of some of the bishops he would

say, "I guess some of you want to
know what an inactive bishop is."
Then he would give the definition:
"An inactive bishop is one who does
not hold a weekly welfare meeting."

Elder Lee often discussed the role
of bishops and was always pleased
with their work. However, he knew
that occasionally a bishop was not
as careful as he should be in his
responsibility to help those in need.
Elder Lee would frequently say that

Elder Harold B. Lee

the *genius* of the welfare program was that the bishop of the
ward is the sole judge in administering welfare. Then he
would quickly add that this could also be the *weakness* of the
welfare program if the bishop did not follow correct principles and listen to the whisperings of the Spirit of the Lord.
Brother Lee felt there was great wisdom and strength in the
position of the bishop. He emphasized that stake presidents
and General Authorities are responsible to help the bishop
understand the basic principles of the welfare program.

Bishop Robert D. Hales said:

"The office of bishop in the Aaronic Priesthood carries
with it a special mandate to care for the poor and needy. The
bishop is the Lord's agent in distributing the resources of
the Lord's storehouse, and he is also a common judge in
Israel. . . .

"How does a bishop decide who to help when it appears
all are poor? Poverty is relative. The Lord, in his infinite wisdom, calls bishops from the people he will serve. The bishop
knows the people of his ward and understands local culture
and conditions. When the bishop is ordained, he receives a
mantle which enables him to discern the difference between
wants and needs."

Bishop Hales then quoted President Marion G. Romney: " 'Whom should I assist? How much assistance should I give? How often and how long should I assist? No hard-and-fast rule will ever be given in answer to these questions. As the common judge, you [the bishop] must live worthy to get the answers for each case from the only source provided— the inspiration of heaven' (in Conference Report, Oct. 1979, p. 140; or *Ensign*, Nov. 1979, p. 96)."

Bishop Hales continued by saying: "General Authorities, Regional Representatives, and stake presidents are less qualified than the bishop in making judgments on these issues. The further away from the local bishop you get, the less able you are to make intelligent judgments, let alone inspired ones, because it is to the bishop the mantle is given. What is the stake president's role? It is to make certain that bishops understand the principles" (Regional Representatives' seminar, 5 Apr. 1991).

Bishop Robert D. Hales

Every bishop who has followed the Lord's instructions to seek out the poor and needy and administer to their relief has received a great spiritual experience. There have been some failures in their efforts, but mostly there have been successes. A bishop's experiences in welfare are among the most spiritual and rewarding of his blessings during the time he serves.

President J. Reuben Clark, Jr., speaking to stake presidencies in 1936, said: "Bishops are the fathers of their wards. They should have with them all of the love and tenderness which a man has for his own children, and he should administer this relief which he is going to give in the same spirit as he would administer it among members of his own family" (J. Reuben Clark, *Selected Papers,* ed. David H. Yarn, Jr. [Provo: BYU Press, 1984], p. 157).

Responsibility for the Lord's Storehouse

The Lord's storehouse has always been the responsibility of the bishop. This storehouse includes all of the resources available in the ward or branch that can be used for serving the poor. The physical bishops' storehouse is an important part of the Lord's storehouse, and this is also the bishop's responsibility. If a storehouse serves just one ward, then the bishop of that ward is in charge. If a storehouse serves an entire stake, the stake president appoints one of the bishops as chairman of the stake bishops' welfare council. That bishop then represents the other bishops of the stake in seeing that the storehouse meets the needs of stake members.

Many years ago, President J. Reuben Clark, Jr., taught a bishop about his role in connection with the storehouse. He telephoned the bishop to tell him that a single mother with three little children had, that very day, moved into the bishop's ward. They were in desperate need, and the Church had some special obligations to help her. President Clark asked the bishop to go as quickly as possible to her new home and do what he could to help her.

Within minutes the bishop and his counselor were in the home. They quickly became aware that there was no food in the home and that there were other needs to be attended to. Within an hour the bishop was back with some groceries and other items to sustain the family for a day or two, and the Relief Society president was asked to help the mother as she worked to reestablish the family.

President Clark told the bishop: "If I could, I would help this sister, but I am only the First Counselor to the President of the Church and do not have authority to write a bishop's order on the storehouse. You have that right and privilege and for that reason I am calling you requesting you to do what you feel should be done in her case."

The bishop reported back to President Clark the next day that through the welfare program, he was in the process of helping this mother with her many problems.

President Ezra Taft Benson taught this same lesson to one of the managers of the Denver welfare facility:

President Ezra Taft
Benson

"In the spring of 1982 President Benson was in Denver visiting a daughter and while there decided to visit and tour the newly built bishops' storehouse and welfare complex.

"President Benson was very gracious and interested in the activities at the complex.

"President Benson shook my hand firmly, looked me straight in my eyes and asked if I understood that 'this is the bishops' storehouse.' President Benson explained that the storehouse is reserved for the bishops of the Church and nobody else. He said that if he were to give me an order for commodities I could not fill it. My response was that if he handed me an order I would fill it. President Benson said that I would be mistaken to do so because even though he was the President of the Quorum of the Twelve, he had no authority to distribute commodities from the bishops' storehouse. A bishop is the only one who has the authority to distribute commodities from the storehouse" (memo sent to the author by Scott Cottam, one of the managers of the Denver welfare facility).

GIVING

Our Responsibility to Give to the Poor

Throughout the years following the establishment of the welfare program, Church leaders have taught that we are to love one another and work to help one another. The principles of love and work are emphasized repeatedly in the scriptures, where the word *love* is found over 400 times and the word *work* appears over 700 times.

The commandment to love one another is so important that the Savior said our observance of it is the way others know we are his disciples (see John 13:35). We are commanded to take care of one another as the way we show our love for him (see Mosiah 2:17). Each member of the Church shows his love for the Savior by caring for the poor and needy, the sons and daughters of God.

This caring must be done in the Lord's own way. In Doctrine and Covenants 104, the Lord explained that he made the earth and everything in it, and everything is his. It is his purpose to provide for his Saints, but "it must needs be done in mine own way" (D&C 104:16). He explained that in his way, "the poor shall be exalted"—lifted up and enabled to live on a higher level—because "the rich are made low"—given an opportunity to be humble and share what they have to lift others (see verse 16). In verse 18 the Lord explained that if any person "take of the abundance which I have made, and impart not his portion, according to the law of my gospel, unto the poor and the needy, he shall, with the wicked, lift up his eyes in hell, being in torment."

President Marion G. Romney many times defined what our "portion" is: "What is the portion of the abundance that the Lord has given us that we are required to give to the poor and the needy? First it is tithing, an honest tenth; and beyond that, it is liberal contributions in time and labor on

290

welfare services projects and a liberal fast offering" (*Learning for the
Eternities,* comp. George J. Romney
[Salt Lake City: Deseret Book Co.,
1977], p. 206).

President Romney also said
about the verses from section 104: "I
understand from them that the Lord
claims the earth as His; that it is not
yours and mine to own and manage
independently of Him. No matter
how many stocks and bonds or how
much land and other properties we

President Marion G.
Romney

possess, they are not wholly ours. They are His. He further
says that He owns and gives to us all the blessings we have
and that He makes us stewards over them. He makes it clear
that it is His purpose to provide for His saints, but He
requires that it be done in His way. *His* way, which way He
explains, is for those who *have* to contribute to those who
have not. Having made us stewards, He gives us our agency
however, and then lays down the condition that if we accept
these blessings and refuse to contribute our share for the
care of the poor, we shall go to—well, He tells us where we
shall go. . . .

"The revelation from which this is taken was given to us
in this dispensation for our guidance. In light of it, do you
think that this matter of taking care of the poor is one that
we can disregard and still obtain the blessings of the Lord?
Not at all. We do it, or we pay the penalty" (Regional
Representatives' seminar, 29 Sept. 1978).

Every Latter-day Saint throughout the world has the
privilege of blessing others by paying tithing. All should
respond to formal assignments to assist in welfare activities
and should give welfare service to the needy without any

assignment. All should understand the principle of fasting and the commandment to give a generous fast offering. In many countries of the world the amount of the offering may be small, but if it is a generous and true fast offering, it will be acceptable to the Lord. All Latter-day Saints have the privilege of showing their love for the Savior by imparting their portion to the care of the needy.

Who Is Worthy to Be Helped?

When members have given generously for the care of the needy, bishops then have the responsibility to see that these offerings are used wisely for the best good of the receivers. The giving of food and clothing to the needy is the most delicate and difficult part of the welfare program. From the beginning Church leaders have taught that it is easier to produce the goods than to get them where they are needed. President J. Reuben Clark, Jr., taught that bishop's orders can be written without solving the problems that need to be solved. Sometimes the needy are despondent or embarrassed or defensive, or they may feel unworthy of help. These people can be harmed spiritually and emotionally if the necessities of life are given without following basic welfare principles and without tenderness of spirit and true charity. "The manner in which assistance is actually administered to the needy determines the success or failure of Church Welfare. . . . The surest guide is the Spirit of the Lord" (*Welfare Plan: Handbook of Instructions* [1952], p. 54).

Harold B. Lee spoke to a Salt Lake regional welfare committee on 3 January 1940. His remarks are summarized as follows:

"Supplying the needs of the people is important, but implanting in them a sense of independence and raising their spiritual morale is even more important. However Bishops should be lenient in judging people. In the cases where men have given freely of their labor—have given all they have—the Bishops should 'loosen up.' He cautioned the committee, however, not to take any definite stand in deciding the classes of people to be helped. The Bishop is the 'common judge in Israel' and with the wisdom he possesses and the inspiration which God gives him, he should decide the matter by giving careful consideration to each case that presents itself. Peoples' needs are not alike. Their food requirements are different. They cannot be judged by the same standard. Leave it to the Bishop."

These guidelines have been a blessing to general Church leaders, to bishops, and to those who have received help.

President J. Reuben Clark, Jr., said this on the subject of who is to be helped:

"Now then, who are to be helped? We have already said primarily the good people who have during all of their lives lived according to the principles of the gospel, who have been good tithepayers—they deserve our first attention. But, you are not going to be able to stop there. We are not going to let anybody starve if we can help it, and we shall not come to the starving stage if we shall work on here in a proper mind and spirit. Starvation is not going to face us. It may if we do not go forward as we should. You are going to help the man who has not always been a full tithe-payer, and particularly, my brethren, where that man has, as he frequently has, a wife and family who are faithful. When I think of the trials and tribulations and the sorrow that must come into the home where the father is not doing just right, and the mother is trying to rear the family in accordance with the principles of the gospel, I feel there is nothing, brethren, that should not be done to help that family. And do not drive the husband, the father, away by harsh word, by unkind treatment; labor with him, work with him. Sometimes in our exuberance and enthusiasm in urging people to keep the commandments of the Lord we may take positions and say things that deeply wound the man who is not doing quite the right thing" (quoted in Albert E. Bowen, *Church Welfare Plan* [Gospel Doctrine manual, 1946], p. 130).

In 1957, a newly appointed member of the General Welfare Committee was assigned to attend the Minidoka Idaho Stake conference with Elder Henry D. Moyle of the Council of the Twelve. After a good welfare meeting in the evening, they followed the stake president to his home. As they drove along, the committee member asked Elder Moyle who is worthy to receive Church welfare assistance. After thinking about it for awhile,

Elder Henry D. Moyle

Brother Moyle said that you couldn't draw a line. The committee member then asked if everybody was worthy and if Elder Moyle had ever met anyone who was unworthy. Elder Moyle said that he was about seventy years old and that he had met only one person in his life who he thought would be unworthy. That person was a man. He said he had never met a mother or a child whom he would classify as being unworthy of welfare assistance.

We cannot draw a line! If a person is in genuine need, then our responsibility is to assist them in one way or another, if we have the means. The Lord intended that we help everyone. Elder Lee discussed this on a number of occasions. He could not draw a line either.

Experience teaches welfare workers that some welfare needs cannot be solved with food or money. A wise bishop can solve many problems just by listening and counseling.

When people need food or other necessities, these should be given to them. A person usually should be given those things that he feels he must have; if his demands are excessive, they will soon decrease. If his requests are legitimate, he will be satisfied. If his wants are fancied, they too will be satisfied and his wants will change.

It is true that some people have unrighteous desires and may not be worthy in every way. But there is no better way to help a person become worthy than to assist him and then carefully work with him to help him identify real needs and long-term solutions. The greatest abuse of the welfare program is to not use it when it is needed to lift a person, to change his or her life. If a person is unrighteous in some way, nothing will help him change more than to have someone be kind and generous, helping him have what he wants and at the same time tactfully assisting him to alter his ways. Although this process is slow, it works.

The Prophet Joseph Smith told the sisters of the Relief Society in the early days: "The best measure or principle to bring the poor to repentance is to administer to their wants. The Ladies' Relief Society is not only to relieve the poor, but to save souls" (*History of the Church*, 5:24–25).

THE IMPORTANCE OF WORK

Most of the things we do in the Church have the word *work* attached to them. We do family history work, temple work, welfare work, and priesthood work. There have likely been more welfare talks given on the importance of work than on any other single topic. Latter-day Saints should know that they are on this earth to *work* out their own salvation. No one will ever be admitted into the celestial kingdom solely through the work of other people. The scriptures are filled with commandments to work and admonitions that idleness should not be found among the Saints. No self-

Hard Labor, a picture that hung in Elder Matthew Cowley's office for
many years, reminding him of the importance of hard work

respecting Church member will voluntarily shift the responsibility of his own maintenance to another.

When the Lord cast Adam and Eve out of the Garden of
Eden, he did not curse *them.* He cursed the land *for their sakes*
and made it possible for them to work and to enjoy the
blessings that come from work. Those who understand
gospel principles have usually learned to love work, and
work has become a vital part of their lives.

In the 1936 October general conference, the First
Presidency said that "work is to be reenthroned as the ruling
principle of the lives of our Church membership" (in
Conference Report, Oct. 1936, p. 3).

Since that time, many other leaders have also taught
about the importance of work. Elder Bruce R. McConkie
wrote, "Work is a blessing that brings salvation, idleness a
curse that assures damnation" (*Mormon Doctrine,* 2nd ed.
[Salt Lake City: Bookcraft, 1966], p. 847). Elder McConkie
also said, "The gospel requires that man work in temporal as
well as spiritual pursuits to gain salvation" (*Mormon Doctrine,*
pp. 224–25). President David O. McKay eloquently taught,

"Let us teach them to work and to realize that the *privilege* to work is a gift, that *power* to work is a blessing, that *love* to work is success" (*True to the Faith,* comp. Llewelyn R. McKay [Salt Lake City: Bookcraft, 1966], p. 287).

THE RELATIONSHIP BETWEEN WORKING AND RECEIVING

Some who assist the needy believe that they should put a dollar value on the work a person contributes. In other words, a recipient should work a certain number of hours for a certain amount of commodities. Some bishops have even said, "I'll give you so much per hour for the work you do." In the true spirit of welfare, this is neither accurate nor fair. An individual's needs will usually far outweigh his abilities. He should receive to the extent of his need. The amount of work given does not have to equal the amount of help received.

To illustrate, a brother drove a city bus for many years and at an advanced age was forced to retire since he could no longer handle the job. He dreaded the thought of being idle. He talked to his bishop, who told him that he would be welcome to work at the bishops' storehouse. He and his wife received a small pension and Social Security payments, and they had limited savings. Their only financial problem would be buying coal when winter came. The bishop agreed to furnish them with coal, and the brother agreed to work to the extent of his ability.

During the first two or three years he worked nearly forty hours a week. He loved his work, and his greatest desire was to serve. His contribution far exceeded what he received from the welfare program. After a few years his health declined so that he could work only three days a week. His savings were depleted and his needs began to increase. The bishop and Relief Society president provided additional bishop's orders for him. Eventually the brother was able to work only one day a week. It was the most he could do. Although as time went by his contributions decreased and his needs increased, he was still giving to the extent of his ability and receiving what he needed—*everything was in perfect balance.*

It would never have worked for the bishop to put a cash value on this brother's contributions or his needs. He was treated in the true spirit of the welfare program.

THE LAW OF THE FAST

On 30 March 1990, Elder James E. Faust spoke to Regional Representatives and summarized the basic principles connected with the law of the fast. This address was presented shortly after the First Presidency announced that Saints in the United States and Canada would no longer be required to make donations in addition to tithes and offerings.

"We are living in a great new era of Church history. The signs of the times are so numerous and compelling that we can hardly conceive of them all. One of the great announcements in our lifetime is that made recently by the First Presidency, indicating that because the Saints in the United States and Canada have been faithful in the payment of their tithes, Saints in these countries will not be assessed for other contributions. Their contribution will only be in the form of tithes and offerings.

"This announcement represents an act of faith on the part of the First Presidency and the Twelve that the Saints themselves in turn will increase in the purity of their spirit and worship by generously returning to the Lord that which is already his in tithes and offerings. . . .

Elder James E. Faust

These freewill offerings will continue to be needed to move forward the many phases of the Lord's work. . . . I wish to emphasize the law of the fast as a form of true worship and the importance of generous fast offerings.

" . . . The law of the fast needs to be continually taught and testified to in the Church. There are separate, supernal blessings available for those who keep the law of the fast. . . .

"President Thomas S. Monson explained that a generous offering is also part of the true fast: 'Remember the principle of the true fast. . . . An honest fast offering, a generous fast offering, will certainly be an indication to our Heavenly Father that we know and abide this particular law' ('Guiding Principles of Personal and Family Welfare,' *Ensign,* Sept. 1986, p. 4). . . .

" . . . President Marion G. Romney stated that 'a maximum fast offering may be measured by the greatness of one's heart' (in Conference Report, Oct. 1950, p. 128).

"For many years, fast offerings contributed to the Church have not been sufficient to entirely care for the needs of the poor. . . .

" . . . The needs of the poor are as great as ever. Has not the day arrived when, with all of the demands all over the world upon the Church for tithing resources, fast offerings should meet the requirement of caring for the poor and the needy?

"Our fast offerings will begin to more fully meet the needs of the poor when every member of the Church observes the fast, is invited to make an offering, and experiences the blessings of giving generously.

"A modest increase in the amount of fast offerings by each member could easily balance donations with expenditures for the whole Church.

"President Harold B. Lee stated: 'And when we presented some statistics to [President Grant] one time, the great increase in the amount of fast offerings, which to us was a very laudable thing, he told us that he was not primarily concerned about the dollars and cents, but that the Church needs blessings, and the only way we can receive the blessings is by keeping the laws on which those blessings are predicated; and the fundamental law pertaining to the welfare of our people was fast offerings. . . . If our people observe the fast and consecrate their fast by paying an offering, we don't need to worry about the amounts of the money' (welfare agricultural meeting, 3 Apr. 1971).

"President Gordon B. Hinckley recently gave renewed emphasis to this principle and the accompanying promise in these powerful words: 'We hope that through the payment of liberal fast offerings there will be more than enough to provide for the needs of the less fortunate. If every member of this Church observed the fast and contributed generously, the poor and the needy not only of the Church, but many others as well, would be blessed and provided for. Every giver would be blessed in body and spirit, and the hungry would be fed, the naked clothed according to need' (Special Budget Fireside, 18 Feb. 1990). . . .

"Our basic challenge is to teach our people to faithfully observe the law of the fast, and invite them to consecrate their fast by making a generous offering. I have the faith to believe that if the saints will do this, they will be greatly blessed and there will be sufficient amounts of money to care for the poor and the needy. This is the spirit in which President Romney promised in 1971, 'If the members of the Church would double their fast-offering contributions, the spirituality in the Church would double' (welfare agricultural meeting, 3 Apr. 1971)."

SPIRITUAL ASPECTS OF THE WELFARE PROGRAM

The spiritual blessings of a properly administered welfare program far exceed the physical blessings. The real vitality of the welfare program is not in its physical accomplishments, but in the love and strength of character members develop as they serve one another and are lifted and blessed by others.

The welfare program today is blessing more lives than ever before. There are more full-tithe payers and more faithful members who appreciate the privilege of paying a generous fast offering. In addition, thousands of willing members give of their time and effort to assist in the canneries, the storehouses, and other welfare facilities. Church members who serve in these ways are blessed abundantly in many aspects of their lives.

President J. Reuben Clark, Jr., said: "The real long term objective of the Welfare Plan is the building of character in the members of the Church, givers and receivers, rescuing all that is finest down deep inside of them, and bringing to flower and fruitage the latent richness of the spirit, which after all is the mission and purpose and reason for being of this Church" (special meeting of stake presidents, 2 Oct. 1936). This objective has been accomplished in the lives of many people.

President Marion G. Romney said: "The principles of the welfare plan, when applied, will lift us out of this worldly life. The welfare plan is the most spiritual program in the Church. It is the final program and preparation for us to live. If and when properly lived, it will usher in the millennium" (regional meeting on Welfare Square, 6 June 1989).

After the Lord visited the Book of Mormon people and taught them, the Saints lived the principles of the welfare program in their fulness. The scriptures record:

"And they had all things common among them; therefore there were not rich and poor, bond and free, but they were all made free, and partakers of the heavenly gift" (4 Nephi 1:3). This heavenly gift is promised to all who will reach out to others in the compassionate way taught by the welfare program.

Providing in the Lord's Way: A Leader's Guide to Welfare

Through the years the Church has produced handbooks and other aids to help leaders and members understand the purposes and processes of the welfare program. Many of these publications are listed in appendix G at the end of this book.

In 1990, a publication titled *Providing in the Lord's Way: A Leader's Guide to Welfare* was prepared and translated for worldwide use. It explains the basic principles that underlie the Church welfare program today. These principles will greatly help members to provide for themselves, their families, and the poor and the needy in the way the Lord has prescribed.

The leader's guide is the first set of welfare guidelines that has been distributed throughout the worldwide Church. Before this publication, Church leaders in some countries had very little information on Church welfare. The concept of a bishops' storehouse was limited to a physical building filled with food, clothing, and other necessary items. This publication introduced another idea of a bishops' storehouse, as explained by President Thomas S. Monson:

"The Lord's storehouse includes the time, talents, skills, compassion, consecrated material, and financial means of faithful Church members. These resources are available to the bishop in assisting those in need" ("Guiding Principles of Personal and Family Welfare," *Ensign,* Sept. 1986, p. 5).

The leader's guide contains five statements prepared by the First Presidency to teach basic welfare principles. They are as follows:

1. *A Definition of the Lord's Storehouse*

"The Lord's storehouse receives, holds in trust, and dispenses consecrated offerings of the Saints. In form and operation, the storehouse is as simple or sophisticated as circumstances require. It may be a list of available services, money in an account, food in a pantry, or commodities in a building. A storehouse is established the moment faithful members give to the bishop of their time, talents, skills, compassion, materials, and financial means in caring for the poor and in building up the kingdom of God on the earth" (p. 11).

2. *The Scope of Welfare*

"Church welfare initiatives by ward and stake leaders should concentrate on helping people overcome those causes of welfare need which the individual or family can remedy.

"Individual Church members, as citizens, may work toward solving economic and political problems by participating in worthy projects sponsored by their communities" (pp. 11–12).

3. *The Bishop's Role*

"Through his priesthood office and calling, the bishop determines to whom, when, how, and how much shall be given to any member of his ward as Church welfare. To enable the bishop to properly discharge his responsibilities, the stake president ensures that the bishop understands welfare principles" (p. 12).

4. *When Assistance Exceeds Donations in the Ward*

"When fast-offering expenditures will exceed donations, the bishop and stake president should counsel together beforehand to ensure that correct principles are being applied" (p. 13).

5. *Public Assistance*

"Latter-day Saints have the responsibility to provide for themselves and their families. Individual members, however, may find it necessary to receive assistance beyond that which the family can provide, in which case they may turn to the Church for help. In some instances, individual members may decide to receive assistance from other sources,

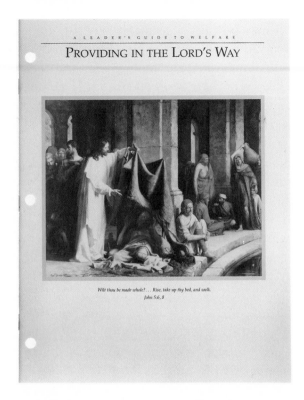

PROVIDING IN THE LORD'S WAY

A LEADER'S GUIDE TO WELFARE

Wilt thou be made whole?... Rise, take up thy bed, and walk.
John 5:6, 8

Providing in the Lord's Way: A Leader's Guide to Welfare

including government. In all such cases, members should avoid becoming dependent upon these sources and strive to become self-reliant. Where possible, they should work in return for assistance rendered" (p. 15).

These five statements address many of the questions that might arise in the administration of welfare today and in the future.

This guide makes clear that no matter where the Church is in the world, a bishops' storehouse exists, and every bishop and branch president can draw upon it to help the poor and needy. For leaders who live where there is a physical bishops' storehouse, a publication titled *Church Welfare Resources for Use in the United States and Canada* (34475) is available.

HAROLD B. LEE ON THE NECESSITY OF THE WELFARE PROGRAM

President Harold B. Lee said the following about those who thought the welfare program would fail:

> There wasn't any beginning to the
> welfare program.
> There isn't any ending of the
> welfare program;
> We are always in the middle of it—
> no beginnings,
> no endings,
> only middles.

"When the welfare program was first announced we had many doubters in the Church. There were those who were predicting that it would be a dismal failure, that it would bankrupt the Church if we set out to try to take care of the needy and unfortunate in the Church, and why should we anyway when we pay taxes, and why didn't we go the way of the government? I was called in by one for whom I have respect. I was a young stake president struggling to take care of my people, and this one said to me, 'Now don't you know that this is a modern age? This matter of churches taking care of their own, that's all passé; this is a modern time when we have been so taught in social welfare that communities get together to take care of their own. This is a laudable effort that you are making down there, but just put it aside and get in line with the modern trend to join with the social agencies and let them join with us in taking care of our own.'

"I said, 'I am sorry; I have read some scriptures and I believe in following what the Lord said.' He said, 'It is my purpose to provide for my saints, for all things are mine . . . ' (D&C 104:15).

"I said, ' . . . I have a responsibility that I am going to try to take care of my people in the Lord's way.'

"Well, fortunately we had a president of the Church who led out in those days when finances were very low and the income was very small; we were struggling in the midst of depression, and it seemed as though we didn't have anywhere to look. I went to the office of the First Presidency with some of my brethren, and he said, in substance, 'We are going to take care of our needy. So don't you worry; we will stand behind you if other things have to go by the board.'

President Harold B. Lee

" . . . One morning as I parked my car out on the parking lot, President Grant was just coming in, and he asked if he could come up with me to my room in the Church office building. And he said something to the effect that, 'I have had some things on my mind.' He said, 'The statistics of the Church and the income of the Church have been gradually increasing, and increasing, and increasing; and that economically is not justified. There was nothing in our communities to make this advance in income.' Then he added that the only way he can explain it is that we are now taking care of our poor and our Heavenly Father is blessing us for it.

"He added that it was miraculous to see that since we started to take care of the needy in the welfare program the income of the Church has increased and increased, and instead as the calamity howlers said that we would fail, we are better off today than we were before because we are taking care of the needy" (welfare agricultural meeting, 3 Apr. 1971).

SPENCER W. KIMBALL'S VISION OF SELF-HELP

"We have had many calamities in this past period. It seems that every day or two there is an earthquake or a flood or a tornado or distress that brings trouble to many people. I am grateful to see that our people and our leaders are beginning to catch the vision of their self-help.

"Let me say that as a stake president long ago, we had a flood in the Duncan Valley in Arizona. As soon as we overcame the excitement of the first report of it, my counselors and I formulated a telegram and sent it to Salt Lake City and said, 'Please send us $10,000 by return mail.' I found that I was learning about welfare programs when no $10,000 came. When President Lee, President Romney and President Moyle came down and took me back in my little office in my business place we sat down around the table and they said, 'This isn't a program of "give me." This is a program of "self-help." ' And so we learned much from those brethren.

"The other stakes in Arizona over the weekend gathered many hundreds of dollars and the presidents of those stakes came rushing in and I remember Lorenzo Wright of the Maricopa Stake in Mesa pulling out of his pocket checks, and bills, and cash, and that was all given to us. After we got in gear and saw that the problem was ours and that we had plenty of people who hadn't been distressed and plenty of people who had the means, we went to work. My office was on Main Street and every day I would see passing my office truckloads of hay and wire and posts going up to Duncan because the flood had washed out

President Spencer W. Kimball

307

the valley fences, barns, and haystacks. It had torn down all the fences, and had left hills where there were hollows and vice versa. Then we got the county to let us use some of their big equipment and it wasn't so very long until the land was leveled; the fences were built; the clothes had been cleaned that were hanging in the closets and covered with mud; and we had helped ourselves; and we had relieved the problems that had brought distress to so many people.

"Now it would have been an easy thing, I think, for the Brethren to have sent us that $10,000 and it wouldn't have been too hard to sit in my office and distribute it; but what a lot of good came to us as we had hundreds of men go to Duncan and build fences and haul the hay and level the ground and do all the things that needed doing. That is self-help" (in Conference Report, Apr. 1974, pp. 183–84).

SPENCER W. KIMBALL'S THOUGHTS ON CARING FOR THE POOR

"Brethren, we hear reports from time to time of older men and women who, in the sunset of their lives, are neglected by their families and their neighbors. Those who are both poor and old often suffer doubly. We hope family members, quorums, Relief Society officers, bishops and others, using the Lord's own way, will make certain that they are not inadvertently neglecting such needy people. The ways the world has of helping the poor are not often the Lord's way. We must render help in the Lord's way, but let us do it!

"We hear reports, too, of some women who are with child but who are not eating well enough for their own health and for the proper development of the child that is about to be born. Please, priesthood leaders, tend the flock. Be certain that we are proceeding appropriately to learn of such instances where people need help of one kind or another.

Please don't assume that such individuals will always make their needs known. Often those who need help most are the last to make it known.

"To be sure, there are some who are poor who seem unconcerned with remedying their situation and there are, of course, some who try to take advantage of every free offer. The ones about whom I am particularly speaking, however, are those who will suffer in silence because they are proud or because they do not know what to do. Surely sensitive home teachers, visiting teachers, quorum leaders, and bishops can be more effective in both ascertaining and responding to the needs of these individuals and meeting them. If we have neighborhoods, wards, or stakes that are overwhelmed by the size of these problems in their midst, there is a way in which they can be assisted under the established procedures of the Church welfare program.

"I do not worry about members of the Church being unresponsive when they learn of the needy as much as I worry about our being unaware of such needs. Moroni warned the affluent of all ages about becoming comfortable and loving the things of this world 'more than ye love the poor and the needy, the sick and the afflicted' (Mormon 8:37). We can sometimes pass by such people and 'notice them not' (Mormon 8:39). Please, priesthood leaders, do not get so busy trying to manage Church programs that you forget about basic duties in what the Apostle James described as 'pure religion and undefiled' (James 1:27)" (Regional Representatives' seminar, 29 Sept. 1978).

GORDON B. HINCKLEY'S VISION OF THE WELFARE PROGRAM

Over fifty years ago, President Gordon B. Hinckley wrote a small pamphlet titled *Helping Others to Help Themselves: The Story of the Mormon Church Welfare Program*. This document is no longer in print, but it is one of the finest explanations of the principles of the Church welfare program. Following are some excerpts:

"In principle the plan is not new among a people who have always believed that whatever pertains to human welfare is the rightful concern of the Church. The prophets and seers of all ages have been champions of the poor and helpless. The Church cannot be less. So

President Gordon B. Hinckley

it has always cared for its needy, but the inroads of unemployment during the thirties demanded more than the customary machinery of relief within the Church if its people were to be kept free and not made wards of the government.

"A man out of work is of special moment to the Church because, deprived of his inheritance, he is on trial as Job was on trial—for his integrity. As days lengthen into weeks and months and even years of adversity, the hurt grows deeper, and he is sorely tempted to 'curse God and die.' Continued economic dependence breaks him; it humiliates him if he is strong, spoils him if he is weak. Sensitive or calloused, despondent or indifferent, rebellious or resigned—either way, he is threatened with spiritual ruin, for the dole is an evil and idleness a curse. He soon becomes the seedbed of discontent, wrong thinking, alien beliefs. The Church cannot hope to save a man on Sunday if during the week it is a complacent witness to the crucifixion of his soul. . . .

"Such is the Mormon belief, and on the strength of it the Church, with courageous and resolute determination, is leading its members to prepare for their own economic security.

Thus has come the widely heralded Welfare Program of the Church.

"The Welfare Program looks three ways:

"First, it looks to the distribution of the necessities of life among the needy. . . .

"Second, it looks to the providing of employment for members out of work, either in private industry or on Church-directed projects. . . .

"Third, it looks to the gradual, progressive improvement of existing conditions among dependent or low-income groups. . . .

"Clearly, such a program gives every man an intensified interest in his brother's welfare. Upon the weak and strong it places an obligation of mutual support. The strong must assist the weak; the weak must seek strength for themselves. There must be abundant charity but no alms-giving. All must produce. All must pay in some way for that which they receive. The program cannot succeed unless helper and helped, in brotherhood, stand shoulder to shoulder in a consecration of effort to banish the inequalities which separate them from each other and threaten their religious solidarity. Opportunity, self-support and mutual goodwill form the foundation of the program. . . .

"When every mouth has been fed, when every able pair of hands has been set to work—when every member has given what he is able and has received in return whatever he needs—the work of the Program has only just begun. There are larger problems, as complex as society itself, demanding attention. . . . Men must have the comforts as well as the necessities of life: education, amusement, cultural pursuits, and above all, opportunity for spiritual growth and joy" (*Helping Others to Help Themselves: The Story of the Mormon Church Welfare Program* [pamphlet, 1941], pp. 3–5, 11–12).

THOMAS S. MONSON'S GUIDELINES FOR PROVIDING ASSISTANCE

"Since [the beginnings of the welfare program], we as a Church have continued to receive divine direction as circumstances have required. Programs and procedures used to implement welfare principles have been modified, and they likely will continue to change from time to time to meet changing needs. But the basic principles do not change. They will not change. They are revealed truths. Direct counsel has been given regarding the application of these revealed truths."

President Monson then reviewed five basic guidelines that bishops should follow when providing welfare assistance:

"First, bishops are to seek out the poor as the Lord has commanded and administer to their needs. Do not suppose that someone else will do it. It is a bishop's priesthood duty. He may call on members to assist, but he is responsible.

"Second, bishops should thoroughly analyze the circumstances surrounding each need for welfare assistance. He wisely calls on his Relief Society president to assist in the evaluation. He exercises discernment, sound judgment, balance, and compassion. Church resources represent a sacred trust which becomes even more sacred as the bishop properly applies these resources in blessing the lives of others.

"Third, those receiving welfare assistance should work to the extent of their abilities for that which is received. There are many creative ways leaders can provide work opportunities. With help from their welfare services committees, bishops will want to provide that work which will enhance the recipient's efforts to become self-reliant.

"Fourth, the assistance given by the bishop is temporary and partial. Remember, Church assistance is designed to help people help themselves. The rehabilitation of members is the responsibility of the individual and the family, aided by the priesthood quorum and Relief Society. We are attempting to develop independence, not dependence. The bishop seeks to build integrity, self-respect, dignity, and soundness of character in each person assisted, leading to complete self-sufficiency.

President Thomas S. Monson

"Fifth, we assist with basic life-sustaining goods and services, not the maintenance of current living standards. Individuals and families may need to alter their standards of living in doing all they can to meet their own needs. A church dole would be worse than a government dole because it would fail in the face of greater light. Church practices portray more honorable aims, more glorious potential.

"Faithful compliance with these revealed welfare principles and practices have preserved lives in times of crises" ("Guiding Principles of Personal and Family Welfare," *Ensign,* Sept. 1986, pp. 3, 5).

GEMS OF PURE RELIGION
◆ ◆ ◆

Who Are the Poor and Needy?

There is a difference between being poor and being needy. The needy might lack money, employment, or some other temporal thing. It is usually easy to solve their need. The poor may be poor in spirit, manner, habits or lifestyle. If they are given money, food, or clothing, they may remain poor.

They have difficulty handling their money or managing their homes. They are usually remiss in their church attendance. Their needs require assistance from compassionate people, and even then, a long healing process is often required.

Jesus said, "Suffer the little children to come unto me, and forbid them not: for of such is the kingdom of God. . . . And he took them up in his arms, put his hands upon them, and blessed them" (Mark 10:14, 16).

The poor of the Church are in some ways like little children. They may be unwise in their judgment, easily distracted, and a little self-centered. Even their faith is like a child's—they go to their bishop when they have a need and expect to get just what they ask for. They are usually unaware of their own responsibilities.

The poor of the Church need leaders who are understanding and patient. Charity, *the pure love of Christ,* must be in the heart of every bishop and Relief Society president.

♦ ♦ ♦

Err on the Side of Generosity

Recently President Monson said to me, "I always considered myself as a bishop who erred on the side of generosity, and if I had it to do again, I would be even more generous."
Author, in talk to Quorums of the Seventy, August 1991

♦ ♦ ♦

Protection against Need

Elder Marion G. Romney said:

"Personally, I believe that the most practical way to protect one's self and family against economic need is to make liberal contributions for the support of the Lord's poor according to the law of the Gospel. I am not promising you riches, but I am telling you that this is the most practical way to protect yourselves and families from actual need.

"I believe that it is consistent with the laws of Heaven that one's right of reliance upon the Lord for protection against want is in direct proportion to his own liberality in sustaining the Lord's poor."

"A Practical Religion," address given to seminary and institute faculty, Brigham Young University, 13 June 1956

Elder Harold B. Lee and President Heber J. Grant working on a welfare project

CHAPTER 12

GREAT WELFARE LEADERS

Many Church leaders and welfare workers have made great contributions to the success of the Church welfare program. Space does not allow all of their contributions to be presented here, but they are remembered by many grateful people.

WELFARE PIONEERS

Elder Thomas S. Monson identified four pioneers who made major contributions to the welfare program: "I am grateful my welfare roots go deep into the soil of the Pioneer Stake and the Pioneer Welfare Region, where giants of our time—Harold B. Lee, Paul C. Child, William F. Perschon, and Jesse M. Drury—taught, testified, and inspired" (Regional Representatives' seminar, 3 Apr. 1981).

Sister Belle S. Spafford should also be recognized as a welfare pioneer. Her dedicated work as the General Relief Society President in the early years of the Church welfare program set a pattern of compassionate service that remains to this day.

President Harold B. Lee

Harold B. Lee had a major influence on the modern-day welfare program of the Church. He grew up in very meager living conditions. His father managed a small farm that provided the necessities, but the family had to live frugally because there was little surplus money to buy things not produced by their own labors. His parents were good Latter-day

Saints, and he was taught by his father and mother how to work hard. He also learned to play the piano and other musical instruments.

Brother Lee finished eight years of grade school and then attended the Oneida Stake Academy in Preston, Idaho. When he was only seventeen, he was employed as a teacher in a small school in southern Idaho. He sent most of the money he made, sixty dollars a month, home to assist his family. At age eighteen he became the principal of a larger school, where he was very active as a debater and a musician.

After filling a mission for the Church and marrying, he and his wife, along with his brother S. Perry Lee and his wife, moved to Salt Lake City. It wasn't long before Brother Lee held important positions in Pioneer Stake. At age thirty he became a member of the stake presidency, then the stake president at age thirty-one.

As soon as Brother Lee recognized the serious unemployment and other welfare needs in his stake brought about by the Great Depression, he couldn't rest until he had organized his high council and bishops to care for the needs of the people of his stake. The events of his youth made him sensitive to the needs of those who struggle with problems.

The welfare work that Brother Lee was doing and his understanding of correct principles caught the attention of the General Authorities. The Pioneer Stake welfare program became the pattern for the welfare program that was later adopted throughout the Church, and Brother Lee became the managing director.

In this position, he traveled extensively for five years before he was called to become a member of the Quorum of the Twelve in 1941. With the new calling he had a greater opportunity to be a leader in welfare matters. He had great vision and knew what the future was going to require. Under the direction of the First Presidency, he organized the

Church welfare program basically as it is today. In 1959 Elder Lee said:

"In those days we learned a bitter lesson, but not as soon as we should. When a man is starving there is no opportunity to feed him spiritually. Only when a man has been fed and clothed and his temporal wants have been satisfied, and only then, can you begin to spiritualize that man. This is one of the first lessons. . . .

"What happened in that day was an interesting thing, and everywhere I went people were always asking questions. They asked, 'Who started the Welfare Program?' I have always answered, and do today, 'The Lord started it.' Many asked how the Welfare Program was getting along—and that got to be such a monotonous question that everywhere I was being asked how the Welfare Program was going—and I used to say, 'Just as fine as the bishops of this Church make it go, and no better' " (Pioneer Region bimonthly welfare meeting, 17 Mar. 1959, held at Welfare Square).

There is no doubt that Harold B. Lee was a teacher of principles, a trainer of leaders, and an inspiration behind much of the welfare work we do today.

President Paul C. Child

Paul C. Child served for many years as the president of Pioneer Stake in Salt Lake City. He was a master teacher who taught Church doctrine and procedures and always used the scriptures. The meetings he conducted were opportunities to teach, not just discussions of Church business. President Child made sure that counselors to bishops were invited into all of the

Paul C. Child

319

monthly bishopric training meetings. He carefully instructed his bishops to take care of their people with a spirit of charity and love.

He was a young boy when his father died, and he then became responsible to help provide for his mother's family. This deprived him of some of the advantages of other children, but because he worked from his childhood on, he knew the true meaning of work.

His life's experiences helped him to become sympathetic to others' problems and appreciative of their contributions. He often spoke about his first ward teacher with high regard. This elderly man had paid special attention to him and helped him become fully active in the Church.

President Child was a great friend to people and had a tremendous influence on priesthood leaders. He taught many newly called bishops how to manage the affairs of the ward, particularly how to take care of the poor and needy. For example, one summer night in 1945, Glen L. Rudd was called to the office of President Child and his counselors. President Child told him that he would be sustained as a bishop on Sunday. President Child testified that the Lord had revealed to him beyond any doubt that Brother Rudd was to fill this position in a ward with a heavy welfare load. He gave the new young bishop detailed instructions about how to care for the poor and needy of the Church, which proved to be of great value in the ten years of service that followed.

President Child became involved in athletic activities and did a considerable amount of coaching. This was one way, among others, in which he was able to bring many young men who lived in his ward boundaries into the Church.

When President Child was released as stake president, he served for many years as a member of the General Welfare Committee. He traveled throughout the Church with the General Authorities, always teaching with the scriptures in his hands and declaring welfare principles from the standard works and from his own experience. He was one of the most able of all the men who served on the General Welfare Committee and was appreciated and respected wherever he went.

He and his wife presided over a mission, allowing him to complete his life on earth as a teacher of the gospel.

Bishop Jesse M. Drury

Jesse M. Drury was bishop of the Fifth Ward in Pioneer Stake, then a counselor to President Paul C. Child in the stake presidency, and then the stake patriarch. He also had Church welfare assignments for over thirty-two years.

In the very early days of the welfare program, Elder Harold B. Lee sent him on a trip to introduce the welfare plan in several Utah counties. He did not have a car, so he traveled from place to place by train

Jesse M. Drury

and by hitchhiking. Sometimes he had to walk in deep snow. He was gone eleven days and spent a total of eleven dollars. He wrote that this was a "wonderful spiritual experience" for him.

He was the storehouse keeper of the original Pierpont Avenue storehouse in Salt Lake City, then the first regional storehouse, and finally the Welfare Square storehouse. In these capacities he touched the lives of hundreds of bishops, Relief Society presidents, and other welfare workers. He was schooled well by his own priesthood leaders and, in a humble and understanding way, was able to teach welfare principles to many other leaders.

A steady flow of people with problems sought out Bishop Drury for advice and council. He helped prepare them to work with their bishops to receive whatever was necessary. His experiences throughout his life increased his understanding and capacity to love those who were struggling with life's problems.

Later in his life several men whom he had taught and trained were appointed as managers over him. He followed their directions and sustained the leaders of the Church. On the day when President David O. McKay called Elder Henry D. Moyle to be a Counselor in the First Presidency, Brother Drury said of the call, "That makes President Moyle one of the three greatest men on the face of the earth."

This faithful spirit motivated Bishop Drury in his service. Few, if any, in the history of welfare have touched more lives than this bishop, who had in his heart the true spirit of love and compassion. President Paul Child said of him: "Of course, there is no way of knowing, but I am certain that Bishop Drury has saved more souls than any other man in the Church." He was referring to the thousands of people who had come to the bishops' storehouse in the years that Bishop Drury served as storehouse keeper.

Bishop William F. Perschon

William F. Perschon, a convert to the Church from Germany, served as bishop over the Fourth Ward of the Pioneer Stake for many years and was an unusually successful leader. In his leadership style, he was both visionary and practical. He took advantage of many opportunities to speak personally to the Aaronic Priesthood boys of his ward. He worked well with men who needed counsel in how to cope with the difficulties caused by the Depression.

Bishop Perschon greatly influenced the lives of many young people. Twenty-nine boys and men who lived in

his ward while he presided became
bishops. Ten became stake presidents or counselors in stake presidencies, and eleven became full-time
mission presidents. Three served as
Regional Representatives, three were
temple presidents, and two were
called as General Authorities of the
Church. He had the ability and took
the time to make men out of boys
and to prepare them for great assignments.

William F. Perschon

In the early 1950s, Bishop Perschon worked less than one
block from where President Harold B. Lee had his office as a
Salt Lake City commissioner. On many occasions during the
early days of the stake welfare program, Brother Lee would
visit with Bishop Perschon at his business. At times Brother
Lee would invite the bishop to come to his office and they
would counsel together. These two men, both of them with
vision, grew very close to each other and sustained each
other in their positions.

In 1960 Bishop Perschon wrote the story of the beginning
of the welfare plan. He said that President Harold B. Lee
"would drop [into my office] from time to time to unburden
his soul to me. I remember in particular the morning he
drove up State Street and when he saw me he stopped his car
and motioned to me to approach him, and this is what he
told me. He said, 'Bishop, this morning the three members
of the Stake Presidency are going to meet with the President
of the Church. Pray for us, so that we may be blessed to
report correctly and effectively the Pioneer Stake Welfare
Plan so that we have their support in our undertaking' "
("The Beginning of the Welfare Plan," written in the early
1960s).

The members who lived in William F. Perschon's ward were greatly influenced by his spirituality and his loyalty to those who presided over him.

President Belle S. Spafford

President Belle S. Spafford

The sisters of the Church have played a vital part in Church welfare activities. As welfare projects were established, in almost every case the sisters were involved. They worked shoulder to shoulder with the men, in addition to providing meals for the workers.

Many sisters could be mentioned, but the work of Belle Smith Spafford stands out. Sister Spafford became a counselor to Amy Brown Lyman, General Relief Society President, in October 1942. She succeeded Sister Brown as General President on 6 April 1945. She served until October 1974, twenty-nine and one-half years.

During this time Sister Spafford visited many bishops' storehouses and Deseret Industries stores. She was particularly interested in the sewing that the Relief Society sisters did for the storehouses. On many occasions, the manager of Welfare Square would call and invite her to come and see the sewing that had been received at the square. She would come and spend an hour or two just admiring the beautiful work of the sisters. She was extremely pleased with the work the sisters did. In her mind, the women did more than the men in filling the shelves of the storehouses. She constantly urged the sisters to sew for themselves and then for others, and particularly for the storehouses of the Church.

Few women ever attended as many general committee and other planning meetings as she did, and she had a comprehensive knowledge of the entire welfare program. She was a vigorous speaker and teacher who could explain welfare principles in a way that everyone could understand.

Her zeal and compassion supported her as she traveled, spoke, and worked constantly over many long years in behalf of others. Others have followed her leadership, and the Church has had valiant service from Relief Society sisters at every level.

OTHER DEDICATED WORKERS

Many faithful welfare workers have received little recognition. Representative of these fine people are Lenore Nitsch and Walter Stover, both of whom recently passed away.

Lenore Nitsch

At the time of her retirement, Lenore Kimball Nitsch had served as an employee in the welfare program longer than any other person. She was born in Salt Lake City and had lived for some years in California. In 1943, when she was twenty-four years old, she came from California to seek a job in Salt Lake City. At that time, she received her temple blessings and resolved to be self-sustaining as much as possible for the rest of her life.

She had little to offer except a beautiful smile and a willing spirit. She was born with spina bifida, a condition that left her paralyzed from the waist down, and she spent her life on crutches or in a wheelchair. She wondered if anyone would hire her. She went to the State Employment Office several times but found nothing. Someone there told her to go to the LDS Church Employment Office. Again, she did not find employment. After several attempts she was told to see Brother Roscoe W. Eardley, who was serving as the first

manager of the welfare program,
working under Harold B. Lee.

Brother Eardley interviewed her
and sent her to see Stewart Eccles
and Jesse M. Drury at Welfare
Square. They told her they would
think about hiring her and get in
touch with her. Lenore knew that
they could make up their minds
right then, and she asked if they
would please do so. The men had a
little meeting and then offered her a
position at seventy-five dollars a month.

Lenore Nitsch

This offer to work at Welfare Square released her from an
existence that had been difficult and protected since her
birth. She had been working in California ironing shirts for
boarders who lived in the family home, where she made
between ten and twenty dollars a month. She was very grateful for this new opportunity. For the next fifty-one years she
gave excellent service at Welfare Square and expressed appreciation for her employment many times. In spite of her
physical handicap, she enjoyed good health and hardly ever
missed a day of work. She was punctual, and she always radi-
ated happiness.

At age twenty-five she married Siegfried Nitsch, and for
the next twenty-four years the two of them lived a life of
great adventure. They took many trips throughout the
United States and were willing to try almost anything.

They both had beautiful voices, and they sang at many
Church functions and funerals. Each year for about twenty-
four years, they sang at the Christmas devotional at Welfare
Square. President Harold B. Lee and President Marion G.
Romney attended most of these devotionals and remarked
several times that they never really got the spirit of

Christmas until they heard Lenore and her husband sing "The Holy City."

After she was widowed, she purchased a car with special hand equipment and learned to drive. She carried on for another twenty-six years.

Those who worked with her will never forget her spirit of love and devotion. Her work as the receptionist and telephone operator near the entrance of Welfare Square allowed her to meet thousands who came to visit, work, or receive assistance. She always greeted them with a radiant smile. Most never knew of her physical handicap. Bishops, stake presidents, and Relief Society presidents loved the "voice of Welfare Square," as she was called by many. Many of the First Presidency and other General Authorities knew and appreciated her.

After forty-five years Lenore retired but never quit her work. She continued to enjoy reasonably good health and a joyful spirit until she died. She was just concluding fifty-one years of service when she passed away.

Walter Stover

Fifty-four brethren had the privilege of serving as members of the General Welfare Committee between 1936 and 1967. One of those who made an outstanding contribution was Walter Stover.

Brother Stover was born in Germany in 1899. His mother died when he was born, and his father died when Walter was eleven years of age. By diligent effort he was able to complete his education. He married at age 22 and shortly afterward opened his first mattress and furniture factory. In 1923, he and his wife accepted the gospel and joined the Church. They immigrated to Utah in 1926 and moved into the Fourth Ward of Pioneer Stake, which was presided over by Bishop William F. Perschon.

In 1929 Walter purchased a mattress factory in Salt Lake City. With few material resources but a lot of faith and hard work, he became very successful and prosperous in his business affairs.

At the end of World War II, the missions in Europe were reopened. Walter Stover was called in 1946 to preside over the East German Mission. In addition to preaching the gospel and organizing branches,

Walter Stover

he was in charge of administering relief to the distressed Saints in Germany. He worked with President Cornelius Zappey in getting the Dutch potatoes and herring into Germany.

President Thomas S. Monson said: "This choice person has done more for the Saints in Germany than perhaps any other individual. He with his own funds erected two chapels in Berlin following the devastation of World War II. On one occasion he personally paid for and chartered an entire train to bring the Saints of the German Democratic Republic to a central meeting place that they might renew their testimonies and receive the sacrament. His eternal reward, I feel, is assured."

Walter did so many generous things that only the Lord has the full record of his kindnesses to others. In America, he freely donated mattresses from his business. He benefited Brigham Young University over a long period of time, including giving to Helaman Halls dormitories the mattresses to be used in each room. He also gave many mattresses to the welfare program, even though he could have sold them to the Church. He contributed $50,000 so that a mattress factory could be established as part of the welfare program and then taught the welfare workers how to make mattresses. Today the welfare program produces thousands of mattresses as a result of his generosity and skill.

Brother Stover lived into his nineties and died recently after a lifetime of generosity. Wherever he went to speak, audiences loved his spirit and message.

There are many faithful workers like Brother Stover and Sister Nitsch who represent one of the reasons for the success of the Church welfare program.

GEMS OF PURE RELIGION

Within the Welfare Program

They say it happened long ago and in a far-off land
Where men and women spoke a tongue we wouldn't
    understand;
The Holy Land, the Christmas Star, the manger where He
    lay—
The ancient streets the Savior walked, are half a world
    away.

Yet spanning land and ocean, with centuries between,
The spirit of the Christ Child lives and permeates this scene;
Within the Welfare Program, He walks and speaks today,
And works His quiet miracles with humble human clay.

'Twas not just in Judea mankind with burdens groped,
It was not just in Bethlehem the Christmas Star brought
    hope;
Today, and here, our fellowmen ofttimes would face despair
Except for those who hear their pleas, and will their
    burdens share.

Within the Welfare Program, throughout the years, you've
ministered for Him;
"Unto the least" you've given aid, and strength where hope
was dim.
When dedicated hearts and hands their daily tasks fulfill,
The earthbound glimpse eternity, and see the Christ Child
still!

Mabel H. Miller

Roger, the husband of Judy, at work in the meat cooler
of the Welfare Square storehouse

CHAPTER 13

WELFARE SUCCESS STORIES

Many individuals and families in serious need have been blessed by the Church welfare program. Most of them have had bishops or other compassionate friends who have intervened to help lift them above the dark and ominous clouds to see the blue sky and feel the warm sun. In many cases, just the opportunity to work or learn how to work was the beginning of the solution to their problems. Not all who received help successfully overcame their problems. Some progressed, faltered, and then finally succeeded.

The following are a few examples of real people who had real problems. Similar experiences are occurring thoughout the Church and have been since the early days of the modern welfare program.

JUDY AND ROGER

Judy was an eighteen-year-old girl living in a stake near Salt Lake City who was born with cerebral palsy. Graduating from high school was a tremendous accomplishment for her. Her family searched for employment for her for several months but found none and became quite discouraged. Being at home every day had become a serious problem for both Judy and her family. The family discussed the problem with their bishop, and the bishop talked with the manager at Welfare Square. "Is there anything she could do here?" the bishop asked. "She needs to be occupied. Her family doesn't need commodities. Their need is to have this girl busy doing something." The manager agreed to let her learn some working skills at the bishops' storehouse.

Her first assignment was to put labels on processed cans. Her wheelchair would allow her to sit at the big table, where she could reach the labels and glue. After some practice she succeeded in labeling a few cans. The first day was difficult, but she cooperated with those who were willing to help her. As she prepared to leave at the end of the day, she was very pleased that she had labeled eleven cases containing 264 cans. She had put in a full day's work, and she felt she had accomplished much. Eleven cases wouldn't have been a great accomplishment for someone with normal physical abilities, but Judy felt that it was one of the best days of her life.

Her supervisors found three or four hundred torn and ruined labels on the floor around her chair after she left. But they felt that the effort was worthwhile and that her mistakes would decrease as time went on. The important thing was what was happening to Judy, a sweet soul whose life was being enriched by doing something worthwhile for others.

Some months later, Judy learned how to candle eggs. Even though she broke a few at first, she could hold the eggs quite well, and she became very expert in this simple but necessary routine.

In 1961 a young boy came through the side door of the storehouse at Welfare Square. It took him fifteen minutes to tell the manager and Bishop Elwynn S. Hewlett, the storehouse keeper, who he was and where he was from. He had spent most of his life in an institution for retarded children in Idaho. When he was eighteen years of age, they discharged him because of his age and because they no longer felt he was retarded. He had great difficulty reading and writing, and he had a speech impediment that made it almost impossible for him to express himself. He was now on his own without relatives or friends, and for some time he had been living alone in the mountains of Idaho. Fortunately he got a ride into Salt Lake City, where he was directed to Welfare Square.

Bishop Hewlett found Roger a place to stay. Through the help of a generous bishop he became active in the Church and worked at Welfare Square as a welfare recipient. The bishop took care of his needs, and Roger worked every day doing many different assignments. He was a willing worker and eager to learn. Fellow workers at Welfare Square helped him to learn to speak better, and after several months almost everyone was able to understand him. He became a strong Church member and was ordained an elder.

Then Roger saw Judy, Judy saw Roger, and they fell in love. Soon they talked about the possibility of getting married. Judy's family agreed that it was a good thing, and many people at Welfare Square took part in helping them make arrangements to be married in the temple.

Roger obtained a steady job in private industry and was able to earn enough money to sustain the two of them. Roger and Judy have lived together happily for many years and blessed each other's lives.

ARTHUR

Some years ago, Arthur, a man who had lived a rough life, moved to Salt Lake City. He had been an excellent carpenter and had done much carpentry work in Pennsylvania. He had even worked as a foreman during the building of the Hoover Dam.

He married a returned sister missionary in her thirties. Their marriage was not pleasant for either of them. He was a crank about cleanliness and needed everything done in a precise and orderly way. She was easy going and not very meticulous, even careless at times. They eventually had

Arthur in his carpenter shop, 1960

three children. By the time they were in their fifties, even though they had been sealed in the temple, they were having a real struggle. Arthur's health was poor, and he was in bed most of the time with severe headaches and a bad back.

The family sometimes needed commodities and other things through the Church welfare program, but it was difficult to get Arthur to do any work in return. He had many excuses for why he couldn't assume responsibility.

One morning around 6:00 A.M. Arthur's wife went to the home of their bishop to talk about her problems. He listened and then went back with her to see her husband. The bishop reprimanded him for fifteen or twenty minutes about his unkindness to his wife. Arthur listened carefully and then said, "Bishop, if you are through, will you now listen to me?" He then told his side of the troubles. He claimed that his wife wasn't as neat as she should be and that he couldn't live in a house that wasn't kept orderly.

With the help of the bishop, they both discussed their faults. They finally agreed to improve their lives and try to live together peacefully. The bishop suggested that Arthur needed to begin working at a large Church welfare center and earn the help they were getting from the welfare program. He was willing but said he couldn't do anything. He claimed he was unable to even lift a hammer anymore.

Arthur was taken to Welfare Square, where he said over and over again that he couldn't do anything. The manager gave him the job of reading the scales at the coal yard. All he had to do was sit on a chair and once or twice a day, when a truck came in to get a load of coal, read the scale and write down the weight. Though necessary, it really wasn't much of a job.

After one week he asked for "something more to do, something more useful." The manager explained that he already had an important job. Arthur said, "Yes, but I can do more." The manager told him that there was plenty of work to do if he would do it and suggested carpentry work. Arthur again stated that he couldn't lift a hammer. What he did not know was that a small carpentry shop had been prepared for him. The manager took him to the shop and said, "Arthur, this is your shop if you want it. We need some things built around the square and there's always repair work to be done. If you will get busy and work here, you can be in charge of this shop."

Arthur immediately came to life. New life flowed into his body and spirit. Within a day or two he seemed to be fifteen or twenty years younger. He regained his skills and did a lot of good work for Welfare Square. The carpentry shop soon needed to be enlarged and some better tools purchased.

Arthur made some lovely desks, bookcases, and other items that were needed in the offices. He proved to be a fine worker. He stayed on for several years until his health failed.

On one occasion Arthur took old pieces of lumber from boxcars and other sources, sanded them, and found the

Sewing
cabinet made
by Arthur

wood to be good. He used this wood to make a beautiful sewing cabinet for his bishop's wife. He said, "I have made this in my spare time, and it has not cost anything except for hinges."

When a person receives a challenge, rediscovers what a marvelous thing work is, and learns that people will love and appreciate him for who he is, he truly becomes a new person.

Arthur and his wife eventually learned to resolve their problems and became faithful temple workers. When Arthur died, he was a high priest, a man of great talent. He responded to a little love, appreciation, and sympathetic understanding when it was most needed. Above all else, the opportunity to *work* changed his life.

Samm, Welfare Square painter, lettering new milk tanker

SAMM

When Samm first came to Welfare Square, he had only one desire—to be able to die. He later said of this time, "I was unemployed and completely broken in spirit, and I felt defeated." In his prayers he asked the Lord to take him if possible.

Samm told the story of his life to the workers at Welfare Square. For thirty-five years he had been active in the Church and seemingly happy. His two older sons had served missions and were married, and he had two teenage sons. Then Samm and his wife began drifting apart and eventually were divorced. Samm's world shattered around him. He went to a doctor who gave him tranquilizers and told him to take them as he needed. He became addicted to these drugs.

Samm moved to a cheap hotel in town. Because of the effect of the drugs and his constant feelings of depression, he would sit day after day in his hotel room and pray to die. Then one day Samm's bishop, who was a medical doctor, came looking for him. The bishop could see that Samm was badly in need of help. The bishop and his wife took Samm some fruit and invited him to go for a ride with them around the city. On his next visit, the bishop took Samm to Welfare Square and asked if there was a job that Samm could do.

Samm was assigned to sweep the floors in the basement of the storehouse. He said, "I looked down at the floors hour after hour for the first few days and just swept." After a week or so, Samm was assigned to help with some painting. With some of his self-confidence returning, Samm expressed a willingness to try.

He began by painting signs to be used around Welfare Square. When transients sought assistance and were able to do some painting, Samm would supervise their efforts. At times Samm would get depressed and stay away. Welfare Square workers would go looking for him and bring him back. It seemed that the only real help Samm ever got was from his bishop and fellow workers at Welfare Square.

Samm slowly turned the corner. His self-confidence continued to grow, and he volunteered to do more and more painting and also some decorating. It was at this time that he said his "life" came back to him. For nearly five years he was in charge of the painting and redecorating at Welfare Square. He had six to ten men under his direction each day, men who often were brought in from alcohol and drug recovery centers.

As Samm's health and outlook improved, his work assignments and responsibilities grew. He became a valuable employee on the square. As a man in his late sixties, he once again enjoyed good health and a positive attitude toward life. He considered the bishop who rescued him to be his greatest friend, and he valued those at Welfare Square who encouraged him and helped with his rehabilitation. "I

wouldn't trade my experience at Welfare Square for anything," he said.

Samm returned to the temple and was sealed to a lovely
sister he met while working at Welfare Square.

HUGENTOBLER AND HOERNICHLE

Some years ago, a member of the British Parliament visited Salt Lake City. He was a member of the Labor party, serving as solicitor general in the cabinet of the prime minister.
He wanted to meet a member of the First Presidency, and he
wanted to learn about the Church welfare program.

President J. Reuben Clark, Jr., who was past ninety years
of age, met with him. He didn't talk about welfare but bore
a strong testimony that the gospel had been restored. He
told the visitor about Joseph Smith and the First Vision and
then said, "Young man, don't you ever forget what I have
told you today because it is true." He again bore his testimony and the interview was over.

The gentleman was escorted to Welfare Square. After he
had seen part of the storehouse, he was bothered by the fact
that older people were working and not being allowed to
enjoy their retirement years. He said to the manager, "Don't
you think that when a man is sixty years of age, he's done
his share of work? This is the only thing that I find difficult
about your welfare program." The manager said, "Well, I'm
not forty years old yet and I really don't know, but we've got
a couple of experts down in the basement working. Let's go
talk to them."

They went down to where there was a huge pile of un-
labeled cans and found Brother Hugentobler and Brother
Hoernichle at work. These men were both converts to the
Church from foreign lands, and they were stalwart labelers.
The manager said to them, "This man has a question he
wants to ask."

341

Brother Hugentobler and Brother Hoernichle
labeling cans at Welfare Square

The solicitor general had the following conversation with Brother Hugentobler:

"Why do you work?"

"I work because I need to."

"Does your bishop make you work?"

"No, my bishop lets me work. I have to sustain my wife and me. It's my responsibility."

"Why don't you stay home and help with the gardening?"

"That's my wife's job and she doesn't want me to help her. Anyway, I need to work. If it weren't for this job, I would have been up in the city cemetery for the past fifteen years."

"How old are you?"

"I'm ninety years old."

Brother Hoernichle was standing by listening to this conversation. He said that he was eighty-nine years old and had tried to stay home but had discovered it was too difficult. He appreciated the great privilege the Church gave him to work in the service of others.

These men both bore testimony of the curse of idleness and the blessing of labor, even at their advanced ages. The answers they gave were far better than any that could have been prepared. As the solicitor general left the storehouse, he had an entirely different point of view on work and old age.

JOHN

John was sent to a welfare center by his bishop. After working a year or so, he quit. He was a poor worker and wouldn't accept responsibility. Then he moved to another ward because he couldn't get along with his bishop.

It wasn't long, however, before John was back at the welfare facility. He was put on the delivery truck. But John was still a slothful worker. He had no desire to do anything more than he was forced to do. He received what was given to him with a greedy hand. After being off and on welfare with three or four different bishops, he dropped out of sight.

Later he came back again and said he wanted to work. This time there was a change in him. He did his work, and his wants and needs seemed to have diminished. He became a cheerful, cooperative worker.

One day John said, "I don't drink much any more, and someday I might give up smoking." As time went by, it was evident that a great change was taking place in John's life. He became active in the Church and began going to the temple.

The change in this man did not happen overnight. It took years of patient help from several bishops and many people at the welfare center before something touched his heart and filled him with appreciation. He became a real Latter-day Saint who loved to work.

John became a high priests group leader, and he said his biggest challenge was getting his high priests out to the temple.

THE PAPER HANGERS

One night a bishop visited a family that was having financial difficulty. After talking about the situation, he turned to the father and said, "Bert, I believe the Church should help you through the welfare program."

All the members of this family were fully active in the Church. They paid their tithing and other offerings and tried to fulfill their duties as well as possible. There was no more worthy family in the ward. But now they had run into serious financial difficulty, and it was apparent to the bishop that they would need commodities from the storehouse for ten or twelve months. No cash would be needed, since their use of storehouse commodities would release the father's earnings to meet the monthly bills.

Bert listened to this plan and said, "Bishop, you can't help me if I don't earn it, and I don't see how I can do that when I am already working full-time."

The bishop said, "Bert, don't you still hang wallpaper occasionally?" Bert said, "Yes, once in a while we pick up a few dollars that way. My wife mixes the paste and puts it on the paper, and I do the hanging."

The bishop asked, "How would the two of you like to help in a special welfare project?" Bert and his wife said they were glad to do whatever they were asked.

The bishop explained: "We have at least twenty-five widows and older people in the ward who could use new wallpaper in their homes. If you two would take the assignment to do the work, you would be performing a fine service."

The bishop and his counselor, who was the ward work director, visited each widow or older couple who needed a room or two repapered. They displayed samples and explained that a friend who was in the wallpaper business felt he needed some special blessings and had offered to donate enough paper to do their rooms. They said that a couple in the ward had volunteered to hang the paper. Those living in the homes never realized that Bert and his wife were doing this work to earn assistance from the welfare program. In fact, no one knew except the ward welfare committee and the couple themselves.

Under the supervision of the ward work director, the couple worked about two nights each week until they had improved the homes of approximately twenty-five widows and elderly couples.

The people who received the new wallpaper were always grateful for the couple's kindness. Bert and his wife were grateful to be able to work for the assistance they received. The only real problem was that in about eight months Bert and his wife no longer needed assistance, but there was wallpapering yet to be done. Bert asked the bishop if they could continue with the work anyway. The bishop agreed and they continued for another six months—happy to be of service.

WORK, THE HOPE FOR HAPPINESS

Ed worked for over forty years with a large national company. When he reached age sixty-five, he asked for permission to put off retirement and he worked for another five years. At age seventy, Ed was told that he must retire. For one full year he stayed at home and puttered about the house. Most of his time was spent in the rocking chair on the front porch. For the first time in fifty years, Ed and his wife began to have squabbles. Idleness was gnawing away at him. He later described this as the most depressing, discouraging period of his life.

One day he went to see his bishop for counsel. He had no financial needs. His pension seemed adequate. However, the bishop contacted the Church welfare center and volunteered Ed's services.

For the next few years Ed worked full-time at the center. There he found companionship with the other workers, and he felt useful again. After the first week he told one of his friends that he was a new man. He said, "I'd like to continue working here as long as I live."

Work prolonged his life, aided in restoring peace in his home, and gave him something to live for. His wish was granted—he was able to work until the day he died.

ORVIL

One day a bishop heard about a family who had moved into his ward. The family included Orvil, his wife, and a young daughter. When the bishop went to the home he noticed there were few lights on. After knocking at the door, the bishop entered the home to find a dejected man sitting at the kitchen table all alone. After the bishop introduced himself, Orvil said, "My wife and little girl have left me. I am having a hard time."

Orvil did the best he could to explain to the bishop that he had not been living the gospel and that he was having some serious heart problems and was unable to work. He was really down. His wife could no longer stand to live this way and had moved away that very day. The bishop was sympathetic because Orvil had a wonderful spirit even though he was not in good condition.

The next day the bishop and one of his counselors located the wife. The couple were willing to try to resolve their problems because they knew the bishop would be there to help them. Within a couple of weeks the bishopric, the Relief Society president, and the family had all become good friends. Orvil and his wife were good people. They were just so far down that they had lost all hope that they could live a normal life. However, they responded to the offered help. Orvil was willing to do what he could, but his health was precarious. The bishop was able to get the medicine he needed and also, through the welfare program, was able to get some food and clothing into the home.

Within two or three weeks Orvil felt that he wanted to try some work, but he was unable to do any lifting or anything strenuous. Through the employment program in the ward and stake, Orvil was able to get a job in a local junkyard as a weigh master. His job was to read the scales for the weight of all junk items that went in and out of the yard. For the next couple of years he was able to work steadily, not full time, but enough to earn the cash needed to sustain his family. The bishop was very thoughtful and was able to get the family some better furniture through Deseret Industries.

Orvil and his wife started going to church, and Orvil was soon able to rid himself of his bad habits. He had always been a good man, but in the depths of his discouragement he had sought relief through substance abuse. The bishop and ward members recognized Orvil as a humble, sweet man with much to offer the Church. Within six or seven months he was an assistant ward clerk and later became the ward clerk. He served faithfully and well during the next few years.

Later Orvil was called to be the first counselor in the bishopric. He served well in that position and became one of the most loved men in the ward. His health was deteriorating, but he persevered in his job at the junkyard and in his duties in the bishopric. A change was made in the bishopric and to the joy of the ward members, Orvil was sustained and set apart as the new bishop of the ward. He presided over the sacrament meeting and the other meetings on the next Sunday. During the following week he quietly passed away.

He served less than ten days as the bishop of the ward, but he was honored, sustained, and loved by all. The blessings of the welfare program had completely changed his and his family's lives.

AXEL

Axel retired early from Kennecott Copper Corporation because of ill health. His doctor told him he had a bad case of emphysema and shouldn't work. Axel couldn't stand being idle, so his bishop sent him to Welfare Square to help during the Christmas season. He stayed for the next twelve years.

As Axel continued working at Welfare Square, his health improved and his abilities increased. He was made a supervisor over fifteen to twenty other welfare recipients, mostly handicapped, who labeled canned milk and then boxed the cans. Axel said, "A man can do twice as much if he enjoys the work and is doing it for the Church, than if he is getting paid for it." He also said, "What I really enjoy most is working with these handicapped people. They need me and when they begin to work, they really begin to change."

Because his heart condition was not good, Axel could not work full-time. His wife asked if she could work with him. The two of them worked side by side, happy and contented welfare workers. They did not need much assistance from the welfare program, but they got what they needed. Both of them gave their full efforts to the important work they did.

MORRIS

Some years ago a good member of the Church was having difficulty keeping full-time employment because he was blind. This father of nine children, several of whom filled missions, volunteered his services to help with the milk plant and other jobs on Welfare Square. Because his outside employment was sporadic, he periodically needed additional assistance. He and his bishop agreed that he would work in the welfare program and, when needed, the bishop would assist him with fast offerings and commodities.

It was soon apparent that Morris had the ability to learn quickly. When the new milk-processing plant was built, he learned how to make butter and cottage cheese. Arrangements were made for him to remain full-time at Welfare Square so that he could receive proper training and have a steady job. For years he made all the butter and cottage cheese used in the welfare program. He worked at nearly all other jobs in the milk plant, even helping to can condensed milk. He was a valued employee.

Throughout his entire adult life he could have lived off public assistance because he was blind. But he finished high school and, in spite of his handicap, he attended one year at a university. He was a skilled craftsman. Behind his success was his tremendous desire to work to earn everything he received.

At age forty-five Morris decided to learn to play the piano. He devoted time each day to practicing his lessons. Today he still practices daily, and by using a braille hymnbook, he commits about one hymn a month to memory.

Morris has developed a chess game for blind people. He has a patent issued by the government and is trying to perfect the game so it can be sold commercially. He is not interested in making a lot of money; his main concern is to make the game available to blind people throughout the world.

MARLENE AND DALE

Marlene was born during the Depression. She was a twin, and her system was affected by toxins when her twin died in the womb. She had serious facial and other physical abnormalities, as well as some mental retardation. As she grew she was unmercifully teased because of her appearance. She finished the tenth grade but didn't complete high school. She lived at home, almost completely dependent on her parents.

When Marlene was twenty-seven years old, her mother died. The family felt that Marlene needed to have an opportunity to earn some of her living. Her bishop helped her get assigned to the Deseret Industries in Murray, Utah. Her work was cutting buttons off old clothing to be used for rags. As time went on, it became evident that Marlene had some hidden talents. She would take old dolls that came into Deseret Industries and sew clothing for them. Soon this was her main work—sewing beautiful clothing for dolls. The dolls, in their fine lace wedding gowns or riding habits or party and everyday dresses, eventually became treasured gifts for little girls.

Working at Deseret Industries gave Marlene some purpose in life. She came to feel that she was contributing to the happiness of other people, especially children.

Because of Marlene's physical appearance and social ineptitude, her family felt that she would never marry. However, at Deseret Industries, she met Dale, who had similar problems. His body had been distorted from infancy and while he seemed to have full mental capabilities, he was socially retarded. As Marlene and Dale associated with each other, they fell in love.

It was a grand and spiritual occasion when two families gathered in the Salt Lake Temple to witness the marriage and sealing of Marlene and Dale—a miraculous event that neither family had expected to see.

Marlene and Dale were together for several years. They continued to work at Deseret Industries and were mostly independent of supervision from their families. Marlene died of lifelong health problems at age forty-nine. A very despondent Dale went back to live with his family. But their separation wasn't to be for very long, for Dale passed away shortly after Marlene's death.

BUILDING CHARACTER

A bishop brought a twenty-eight-year-old man to a bishops' storehouse one day. He reported to the manager that the young man was planning to leave his wife and children, and the bishop said: "I absolutely won't allow that. I am going to help them. I'm going to help them out of the financial mess they are in."

The bishop asked the storehouse keeper to give the man some work so that he could earn the assistance he and his family needed. This young father was not very willing to work, but he stayed and worked until the bishop came to pick him up that night. The bishop brought him to work every morning for a week and picked him up each evening. After a while the young man was able to find his own way to work. He became embarrassed to think that his bishop was spending so much time trying to make sure he was earning the help his family received. This young man became a fine worker when he realized that he had some talents that could be of value and that he was needed.

Fortunately he had a good supervisor, and within a year's time he had been rehabilitated. The family received assistance for over two years. He was then offered a good job and was able to sustain his own family. He provided for his family for the next thirty-five years, and then he retired.

This man grew in his ability and spirituality and became totally active in the Church. He was the Scoutmaster one year after he started working at the storehouse. A year later he became a counselor to the very bishop who had assisted him. He has now had the privilege of serving as a bishop himself. After his release as bishop, he and his wife were called on a mission, where they served faithfully and well.

What would have happened to that man and his family if the bishop had not been consistent and firm in his approach to helping them, and if the welfare program had not been available to help lift him out of his problems?

A BOWL OF OATMEAL

On the morning before Christmas in 1970, a bishops' storehouse received a telephone call. The caller told of a family in desperate need who had just arrived in the city and moved into a small apartment.

About noontime, the storehouse manager visited the home where the family was staying. The mother and four young children, all under the age of ten, were obviously living in poverty. They were members of the Church but had not been in the city long enough to contact a bishop. She discussed their condition openly and said that they needed food and a few other items. As she talked, it became obvious that the children were not planning to have a Christmas.

That very morning, a generous member of the Church had given the storehouse manager fifty dollars "for someone in need." Because a transient order could provide the family with food and clothing through the storehouse, the manager felt that the money could be used to provide some kind of a Christmas for the family. He asked the mother what she thought they would like. She said they were prepared to go without and would manage quite well, but she did agree that a small Christmas tree would be appreciated.

The little girls responded that they would like a doll or stuffed animal. The little boy, who was about six years of age, simply said, "I would like a bowl of oatmeal." How hungry he must have been. The manager told him he would get some good oatmeal, and maybe something else too.

Back at the storehouse, a bishop's order was filled to take care of some of the family's immediate needs. The manager went home and told three of his young children about the needy family. They decided to go shopping together to purchase some toys. The children selected toys for each of the children of the needy family. They also went to a wholesale jewelry store owned by a friend, who gave them a watch and several other inexpensive gifts. Finally they purchased a nice tree and some ornaments. It was a humbling experience for the manager's children, who had never before been involved in this sort of Christmas Eve activity.

The four drove out to the home of the family. They took in the tree, helped the family set it up, and delivered the food and clothing, making sure that the little boy received a large package of oatmeal. Then they brought in the toys and put them under the tree. The mother was in tears, and her children were overjoyed. The children sang a Christmas song, and the visitors left the happy family with good wishes.

That night as the storehouse manager's family gathered around their dinner table laden with good food, they gave thanks that a little boy had received his bowl of oatmeal.

WYNN

Edna and her husband, Wynn, lived in California. Edna's mother lived in Utah and had become unable to care for herself. The mother's bishop asked Edna to move to Utah, and at great sacrifice she and her husband did so.

After being in Utah for some time, Edna went to counsel with her bishop. She said that she and her husband, who was inactive in the Church, were struggling financially. Wynn was an excellent painter who did work for various people, but he was unable to collect all the money owed to him. Edna asked if there was some way the welfare program could help them through this difficult period. The bishop told her that a painter was very much needed at Welfare Square.

Wynn met with the manager of Welfare Square and agreed that he would work all day as a professional painter, earning as much as he could. About 5:00 P.M. he would come to Welfare Square to mix the paint and prepare the brushes for the volunteer work crews that came each evening to paint. Then he would go home, have his evening meal with his family, and return to Welfare Square around 8:00 to work with the men until their assignments were completed about 9:00. He would then clean up the brushes and put things away until the next day.

This went on for a while. Wynn began to come earlier to Welfare Square, and sometimes he was there all afternoon. He said that he didn't have much professional work to do and he liked working at the square. The manager explained that he should earn as much money as he could in his private business to sustain his family. But his business was dwindling, and his family was still being helped with food and clothing and other necessary things.

Wynn was an excellent worker. His oldest son came to the square to assist him in the evening. They honestly earned more than they were taking from the program.

A few months passed and the salaried work director left employment at Welfare Square to pursue other work. Wynn immediately applied for the vacancy. The manager took Wynn for a walk around the square and told him that he could not hire a person who was inactive in the Church as a Church employee. He told Wynn of an incident that had happened years ago in New Zealand.

The mission president, Matthew Cowley, visited the home of an old friend named Syd, who was a fine Latter-day Saint in many ways but had fallen away from the Church because of one bad habit—he enjoyed his cigar. President

Cowley sat beside Syd on the steps of his front porch, with Syd smoking a big cigar. President Cowley told Syd that he wanted him to be in church the next day because there was going to be a change in the branch presidency. Syd said, "Why don't you just tell me who it is going to be so I won't have to clean up and go." President Cowley said, "Tomorrow I am releasing the branch president and I want to sustain you as the new branch president." Syd took one look at his cigar and said, "You mean me and my cigar?" President Cowley said, "No, just you; we don't need your cigar." After a minute of thought, Syd threw his cigar on the ground and said, "Tumuaki (meaning president), I don't break the Word of Wisdom any more, I am a full-tithe payer, I'm totally active in the Church, I will accept the call to be branch president, and I will be the best in all of New Zealand." He became a stalwart in the Church.

As Wynn and the manager continued their walk around Welfare Square, there was a little pause in the conversation and then Wynn said, "Bishop, I don't smoke any more—I live the Word of Wisdom one hundred percent." The manager asked, "When did you quit smoking?" "Right now," Wynn said, "but I'm through. I am also a full-tithe payer, and I am fully active. Please give me the job as work director." The manager hired him on the spot, and Wynn was completely true to his word.

Wynn became a counselor in his ward bishopric and was later sustained as bishop. He was an excellent bishop who could understand the people and their problems. He was very kind and generous to those in need, and he took care of all the widows in a marvelous way. He continued as a valuable Welfare Square employee and became the storehouse keeper and the assistant to the manager before he retired. His three sons served missions, and his wife served as stake Relief Society president for seventeen years. He has never stopped serving in the Church. The welfare program truly blessed the lives of this family.

HEAVILY IN DEBT

A divorced mother and her two teenaged sons lived in an inexpensive apartment in a large western city with little to sustain them. She had just moved from a small town in another part of the state where she had run into financial difficulties and unwisely gone into debt with many different businesses. She went to her bishop and gave him a list of all the people to whom she owed money—several hundred dollars to sixteen different doctors and businesses. In her present circumstances she could not possibly pay off her debts.

She was a willing worker and immediately went to work in the welfare program to earn food and other necessities. The bishop wrote to each of the sixteen creditors. He explained that the woman wanted to pay her debts but was unable to do so and that the Church was helping her with commodities and fast-offering funds. He asked them if they could discount her debt as much as possible and submit their bills to the bishop.

Within the next couple of weeks, the bishop received encouraging letters from nearly all the creditors. The grocer said he would settle for 25 percent, as did most of the others. One or two said the woman did not have to pay any money and sent their best wishes. Only one company said it wanted every penny. Within a few months, the bills were all taken care of.

A highlight of this story was a letter from a doctor to whom the woman owed money:

"Dear Bishop:

"I am a nonmember of the Church. I live here among all of these Latter-day Saints. I have come to respect and love them. I am living here for a very unusual reason. A few years ago my sister was traveling through Utah and had a very severe accident. She was in the hospital for a while and then was taken into the home of some Latter-day Saints, who nursed her and helped her back to health. She was not able to repay them and when I tried the people refused any payment from me. When my sister was well enough, we made arrangements to transport her back to her home.

"I have always felt that I would like to do something for the Latter-day Saints in Utah, but they have never asked me for anything. As a result of the kindness of your Church members, I moved here from the East to begin my medical practice with these wonderful people. I have been good and kind to them when they have been my patients, but for years I have wanted to make some kind of payment. Now the opportunity comes. Probably the largest bill your member has is the one from me. You will find a copy of her statement marked 'paid in full,' which I am grateful to do. At long last I have the opportunity of repaying in part to the Church the wonderful Christian service they gave to my sister in her time of need."

It wasn't long before this family was completely able to sustain itself. Both boys filled honorable missions, and all have remained faithful partly because a bishop was willing to help them through their serious problems using the resources of the welfare program.

THE KINCAIDS' CONVERSION

In 1964 a couple visited in Salt Lake City for three days. They intended to leave for home on the morning of the fourth day, but for some reason the husband wanted to go back to Temple Square. His wife said she was too tired to walk around Temple Square another day, even though they both had enjoyed everything they had seen. Mr. Kincaid told his wife to stay in bed and rest and he would go out for a

Daisy and Herbert Kincaid

while and be back around noon. As he walked across the street from the hotel to Temple Square, he saw the bus that was just leaving for Welfare Square. He hailed it down and asked if he could go, not knowing where or what Welfare Square was, but being assured they would return by noon.

He took the tour of Welfare Square and at the conclusion, one of the guides brought him into the office of the manager. He introduced himself as Herbert Kincaid. Mr. Kincaid had been a Methodist minister for more than thirty years and had spent a considerable amount of time helping people with welfare problems. He had many questions, which the manager answered, and he missed the bus returning to Temple Square because he was so interested in the discussion.

He said that he was thrilled to see real welfare work being done and wanted to know more about the Church. The manager told him that two young missionaries would be happy to come to his home. The minister said that he and his wife would love to have them and agreed to have them for supper and an evening of gospel discussion. After more than two hours on Welfare Square visiting and asking questions, Mr. Kincaid was thoroughly inspired. When he went back to the hotel, he had a great announcement to make to his wife.

He planned to open the door and say to his wife, "Now, Daisy, don't say a word. I want to tell you something important." As he opened the door and entered, she said, "Herbert, I've found the true church! All morning, I've been here in bed reading this book. It's called the Book of Mormon. I have read it now for three hours, and this book is true. There is a true church on the earth, and I think at long last we have found it."

When he had composed himself, he said, "Daisy, I too found the true church today. I have seen the true church in action, and the Mormon Church is true." On that marvelous morning, each member of this couple was converted to the Church.

They went back to their home in Utica, New York. About four weeks later, the manager received a short letter from two missionaries stating that they were now teaching Mr. and Mrs. Kincaid. Although the Kincaids were actually converted in Utah, they needed to be taught the discussions and attend church before being baptized.

A year later they visited Salt Lake City to receive the blessings of the temple. The guide who took them through Welfare Square was able to go with them. They went home to carry on as worthy, active Latter-day Saints.

Another year passed, and the manager of Welfare Square had been called to preside over a mission. One day as he was opening mail from the Missionary Department, he received the missionary recommendation forms for Herbert and Daisy Kincaid, who had been called to serve in his mission. This was a thrill for both the mission president and the

Kincaids. The Kincaids were assigned to labor in Madison, Florida, and later in Live Oak, where they filled honorable missions.

Both husband and wife remained faithful members of the Church throughout their lives.

"And inasmuch as ye impart of your substance unto the poor,
ye will do it unto me" (D&C 42:31).

PROPHETIC QUOTATIONS

The following are selected inspirational statements from members of the First Presidency and Quorum of the Twelve about welfare principles and activities.

JOSEPH SMITH

"Respecting how much a man of property shall give annually we have no special instructions to give; he is to feed the hungry, to clothe the naked, to provide for the widow, to dry up the tear of the orphan, to comfort the afflicted, whether in this church, or in any other, or in no church at all, wherever he finds them, to believe and obey all that God has revealed, does reveal, or will reveal, to do good unto all men, to be a member in good standing in the Church of Jesus Christ of Latter-day Saints" (*Times and Seasons*, 15 Mar. 1842, p. 732).

◆ ◆ ◆

"I attended by request the Female Relief Society, whose object is the relief of the poor, the destitute, the widow and the orphan, and for the exercise of all benevolent purposes. . . . We are well assured . . . that with the resources they will have at command, they will fly to the relief of the stranger; they will pour in oil and wine to the wounded heart of the distressed; they will dry up the tears of the orphan and make the widow's heart to rejoice" (*History of the Church*, 4:567).

Brigham Young

"I will give you a piece of counsel. Do good to all. It is better to feed nine unworthy persons than to let one worthy person—the tenth, go hungry. Follow this rule and you will be apt to be found on the right side of doing good" (in *Journal of Discourses*, 16:44).

♦ ♦ ♦

"True charity to a poor family or person consists of placing them in a situation in which they can support themselves" (James R. Clark, comp., *Messages of the First Presidency of The Church of Jesus Christ of Latter-day Saints*, 6 vols. [Salt Lake City: Bookcraft, 1965–75), 2:134).

♦ ♦ ♦

"The first year that I came into this valley I had not flour enough to last my family until harvest, . . . and persons were coming to my house every day for bread. I had the blues about [it] one day; I went down to the old fort, and by the time I got back to my house I was completely cured. I said to my wife, 'Do not let a person come here for food and go away empty handed, for if you do we shall suffer before harvest; but if you give to every individual that comes we shall have enough to last us through.'

"I intend to keep doing so, that my bread may hold out, for if I do not I shall come short.

"Do you believe that principle? I know it is true, because I have proven it so many times" (in *Journal of Discourses*, 3:332–33).

♦ ♦ ♦

"If you wish to get rich, save what you get. A fool can earn money, but it takes a wise man to save and dispose of it to his own advantage" (*Discourses of Brigham Young*, sel. John A. Widtsoe [Salt Lake City: Deseret Book Co., 1954], p. 292).

JOHN TAYLOR

"If a man were poor or hungry, [some] would say, let us pray for him. I would suggest a little different regiment for a person in this condition: rather take him a bag of flour and a little beef or pork, and a little sugar and butter. A few such comforts will do him more good than your prayers. And I would be ashamed to ask the Lord to do something that I would not do myself. Then go to work and help the poor yourselves first, and do all you can for them, and then call upon God to do the balance" (in *Journal of Discourses,* 19:340).

WILFORD WOODRUFF

"We feel led to caution the Latter-day Saints against forming the bad habit of incurring debt and taking upon themselves obligations which frequently burden them heavier than they can bear, and lead to the loss of their homes and other possessions. We know it is the fashion of the age to use credit to the utmost limit. . . . We, therefore, repeat our counsel to the Latter-day Saints, to shun debt. Be content with moderate gains, and be not misled by illusory hopes of acquiring wealth. . . . Let our children also be taught habits of economy, and not to indulge in tastes which they cannot gratify without running into debt" (James R. Clark, *Messages of the First Presidency,* 3:144–45).

LORENZO SNOW

"Men and women of wealth, use your riches to give employment to the laborer! Take the idle from the crowded centres of population and place them on the untilled areas that await the hand of industry. Unlock your vaults, unloose your purses, and embark in enterprises that will give work to the unemployed, and relieve the wretchedness that leads to the vice and crime which curse your great cities, and that poison the moral atmosphere around you. Make others happy, and you will be happy yourselves" (James R. Clark, *Messages of the First Presidency*, 3:334).

DANIEL H. WELLS

"You may give a piece of bread to a hungry person, and when the cravings of hunger return some one else must administer to his wants again; to put that person in a position to earn his own subsistence is true charity; in this way you direct his feet in the path of true independence, he is then only dependent on his own exertions and on the blessings of his God" (in *Journal of Discourses*, 10:196–97).

JOSEPH F. SMITH

"It has always been a cardinal teaching with the Latter-day Saints, that a religion which has not the power to save people temporally and make them prosperous and happy here, cannot be depended upon to save them spiritually, to exalt them in the life to come" ("The Truth about Mormonism," *Out West* magazine, Sept. 1905, p. 242).

HEBER J. GRANT

"[The welfare program] is one of the greatest and most important things the Church has ever undertaken to put over, and it will be put over because we have the ability and the power to do it" (quoted in Albert E. Bowen, *Church Welfare Plan* [Gospel Doctrine course of study, 1946], p. 3).

♦ ♦ ♦

"No pains must be spared to wipe out all feeling of diffidence, embarrassment, or shame on the part of those receiving relief; the Ward must be one great family of equals. The spiritual welfare of those on relief must receive especial care and be earnestly and prayerfully fostered. A system which gives relief for work or service will go far to reaching these ends" (Heber J. Grant, J. Reuben Clark, Jr., David O. McKay, "An Important Message," *Deseret News*, 7 Apr. 1936).

GEORGE ALBERT SMITH

"We are most grateful unto Thee that Thou didst inspire Thy servants to institute the Welfare Program of the Church through which it is made possible that the poor and unfortunate might be provided for without the forfeiture of self-respect. May Thy servants continue in Thy favor that they may thereby merit Thy inspiration in developing this Welfare Program until it becomes perfect in all respects to the care and blessing of Thy people" (dedicatory prayer, Idaho Falls Temple, 23 Sept. 1945, quoted in Albert E. Bowen, *Church Welfare Plan*, p. 67).

DAVID O. McKAY

"It is something to supply clothing to the scantily clad, to furnish ample food to those whose table is thinly spread, to give activity to those who are fighting desperately the despair that comes from enforced idleness, but after all is said and done, the greatest blessings that will accrue from the Church Security Plan are spiritual. Outwardly, every act seems to be directed toward the physical: re-making of dresses and suits of clothes, canning fruits and vegetables, storing foodstuffs, choosing of fertile fields for settlement— all seem strictly temporal, but permeating all these acts, inspiring and sanctifying them, is the element of spirituality" (in Conference Report, Oct. 1936, p. 103).

JOSEPH FIELDING SMITH

"[After World War II] the authorities of the Church took steps immediately when the way was opened to succor and alleviate the suffering of all the members of the Church.

Through the Welfare organization of the Church, thousands of boxes of provisions, clothing and other necessities were sent to the Saints in Europe so that all received some relief which helped to tide them over. . . . It was fortunate that the Church was in a position to care for its own, and with the privileges granted by the government was able to accomplish this great work for its members" (*Essentials in Church History* [Salt Lake City: Deseret Book Co., 1950], p. 535).

J. REUBEN CLARK, JR.

"It has always been interesting to me that the Lord revealed the Welfare Program just 100 years after he had given the law of the United Order. . . . The Lord took the commandment from the people to live the United Order because of their selfishness, and their greed, and their love of idleness. Had they lived it, they would have brought in the Millennium. . . . If we don't live the Welfare Program, the Lord will take from us the requirement to live it, and if he does, it will be because of our selfishness and greed and love of idleness. If that should happen, 100 years from now the people will look back at us as we look back on the people who were given the United Order law, and they will say of us, 'They had the Welfare Program. If they had lived it, they would have brought in the Millennium' " (regional welfare meeting, Feb. 1944; quoted by Marion G. Romney, address given at Brigham Young University, 17 June 1953). (Author's note: Fifty years of the one hundred mentioned by President Clark have already passed.)

♦ ♦ ♦

"Let us avoid debt as we would avoid a plague; where we are now in debt let us get out of debt; if not today, then tomorrow.

"Let us straitly and strictly live within our incomes, and save a little.

"Let every head of every household see to it that he has on hand enough food and clothing, and, where possible, fuel also, for at least a year ahead. . . . Let every head of every household aim to own his own home, free from mortgage. Let every man who has a garden spot, garden it; every man who owns a farm, farm it.

"Let us again clothe ourselves with these proved and sterling virtues—honesty, truthfulness, chastity, sobriety, temperance, industry and thrift; let us discard all covetousness and greed" (in Conference Report, Apr. 1937, p. 26).

◆ ◆ ◆

"Basic to this Plan are deep, sincere, religious convictions built on God's universal command given to all men through ancient Israel in the Wilderness: 'Thou shalt love thy neighbour as thyself' (Lev. 19:18)" (*Church Welfare Plan: A Discussion* [pamphlet, address given at Estes Park, Colo., 20 June 1939], p. 3).

◆ ◆ ◆

"The welfare plan is a permanent plan for the purpose of extending temporary assistance to the individual, so far as his temporal needs are concerned, but permanent benefits so far as his spiritual welfare is involved. That is all there is to it" (special welfare meeting, 5 Apr. 1949).

ALBERT E. BOWEN

"The only way the Church can stand independent is for its members to stand independent, for the Church IS its members. It is not possible to conceive of an independent Church made up of dependent members—members who are under the inescapable obligation of dependency" (*Church Welfare Plan* [Gospel Doctrine course of study, 1946], p. 77).

◆ ◆ ◆

" 'Bishops should exercise fatherly and kind consideration to the needs of the worthy poor in their midst whether

Latter-day Saints or not.' [Joseph F. Smith, in Conference Report, Oct. 1914, p. 3.] Thus it is seen that 'worthy' is given a wider connotation. It might embrace any one who is living decently and doing the best he can to help himself even though not a Church member" (*Church Welfare Plan* [Gospel Doctrine course of study, 1946], p. 130).

HAROLD B. LEE

"We are tested, we are tried, we are going through some of the severest tests today and we don't realize perhaps the severity of the tests that we are going through. In those [early] days there were murders, there were mobbings, there were drivings. They were driven out into the desert; they were starving and they were unclad; they were cold. They came here to this favored land. We are the inheritors of what they gave to us. But what are we doing with it? Today we are basking in the lap of luxury, the like of which we've never seen before in the history of the world. . . .

"As I read the papers today and the talk about food shortage, energy crises, the talk of war and the possibility of entering into a world conflict if things don't change, I wonder now if we are beginning to see the tip of the iceberg as it were. I'm wondering if we are beginning to see what the brethren were talking about when they said, way back in 1937, to put aside in storage for at least a year food, fuel, clothing and enough to tide one over during an emergency. And we've said, 'Now don't think of storing all that you are accustomed to having. But store enough of what would keep you alive if you didn't have anything else to eat. Think of storing that for a year's supply.'

"How many of our Saints listen to that counsel? Do all of you folks . . . listen to the Brethren who said that to you, and have been trying to urge you to do that? Have you done that today?" (Christmas devotional for Church employees, 13

Dec. 1973). (Author's note: This was one of President Lee's last public addresses, for he died thirteen days later.)

♦ ♦ ♦

"The idle person of the present must be provided with the opportunity of rendering some service of which he is capable so that if and when he needs assistance it may be given not as a dole to sustain him in idleness but as a partial compensation for the work he has done or the services he has rendered" ("Church Security: Retrospect, Introspect, Prospect," *Improvement Era*, Apr. 1937, p. 208).

♦ ♦ ♦

"We have been asked, again and again, can the Church take care of its needy? . . .

"It is my humble conviction, and I think everyone here who has had any experience will bear me out, that the answer to that question will not be in dollars or pounds, but in the amount of coordinated, courageous brotherhood that we can stimulate in this Church. If we stimulate brotherhood, the answer to the question can only be one answer: Yes. By the power of the living God we can and we will be self-sustaining and be the most independent creatures under the celestial world" (*Church News*, 12 Feb. 1944, p. 8).

♦ ♦ ♦

"Should there be a woman left in widowhood who has to work, she should go to her bishop and Relief Society president. Relief Society sisters should stay close to such a home and see that when that mother is away there are provided those essential elements that safeguard her home and take care of her little ones. Perchance there may be a season when her children are small that maybe there could be full enough material support so she wouldn't have to leave her children. Remember, these are days when we must think first of the welfare of the children in the home" (stake conference welfare meeting; from author's notes).

◆ ◆ ◆

"The president of [a] company . . . said to me [one] day, 'Harold, I listened to you last night with great interest, how you produce, store, and distribute all this to needy families, and so on; but wouldn't it be much more efficient and labor-saving if you were to sell all that produce and give the money to the poor? Wouldn't it be more efficient?'

"I said, 'Yes, yes, I think so—just like a dictatorship is more efficient than a democracy, the republican form of government.' He said, 'I get your point.'

"I said, 'We're not just concerned in making money; that isn't the prime consideration. We're trying to save souls, and to involve all these people, when they need help, in a productive activity. It's teaching them a way to a temporal salvation here, that they don't have to buy to get; and it is leading them on the trail to eternal salvation. Of course, it would be more efficient; but we're not thinking of efficiency. We're thinking of an activity that saves the souls of those whom we take care of.'

"Then I said, 'It's the keeping of these people happy by giving them the opportunity to give what service they can in return for what they need. That's an age-old religious principle' " (welfare representatives' seminar, 29 Nov. 1966).

Spencer W. Kimball

"As givers gain control of their desires and properly see other needs in light of their own wants, then the powers of the gospel are released in their lives. They learn that by living the great law of consecration they insure not only temporal salvation but also spiritual sanctification. And as a recipient receives with thanksgiving, he rejoices in knowing that in its purest form—in the true Zion—one may partake of both temporal and spiritual salvation. Then they are motivated to become self-sustaining and able to share with others.

"Isn't the plan beautiful? Don't you thrill to this part of the gospel that causes Zion to put on her beautiful garments? When viewed in this light, we can see that Welfare Services is not a program, but the essence of the gospel. *It is the gospel in action.*

"It is the crowning principle of a Christian life" (in Conference Report, Oct. 1977, p. 123; or *Ensign,* Nov. 1977, p. 77).

♦ ♦ ♦

"Sometimes we have been a bit penurious and figured that we had for breakfast one egg and that cost so many cents and then we give that to the Lord. I think that when we are affluent, as many of us are, we ought to be very, very generous. . . .

"I think we should be very generous and give, instead of the amount we saved by our two meals of fasting, perhaps much, much more—ten times more where we are in a position to do it" (in Conference Report, Apr. 1974, p. 184).

♦ ♦ ♦

"We wish to remind all the Saints of the blessings that come from observing the regular fast and contributing as generous a fast offering as we can, and as we are in a position to give. Wherever we can, we should give many times the value of the meals from which we abstained.

"This principle of promise, when lived in the spirit thereof, greatly blesses both giver and receiver. Upon practicing the law of the fast, one finds a personal well-spring of power to overcome self-indulgence and selfishness" (in Conference Report, Apr. 1978, p. 121; or *Ensign,* May 1978, p. 80).

♦ ♦ ♦

"My thoughts went back to old Israel, who, becoming hungry, went south to Egypt and found corn. That corn tasted so good to them that they continued eating the corn of another people. Eventually they accepted the grain and the security it symbolized in full payment for their liberty. Chains and abject slavery came to them and to their children and their children's children. Their suffering accelerated in intensity until a great Moses, under God, came to emancipate them. Thank the Lord for a deliverer! But how much nobler if people could accept the advice of God's leaders before the bondage comes!" (*The Teachings of Spencer W. Kimball,* ed. Edward L. Kimball [Salt Lake City: Bookcraft, 1982], pp. 368–69).

EZRA TAFT BENSON

"Twenty-seven years ago I attended my first welfare meeting conducted by Elder Melvin J. Ballard and Elder Harold B. Lee. I am more convinced now than ever before that the basic principles of the Welfare Plan are true and eternal principles. The laws of economy are as immutable as the laws of morality. I am grateful for President Heber J. Grant, who instituted this program" (Great Falls Montana Stake welfare meeting, 2 Feb. 1963; from author's notes).

♦ ♦ ♦

"The Welfare Program is the greatest insurance program on earth. It is sound economically, socially, and physically" (Great Falls Montana Stake welfare meeting, 2 Feb. 1963; from author's notes).

♦ ♦ ♦

"More than ever before, we need to learn and apply the principles of economic self-reliance. We do not know when the crisis involving sickness or unemployment may affect our own circumstances. We do know that the Lord has decreed global calamities for the future and has warned and forewarned us to be prepared. For this reason the Brethren have repeatedly stressed a 'back to basics' program for temporal and spiritual welfare" (in Conference Report, Oct. 1980, p. 46; or *Ensign,* Nov. 1980, p. 32).

♦ ♦ ♦

"From the standpoint of food production, storage, handling, and the Lord's counsel, wheat should have high priority. . . . Water, of course, is essential. Other basics could include honey or sugar, legumes, milk products or substitutes, and salt or its equivalent. The revelation to produce and store food may be as essential to our temporal welfare today as boarding the ark was to the people in the days of Noah" (in Conference Report, Oct. 1980, p. 46; or *Ensign,* Nov. 1980, p. 33).

MATTHEW COWLEY

"Now you can't have peace of mind and be in want materially. You can't have the spirit of the gospel in your hearts with an empty stomach, and so in the plan of the Master there is provision not only for the salvation of the spirit of man, but also for his physical being. And to me the greatest movement in the history of this Church, to bring a sense of security and a spirit of peace into the hearts of the members of this Church, is what we call the welfare plan. Once we grasp fully the spirit and genius of that plan, then all of us can divest our minds of worry and anxiety, not only pertaining to the spiritual things, but also to the material things of life" (*Matthew Cowley Speaks* [Salt Lake City: Deseret Book Co., 1954], pp. 299–300).

HENRY D. MOYLE

"Our ultimate aim in this welfare work is to help Church members to become self-supporting, and to obtain work they can do best. The Church, with its members independent and free from debt, with time to labor in the ministry, can then successfully carry on the work of the Lord here on earth" ("Practical Christianity," address given on CBS "Church on the Air," 2 Nov. 1941).

♦ ♦ ♦

"Brethren, I plead with you, seriously, we are living in a very precarious, dangerous, serious economic age, and the Presidency, when they were inspired to inaugurate this Program in 1936, were speaking the mind and the will of the Lord. About that, there can be no question. I say to myself every day, it is not the poor and the needy of the Church of today that I am worrying about, because we are so amply able to take care of their needs, but, Brethren, it is the men who are still contributing to the Welfare Program and getting themselves further and further involved in the intricacies of our civilization today about which I worry, and sometimes it involves bishops and stake presidents" (welfare agricultural meeting, 8 Apr. 1961).

MARION G. ROMNEY

"The welfare program will not be completely successful until the bishop gives more than the people ask for and the people take less than the bishops give" (stake conference welfare meeting; from author's notes).

♦ ♦ ♦

"I am persuaded that one can find charity, the pure love of Christ, in building up the unfortunate quicker than in any other way. I firmly believe that the development of this phase of our work (I mean giving more of ourselves in exalting the poor), stands between us and the glorious millennium for which we pray" ("Relief Society and the Church Welfare Program," general Relief Society conference, 4 Oct. 1951).

♦ ♦ ♦

"Everything we do in welfare services must be measured by its accomplishment in spiritual terms. Givers must give out of a righteous heart and with a willing spirit. Receivers must receive with thankfulness and gladness of heart" (in Conference Report, Apr. 1980, p. 115; or *Ensign,* May 1980, p. 84).

♦ ♦ ♦

"Be liberal in your giving, that you may grow yourselves. Don't give just for the benefit of the poor, but give for your own welfare. Give enough so that you can give yourself into the kingdom of God through consecrating of your means and your time. Pay an honest tithing and double your fast offerings, if you want the blessings of heaven: I promise every one of you who will do it that you will increase your income. The Lord will reward you according to your deeds" (welfare agricultural meeting, 30 Sept. 1967).

♦ ♦ ♦

"If the members of the Church would double their fast-offering contributions, the spirituality in the Church would double. We need to keep that in mind and be liberal in our contributions" (welfare agricultural meeting, 3 Apr. 1971).

♦ ♦ ♦

"I suppose I've said enough to establish the fact that caring for the poor is a covenantal obligation. It follows, then, that we look after our poor and distressed not only because it is convenient, or exciting, or socially acceptable; we should do it first and foremost in fulfillment of our covenant with the Lord that we will do so" (in Conference Report, Oct. 1978, p. 131; or *Ensign,* Nov. 1978, p. 88).

♦ ♦ ♦

"Few evils has the Lord denounced with more vehemence than idleness. 'Thou shalt not be idle;' he said to the Church on February 9, 1831, 'for he that is idle shall not eat the bread nor wear the garments of the laborer' (D&C 42:42). In November of the same year, he said, 'And the idler shall not have place in the Church, except he repent and mend his ways' (D&C 75:29)" (*Welfare Handbook* [1952], p. 2). (Author's note: Although this statement comes from the *Welfare Handbook,* Elder Romney quoted it repeatedly and made it one of his major themes.)

♦ ♦ ♦

"Some members become financially or emotionally dependent on their bishops. A dole is a dole whatever its source. All of our Church and family actions should be directed toward making our children and members self-reliant. We can't always control government programs, but we can control our own homes and congregations" (in Conference Report, Oct. 1982, p. 133; or *Ensign*, Nov. 1982, p. 92).

RICHARD L. EVANS

"This is the essence of the Church Security Program—not merely that men shall be fed and clothed, though that is important—but that eternal man shall be built up by self-reliance, by creative activity, by honorable labor, by service. A generation reared in idleness cannot maintain its integrity" ("Editorial," *Improvement Era*, Dec. 1936, p. 768).

GEORGE Q. MORRIS

"Maybe if we pay our tithing and fast offerings, the Lord will give us enough sense not to buy the things we don't need" (West Boise Stake conference, 20 Feb. 1960; from author's notes).

HOWARD W. HUNTER

"There are some who ask why the Church is concerned with temporal affairs. The Church is interested in the welfare of each of its members. This interest therefore cannot be limited to man's spiritual needs alone but extends to every phase of his life. Social and economic needs are important to everyone. Man also has need for physical, mental, and moral guidance. Our lives cannot be one-sided, nor can we separate the spiritual from the temporal" (in Conference Report, Oct. 1961, p. 108; or *Improvement Era*, Dec. 1951, p. 962).

◆ ◆ ◆

"I have never been on a gloomy welfare project. I have climbed trees and picked lemons, peeled fruit, tended boiler, carried boxes, unloaded trucks, cleaned the cannery, and a thousand and one other things, but the things I remember most are the laughing and the singing and the good fellowship of people engaged in the service of the Lord" ("Welfare and the Relief Society," *Relief Society Magazine,* Apr. 1962, p. 238).

◆ ◆ ◆

"We often refer to the Welfare work of the Church. The word *work* creeps in with the word *Welfare,* and the two seem to be associated together. We know we must work for the things that are worthwhile in life, and if the Welfare Program is to be worthwhile and succeed, we must couple work with high ideals. Faith without works is dead. In the same sense, our success in our Welfare endeavors can only be accomplished by work" ("Welfare and the Relief Society," p. 237).

◆ ◆ ◆

"There is nothing old or old-fashioned about the Welfare Program. The principles are old, but the challenges are new. . . . I bear witness that the Welfare Program comes to us by inspiration and revelation. It is part of living the gospel" ("Welfare and the Relief Society," pp. 236, 239).

GORDON B. HINCKLEY

"I recall that when I was a boy I raised a question with my father, who was my stake president, concerning the expenditure of Church funds. He reminded me that mine is the God-given obligation to pay my tithes and offerings. When I do so, that which I give is no longer mine. It belongs to the Lord to whom I consecrate it. What the authorities of the Church do with it need not concern me. They are answerable to the Lord, who will require an accounting at their hands" ("Member Finances Fireside," *Ensign,* May 1990, p. 96).

◆ ◆ ◆

"In remembering together before the Lord the poor, the needy, and the oppressed, there is developed, unconsciously but realistically, a love for others above self, a respect for others, a desire to serve the needs of others" (in Conference Report, Apr. 1963, p. 127; or *Improvement Era,* June 1963, p. 530).

◆ ◆ ◆

"It is the responsibility of the bishop to give emergency help to see that neither the individual nor his family suffers. It is the obligation of the priesthood quorum to set in motion those forces and facilities which will equip the needy member to provide on a continuing basis for himself and his family" *(Ensign,* Nov. 1977, p. 86).

◆ ◆ ◆

"In the environment in which we live today, we all should be looking to greater self-sufficiency, a greater spirit of self-reliance, a greater desire to take care of ourselves and our own" (in Conference Report, Oct. 1982, p. 111; or *Ensign,* Nov. 1982, p. 76).

◆ ◆ ◆

"I am confident that the Lord loves His people for the goodness of their lives and the generosity of their hearts as they consecrate of their means in the payment of tithes and offerings. I am grateful for the faith of the wealthy who give generously of their abundance. I am equally grateful for the faith of the poor who likewise contribute with a great spirit of consecration" ("Member Finances Fireside," p. 95).

◆ ◆ ◆

"We hope that through the payment of liberal fast offerings there will be more than enough to provide for the needs of the less fortunate. If every member of this church observed the fast and contributed generously, the poor and the needy—not only of the Church, but many others as well, would be blessed and provided for" ("Member Finances Fireside," p. 97).

Thomas S. Monson

"No member of The Church of Jesus Christ of Latter-day Saints who has canned peas, topped beets, hauled hay, or shoveled coal in [the welfare] cause ever forgets or regrets the experience of helping provide for those in need" (in Conference Report, Oct. 1977, p. 9; or *Ensign*, Nov. 1977, p. 7).

♦ ♦ ♦

"Latter-day Saints are advised to maintain gardens, to sew, and to make household items. They are also taught how to can, freeze, and dry foods. Where legally permitted, and physically and economically possible, they are urged to store a year's supply of food, clothing, and where possible, fuel" (*"Mormon" Church Welfare Services: An Overview of the Welfare Effort of The Church of Jesus Christ of Latter-day Saints* [pamphlet, 1982], p. 2).

♦ ♦ ♦

"While [bishops'] storehouses provide many of the same services as any retail food store, not one has a cash register. The only way a person can obtain commodities from a storehouse is through a bishop's requisition order. These are goods that money cannot buy. No price tag is put on the time, effort, and love so generously contributed to the common good of those in need" (*"Mormon" Church Welfare Services*, p. 4).

♦ ♦ ♦

"As has been said so often, the best storehouse system that the Church could devise would be for every family to store a year's supply of needed food, clothing, and, where possible, the other necessities of life" ("Guiding Principles of Personal and Family Welfare," *Ensign,* Sept. 1986, p. 4).

BOYD K. PACKER

"[The welfare program] is a self-help system, not a quick handout system. . . .

"It is not an unkind or an unfeeling bishop who requires a member to work to the fullest extent he can for what he receives from Church welfare.

"There should not be the slightest embarrassment for any member to be assisted by the Church. *Provided,* that is, that he has contributed all that he can" (in Conference Report, Apr. 1978, p. 136; or *Ensign,* May 1978, p. 91).

◆ ◆ ◆

"We have been taught to store a year's supply of food, clothing, and, if possible, fuel—at home. There has been no attempt to set up storerooms in every chapel. We know that in the crunch our members may not be able to get to the chapel for supplies" (in Conference Report, Apr. 1978, p. 136; or *Ensign,* May 1978, p. 91).

MARVIN J. ASHTON

"There are those who would have us believe that the present Welfare Services principles are outdated, overemphasized, and impossible under existing world conditions. To them we would declare it is easier for some skeptics to give up than to learn. It is no doubt easier to be a critic than a servant. In the uncertain days of the present and of the future, welfare services will remain a beacon for the world to see. Its very foundation continues to be built on the rock of helping people to help themselves. Properly implemented, most human needs can be met through this important program of the Church" (in Conference Report, Oct. 1981, p. 126; or *Ensign,* Nov. 1981, pp. 89–90).

L. Tom Perry

"The principle of self-reliance is spiritual as well as temporal. It is not a doomsday program; it is something to be practiced each and every day of our lives" (in Conference Report, Oct. 1991, p. 90; or *Ensign,* Nov. 1991, p. 66).

♦ ♦ ♦

"Love and service, work and self-reliance, stewardship and consecration, the provident living that comes from personal and family preparedness, caring for the poor and the needy—these are principles members must learn and practice if they would live celestial lives in a telestial world. These same teachings must come down through quorum leaders as well" (*Ensign,* May 1977, p. 88).

David B. Haight

"It is significant to note that about this same time, when the Lord established his way of caring for those in need, the 'world,' or government, introduced its form of dole assistance—a counterfeit alternative to the Lord's way. In most instances, the world's way dismissed the principle of individual work and family responsibility and adopted the philosophy that 'the government will take care of our needs' or 'the government owes us a living.' Individual and family initiative was supplanted by government handouts. The true spirit of love for our neighbor and concern for others as taught by the Savior had been generally ignored. . . .

"The Lord's way is different from government programs. The inspired Church welfare plan is administered on the principle that an individual is responsible to care for himself; where his resources are not adequate, family members are to assist. Where the family is unable to meet the needs of the individual, the Church stands ready to help. The Lord's way emphasizes individual work and responsibility and encourages people to help themselves" (in Conference Report, Oct. 1978, pp. 126–27; or *Ensign*, Nov. 1978, pp. 85–86).

◆ ◆ ◆

"The heart of our welfare services work [is] to lift, to sanctify, to bless so that individuals who have been helped can become more like God" (in Conference Report, Oct. 1978, p. 126; or *Ensign*, Nov. 1978, p. 85).

JAMES E. FAUST

"Strive to have a year's supply of food and clothing. The counsel to have a year's supply of basic food, clothing, and commodities was given fifty years ago and has been repeated many times since. Every father and mother are the family's storekeepers. They should store whatever their own family would like to have in the case of an emergency. . . .

"The Church cannot be expected to provide for every one of its millions of members in case of public or personal disaster. It is therefore necessary that each home and family do what they can to assume the responsibility for their own hour of need. . . . I believe if we are provident and wise in the management of our personal and family affairs and are faithful, God will sustain us through our trials" (in Conference Report, Apr. 1986, p. 26; or *Ensign*, May 1986, p. 22).

◆ ◆ ◆

"Who determines who is poor in Utah, Peru, Nigeria, Samoa, Germany, and elsewhere? Conditions are so different around the world that the local bishop in each area determines which of his people, according to their local circumstances, are poor" (Regional Representatives' seminar, 15 Apr. 1991).

NEAL A. MAXWELL

"The Church . . . wisely places great emphasis upon its members learning to be righteously self-reliant. Having oil in our own lamps, as a matter of fact, entitles us to be partakers of the essential gift of personal revelation" (*We Will Prove Them Herewith* [Salt Lake City: Deseret Book Co., 1982], p. 19).

RUSSELL M. NELSON

"An important part of the Lord's storehouse is maintained as a year's supply, stored, where possible, in the homes of faithful families of the Church" (in Conference Report, Apr. 1986, p. 33; or *Ensign*, May 1986, p. 27).

DALLIN H. OAKS

"We know from these inspired words [see 1 Corinthians 13:1–3] that even the most extreme acts of service—such as giving all of our goods to feed the poor—profit us nothing unless our service is motivated by the pure love of Christ" (in Conference Report, Oct. 1984, p. 16; or *Ensign*, Nov. 1984, p. 14).

♦ ♦ ♦

"The prophets of the Book of Mormon taught that the care of the poor was the only way we could obtain essential blessings. The prophet/king Benjamin declared that we must impart of our substance to the poor, 'such as feeding the hungry, clothing the naked, visiting the sick and administering to their relief' for the sake of 'retaining a remission of [our] sins from day to day, that [we] may walk guiltless before God' (Mosiah 4:26.)" (*The Lord's Way* [Salt Lake City: Deseret Book Co., 1991], p. 103).

M. RUSSELL BALLARD

"The love of work is an attitude that members of the Church must develop. In some ways, we have gone through a period of great prosperity which may, when history is written, prove to be as devastating as the Great Depression in its effect upon the attitudes of the people. . . .

"The love for work needs to be reenthroned in our lives. Every family should have a plan for work that touches the lives of each family member so that this eternal principle will be ingrained in their lives" (in Conference Report, Apr. 1981, p. 116; or *Ensign*, May 1981, p. 86).

JOSEPH B. WIRTHLIN

"The Church does substantial but perhaps little-known humanitarian work in many places in the world. Our ability to reach out to others is made possible only to the extent that we are self-reliant. When we are self-reliant, we will use material blessings we receive from God to take care of ourselves and our families and to be in a position to help others" (in Conference Report, Oct. 1991, p. 20; or *Ensign*, Nov. 1991, p. 16).

♦ ♦ ♦

"Members throughout the Church face many challenges in becoming self-reliant. Changing economic and political conditions, the prevalence of one-parent families, working mothers, political refugees, and natural disasters overwhelm the abilities of some to care for themselves and their families. . . .

"We must act to help our members everywhere to overcome these challenges as they strive to apply revealed welfare principles in their lives. . . . Members should be taught to provide for themselves and their families. That is the Lord's way. When they are caring for their own they are in a better position to help others as the gospel requires" (talk given to General Authorities, 30 Sept. 1988; from author's notes).

RICHARD G. SCOTT

"When our interest is first in serving, building, edifying, strengthening without thought of self; when we do not expect an automatic return for each act of kindness, generosity, or sincere effort to help; when we are not concerned about what we will receive or what others will say or whether our own burdens will be diminished, but selflessly seek to build another, the miracle of the power of the gospel is released in our lives. When we permit the Lord to work through us to bless others, that sacred experience releases power in our own lives, and miracles occur. Well did the Master say, 'For inasmuch as ye do it unto the least of these, ye do it unto me' (D&C 42:38)" (in Conference Report, Oct. 1983, p. 103; or *Ensign*, Nov. 1983, p. 71).

ROBERT D. HALES

"Members who receive Church welfare assistance should be expected to work to the extent of their ability for what they receive. Bishops who do not provide this opportunity or fail to expect it do the recipient a disservice in terms of retaining their industriousness, maintaining their self-respect, and increasing their ability to be self-reliant" (Regional Representatives' seminar, 5 Apr. 1991).

JEFFREY R. HOLLAND

"I have always loved—and take literally—King Benjamin's teaching that the only way we can *retain a remission of our sins* is to 'impart of [our] substance to the poor, every man according to that which he hath, such as feeding the hungry, clothing the naked, visiting the sick and administering to their relief, both spiritually and temporally, according to their wants' (Mosiah 4:26). No gospel theme seems to be more fundamental than this one" (statement made to author, 5 Aug. 1994).

◆ ◆ ◆

"Surely no man or woman in this Church can stand fully blameless before the Lord who has turned away the needy or been unmindful of the poor. To resolve those inequities has always been one of the chief tasks of those who would build Zion. Surely it will continue to be so" (statement made to author, 5 Aug. 1994).

HENRY B. EYRING

"The people of God always organize under the direction of the priesthood to care for the poor among them. The desire to reach out to those in need follows naturally from the effects of the gospel of Jesus Christ. As we live it, it creates in us feelings of charity and desires to be productive so that we can not only care for ourselves but share the fruits of our labors with others" (statement made to author, Apr. 1995).

"I, the Lord, stretched out the heavens, and built the earth, my very handiwork; and all things therein are mine. And it is my purpose to provide for my saints, . . . For the earth is full, and there is enough and to spare" (D&C 104:14–15, 17).

CHAPTER 15

THE FUTURE OF
CHURCH WELFARE

The scriptures provide us a glimpse of the ultimate future of the Church welfare program. In Fourth Nephi we read of the happiness of the people who lived following Christ's visit to the Americas:

"The people were all converted unto the Lord, upon all the face of the land, both Nephites and Lamanites, and there were no contentions and disputations among them, and every man did deal justly one with another.

"And they had all things common among them; therefore there were not rich and poor, bond and free, but they were all made free, and partakers of the heavenly gift.

" . . . And surely there could not be a happier people among all the people who had been created by the hand of God" (4 Nephi 1:2, 3, 16).

In Moses we also read about the great peace and joy of the people of Enoch:

"And the Lord called his people Zion, because they were of one heart and one mind, and dwelt in righteousness; and there was no poor among them" (Moses 7:18).

There is no doubt that the Church welfare program will continue to bless the lives of people throughout the world in the years to come. It will ultimately help to bring peace and happiness to those who accept and following the teachings of the Savior. The following excerpts describe the vision that some of our leaders have for the future of this program.

GORDON B. HINCKLEY

"The Mormon Welfare Program is young and looks forward. There will never be a time when what it stands for is not needed, for the poor who are always with us are not the same poor; as some rise, others fall and must be assisted to build again. The plan, still growing as experience points the way, is as valid in times of prosperity as it is in times of stress; in days of plenty it teaches thrift and industry; in days of scarcity it sets an example of self-help and brotherly kindness. The plan is having a chastening influence on the whole Church. . . . In the name of religion, the faith which moves mountains has been set to work solving questions growing out of life. . . .

"The Welfare Plan works. . . . Through it the Church stands, as it has always stood, ready and willing when men cry for bread, to give them a loaf instead of a stone; and the bread thus offered will be made sweet with the divine spirit of love and helpfulness" (*Helping Others to Help Themselves: The Story of the Mormon Church Welfare Program* [pamphlet, 1941], pp. 14–15).

MARION G. ROMNEY

"I have visions of the Welfare Program of the future. I am sure that we are just in the beginning of welfare work. I have certain knowledge, as you do, that the Savior will come soon. The Lord said 130 years ago that His coming was nigh, and it is 130 years nigher now than it was then. Before He comes, this world is going to have some experiences that we can't quite appreciate, even though we read the scriptures and see the writings in the books and see the signs of the times. This people will have to stand on their own feet when the world is shaken down, as sin and corruption and wickedness are wiped off the earth. The Lord can't come to a filthy world. The Welfare Program is to help prepare us to live the United Order" (address given at the dedication of the bishops' storehouse on Welfare Square, 25 May 1976).

"As we prepare for the building of Zion, we must not and we shall not abandon the basic principles upon which our Church Welfare Services are founded: *love*—love of God and neighbor—and *work,* or labor.

"We shall persevere by helping people to help themselves until 'the curse of idleness [is] done away with, the evils of a dole abolished, and independence, industry, thrift and self respect [are] once more established amongst our people' " (in Conference Report, Apr. 1976, p. 169; or *Ensign,* May 1976, p. 123).

"If you will think of the most holy, sacred place you ever have been, you will remember that the final thing we are to do is to be able and willing to consecrate all that we have to the building up of the kingdom of God—which includes caring for our fellowmen. Doing this, we will hasten the advent of the Millennium" (in Conference Report, Oct. 1981, p. 133; or *Ensign,* Nov. 1981, p. 93).

HAROLD B. LEE

"Today we are witnessing the results of schemes and philosophies of uninspired men given out as socialistic, communistic or as civic and community programs in vain attempt to stay the ruthless hand of want, depression, and bloodshed. The time is about ripe for the demonstration of the power and efficacy of the Lord's Plan which He designed as 'a light to the world, and to be a standard for my people, and for the Gentiles to seek to it.' (D.&C. 45:9)

"During the last eleven years, there have been occasional 'dress rehearsals' in the Welfare Program with floods and disasters, wars, and overwhelming destruction, all no doubt, looking to a day when greater problems confronting this people may demand greater abilities and facilities to meet them. The application of the principles of the Welfare Program directed by intelligent and inspired leaders has brought phenomenal results in the blessings of brotherhood and benefits fully as much or more to the givers as to the receivers.

"We must ever have in mind the promise of the Lord in the day when His judgments would descend in full fury upon an unrighteous and unrepentant world, that 'the Lord shall have power over his saints, and shall reign in their midst. . . .' [D&C 1:36]

"Who is there to say but that the Welfare Program when fully developed might not mean the temporal salvation of the Latter-day Saints and be an example to the world of a temporal security in the New Jerusalem spoken of in the scriptures which the Lord declared was to be, 'a land of peace, a city of refuge, a place of safety for the saints of the Most High God' [D&C 45:66]—Who is there to say, if that day comes, the nations of the world may not say, 'Come ye, and let us go up to the mountain of the Lord, . . . and he will teach us of his ways, and we will walk in his paths'? [Isaiah 2:3]

"God grant that we may make sufficient preparation for those days of demonstration while it is yet day and the time for men to perform their labors!" (*Church News*, 20 Dec. 1947, p. 7).

THOMAS S. MONSON

"In reviewing the history of the welfare program, we note that the procedures were revealed to fit a particular time. During the life of Joseph who was sold into Egypt, inspiration directed the Lord's servant to counsel that during the years of plenty, precious grain was to be stored to sustain life during the years of famine that followed. Just a year after the

Church was organized, the Saints were given the united order as the welfare plan. Subsequently, although the united order was not practiced in Nauvoo, the principles were used in new programs in an effort to accomplish the same objectives. . . . The objective of the welfare program then, as now, was to help people become self-reliant.

"In early Utah history, the Church was the economy, and jobs were available through many of its enterprises. However, as the Utah economy became an integral part of the national economy, the welfare program was modified to fit the existing circumstances.

"Helping people find jobs was the primary thrust of the effort in the early 1900s, but when the Depression of 1930 came along, there were no jobs. It was in this setting that the 1936 program pronouncements were made. Restored was the old system of the bishops' storehouse, for many years the economic salvation of the pioneers.

"In recent years more change has taken place. An urban society replaced a rural society, and farming became capital intensive rather than labor intensive. Also, the international growth of the Church has caused no small amount of thought as to how the welfare program should be modified to meet international needs.

"Today the welfare program of this Church is not hidden in a canyon of obscurity, unknown, unappreciated, or unpraised. It is as a city upon a hill which cannot be hid. Presidents of the United States and leaders of nations worldwide seek audience with the leaders of the Church to learn and later to praise the basic principles of the welfare program.

"Reviewing the past, examining the present, and looking to the future, the welfare program of the Church continues to comfort the widow and orphan, feed the hungry, clothe the naked, visit the sick, and come to the rescue of those who are in need. Its procedures may change to meet a particular need at a given time. However, the fundamental doctrines and purposes of the welfare program remain unchanged, for they are scripturally sound, prophetically proclaimed, and time-tested; indeed, they are God-given" ("New Policies in Perspective," address given at special session for Regional Representatives and stake presidents, Apr. 1983).

CONCLUSION

The Church will continue to help those in need. The Savior taught, "For ye have the poor always with you" (Matthew 26:11). He has given many commandments to his Church to seek out and administer to those in need, whether in or out of the Church.

The Lord sent great men to the earth to establish his modern-day welfare program. They had the vision and courage to organize the Church so that the poor and needy could be properly cared for. Their work on earth is completed. However, others who are current leaders were taught by them, and they in turn are training future leaders. Thus correct welfare principles are being perpetuated and, as needed, improved to meet the circumstances of the day. We can rest assured that those who preside over the Church today will move forward the work of Church welfare to bless the sons and daughters of God.

Much of this book has discussed the welfare activities that blessed the lives of people who lived in Utah many years ago. But welfare work is blessing lives today throughout the worldwide Church. Thousands of bishops and branch presidents seek out the poor and administer to their temporal and spiritual needs. Welfare work continues without interruption, building character in those who are willing to work for the good of themselves and others.

The primary purpose of the welfare program, established in 1936, is still the purpose today. The *curse of idleness* still persists in the world, but not in the lives of millions of Church members. The *evils of the dole* have not been abolished in the world, but they have in the lives of millions of Church members. *Independence, industry, thrift, and self-respect* have not been established in the world, but they have been in the lives of many members of the Church. *Work* has been reenthroned as a ruling principle in the lives of millions of people who understand that work is not a curse but an opportunity to bless themselves and others. The aim of the Church is to help people to help themselves, and this aim does not change.

The welfare program of The Church of Jesus Christ of Latter-day Saints is the Lord's plan to take care of the poor and the needy. The Lord inspired President Heber J. Grant to initiate this great work. He has continued to inspire the prophets, seers, and revelators who have presided over the Church and over this program since that time. This work will continue, and lives will be blessed through the united efforts of faithful, charitable members of the Lord's living Church.

Elder Harold B. Lee, in the very early years of the Church welfare program, wrote on the front page of his journal these memorable words: "This program will last as long as this Church exists as a Church" (quoted in L. Brent Goates, *Harold B. Lee: Prophet and Seer* [Salt Lake City: Bookcraft, 1985], p. 141).

APPENDIX A: STAKE PRESIDENTS IN THE SALT LAKE CITY AREA, 1930–1936

Stake	Stake President(s), Years in Service
Salt Lake	Wilford Beesley, 1930–1936
Ensign	Winslow Smith, 1930–1936
Liberty	Bryant S. Hinckley, 1930–1935; J. Percy Goddard, 1936
Pioneer	D. E. Hammond, 1930; Harold B. Lee, 1930–1936; Paul C. Child, 1936
Grant	Joseph Daynes, 1930–1935; Charles Fagg, 1936
Granite	Hugh B. Brown, 1930–1935; Lorenzo Hatch, 1936
Cottonwood	Henry D. Moyle, 1930–1935; Samuel Binghurst, 1936
Highland	(Created 9/8/35) Marvin O. Ashton, 1935–1936
Bonneville	(Created 10/27/35) Joseph L. Wirthlin, 1935–1936

The stake presidents in the Salt Lake City area from 1930 to 1936 led their stakes in caring for the temporal needs of the people. They each participated in one or more welfare activities, such as employment centers, production projects, social services, grain storage, and bishops' storehouses.

APPENDIX B: WELFARE REGIONS IN THE WESTERN UNITED STATES, 1936

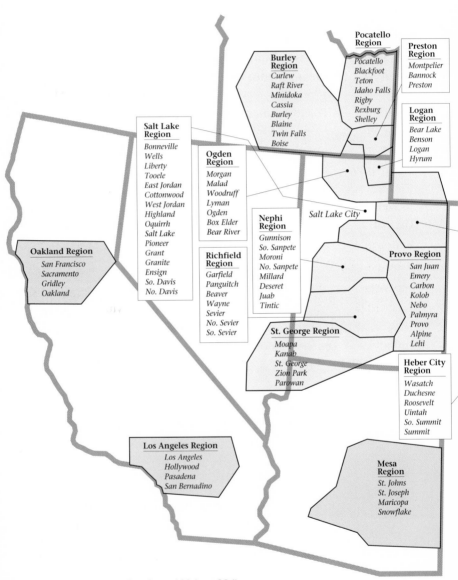

Pocatello Region
Pocatello
Blackfoot
Teton
Idaho Falls
Rigby
Rexburg
Shelley

Preston Region
Montpelier
Bannock
Preston

Burley Region
Curlew
Raft River
Minidoka
Cassia
Burley
Blaine
Twin Falls
Boise

Logan Region
Bear Lake
Benson
Logan
Hyrum

Salt Lake Region
Bonneville
Wells
Liberty
Tooele
East Jordan
Cottonwood
West Jordan
Highland
Oquirrh
Salt Lake
Pioneer
Grant
Granite
Ensign
So. Davis
No. Davis

Ogden Region
Morgan
Malad
Woodruff
Lyman
Ogden
Box Elder
Bear River

Salt Lake City

Nephi Region
Gunnison
So. Sanpete
Moroni
No. Sanpete
Millard
Deseret
Juab
Tintic

Provo Region
San Juan
Emery
Carbon
Kolob
Nebo
Palmyra
Provo
Alpine
Lehi

Oakland Region
San Francisco
Sacramento
Gridley
Oakland

Richfield Region
Garfield
Panguitch
Beaver
Wayne
Sevier
No. Sevier
So. Sevier

St. George Region
Moapa
Kanab
St. George
Zion Park
Parowan

Heber City Region
Wasatch
Duchesne
Roosevelt
Uintah
So. Summit
Summit

Los Angeles Region
Los Angeles
Hollywood
Pasadena
San Bernardino

Mesa Region
St. Johns
St. Joseph
Maricopa
Snowflake

(Taken from *Improvement Era*, June 1936, p. 336)

APPENDIX C: ADMINISTRATORS IN THE GENERAL WELFARE COMMITTEE

Date	Chairman	Managing Director
April 1936	Melvin J. Ballard	Harold B. Lee
April 1938	Henry D. Moyle	Harold B. Lee
June 1941	Henry D. Moyle	Harold B. Lee and Marion G. Romney (asst.)
July 1959	Marion G. Romney	Henry D. Taylor
March 1963	John H. Vandenberg	Henry D. Taylor
April 1972	Victor L. Brown	Junior Wright Child
August 1976	Victor L. Brown	James O. Mason and R. Quinn Gardner
January 1977	Spencer W. Kimball	R. Quinn Gardner
July 1981	Spencer W. Kimball	Glenn L. Pace
May 1985	Spencer W. Kimball	Keith B. McMullin
November 1985	Ezra Taft Benson	Keith B. McMullin
June 1994	Howard W. Hunter	Keith B. McMullin
March 1995	Gordon B. Hinckley	Keith B. McMullin

APPENDIX D

THE IMPROVEMENT ERA, JUNE, 1936

A MESSAGE FROM THE PRESIDENT OF THE CHURCH
THE PRESIDENCIES OF STAKES AND BISHOPRICS OF WARDS
CONCERNING THE MAKE-WORK PROJECT IN THE BEET-GROWING DISTRICTS

Salt Lake City, Utah.
April 21, 1936.

To Presidencies of Stakes and Bishoprics of Wards—
Dear Brethren:

THE FOLLOWING is a suggestive outline for a Make-Work Project for each ward in the Church in the beet-growing districts of Utah and Idaho, which has been submitted to me by Elders Melvin J. Ballard, Mark Austin, and Harold B. Lee, a committee that has been appointed—and other members will be added— to take care of the unemployed members of the Church:

That the bishopric of each ward be requested to select and secure at once one hundred or more acres of land suitable for sugar beets from the various farmers of his ward in tracts of not less than one acre for each farmer and more where possible and suitable, that would not otherwise be planted to beets, for which the farmer is to receive as rent on the land one dollar a ton for each ton of beets raised and a minimum of not less than ten dollars an acre for the use of the land and water.

Just as soon as the land is selected, a day should be set apart at once for the farmers with equipment to donate one or more days to prepare properly and plant the beets by manuring the land where necessary and where the manure is available. If the land, when prepared for planting, has not sufficient moisture, then it should be irrigated and reworked before planting. No beets should be planted in dry ground.

While we realize it is a little late, at least a reasonable tonnage may be secured if the land is selected, prepared, and planted within the next week or ten days, the quicker the better.

When the beets are ready to cultivate, the farmer with a suitable cultivator, and who is used to the work, should be selected to cultivate about ten acres of those beets as many times during the season as is necessary to properly take care of the crop. He is to donate this part of the work.

When the time comes to harvest, another day should be set apart for the farmers of the ward (a sufficient number) to plow out and haul the beets to market, free of charge. One group of farmers could prepare the soil with their teams and equipment; another group could do the cultivating; and another group could do the plowing out of the beets with a beet puller; and another group could haul the beets so that the work could be distributed in order that no farmer would be asked to donate more than a few days' work during the season to help out those who have no employment.

Then the bishopric could divide up the acreage, ranging from five to ten acres to a family, according to the size of the family, to do the hand work; namely, the thinning, the hoeing, irrigating, keeping the beets clean, the pulling and topping, and loading the same into the wagon at the time of harvesting. These families should be selected where available who are suitable for this kind of work so that proper work will be done to secure the highest possible tonnage, even though the lands are not very choice and the season is a little late.

At least ten to twelve tons to the acre should be secured if proper selection and work is done at the right time and in the right way under the direction of the bishopric of the ward, or some suitable man whom they may appoint who is a good farmer and understands the growing of beets.

The laborers should receive an advance payment at the time of thinning, hoeing, the irrigating, and when the work is done so that they may be able to live during the summer while the crop is growing. If ten tons of beets are grown an acre, or a minimum of fifty dollars an acre, after the rent of a minimum of ten dollars an acre and the cost of seed, phosphate, and fertilizer has been deducted of five dollars to six dollars an acre, making a total of sixteen dollars an acre, the laborer should have at least about thirty dollars an acre, or one hundred fifty for the hand work on five acres, or three hundred for the hand work on ten acres where the team work, as above mentioned, has been donated by the people, which would help these people who are out of employment. This co-operative work will be helpful both to the people who donate the team work and the people who receive the benefit of the same through this plan of co-operation.

If this unemployment is to be solved, it must be done by all the people working together and helping each other to find employment, and if the start is made this season, more preparation can be made for another season and the project extended so that it will become a material benefit and absorb a large percentage of the unemployed. There is a market for all the sugar that can be grown and plenty of factories to extract the sugar.

Sincerely your brother,

Heber J. Grant

APPENDIX E: GENERAL WELFARE COMMITTEE MEMBERS, 1936–1967

First Presidency

Quorum of the Twelve

Presiding Bishopric

Relief Society General Presidency

The following is a list of others who served on the General Welfare Committee at some time between 1936 and 1967. They were assigned to visit stake conferences with General Authorities to teach welfare principles. Those marked with an asterisk later became General Authorities.

Leonard Adams	Stewart B. Eccles	Sterling H. Nelson
*Marvin O. Ashton	Clyde C. Edmonds	Irvin B. Nydegger
Mark Austin	A. Louis Elgrenn	*Spencer H. Osborn
Donald M. Bagley	Donald Ellsworth	Casper Parker
Howard Barker	Mark B. Garff	Jack H. Prince
*William H. Bennett	A. Reed Halverson	*Glen L. Rudd
Daken K. Broadhead	Lorenzo H. Hatch	John M. Russon
Campbell M. Brown	Sidney M. Horman	William Eric Ryberg
Clyde J. Brown	Fontleroy Hunsaker	Alfred B. Smith
Grant M. Burbidge	Owen S. Jacobs	T. C. Stayner
Ara C. Call	Phil D. Jensen	Stringham A. Stevens
Paul C. Child	Henry Jorgenson	Walter Stover
Arben O. Clark	Robert L. Judd	Alfred Uhrhan
*James A. Cullimore	Ezra Knowlton	Rudger H. Walker
Walter Dansie	William T. Lawrence	William M. Walsh
Donald Davis	*John Longden	J. Frank Ward
Lionel L. Dradge	J. Leonard Love	George R. Watkins
Roscoe W. Eardley	*Henry D. Moyle	LeRoy A. Wirthlin

When the position of Regional Representative was created in 1967, the persons on the above list were released. Some were called to serve as Regional Representatives.

GENERAL CHURCH WELFARE COMMITTEE MEMBERS SINCE 1967

First Presidency

Quorum of the Twelve

Presiding Bishopric

Relief Society General Presidency

The Presidents of the Seventy and the managing director of the Welfare Department, while not members of the General Welfare Committee, attend the committee meetings to provide and receive information.

APPENDIX F: EARLY WELFARE WORKERS

Between 1936 and 1966, many people served faithfully in help-ing to firmly establish the Church welfare program. Some of them worked at Church headquarters and others at the regional level. They made great contributions to the success of this inspired pro-gram. Some of these people and their assignments are as follows:

General Welfare Office Staff

Lynn Bridges	Supervisor, Garage and Transportation Fleet
John Campbell	Supervisor, Church Canneries
Fenno Casto	Accountant and Statistician
Arben O. Clark	Manager, Central Office
Donald Davis	Employment and Work Director
Roscoe W. Eardley	Assistant to Harold B. Lee and First Coordinator of Bishops' Storehouses
Stewart B. Eccles	Manager, Deseret Industries
Lawrence Harman	Manager, Clothing Factory
Charles Knighton	Manager, Bishops' Central Storehouse and Transportation Fleet
Holgar Larson	Assistant Manager, Deseret Industries
Irvin B. Nydegger	Administrator, Production Projects and Budget
Alice Rentmeister	Secretary, General Welfare Committee
Alfred W. Uhrhan	Secretary, Finance Committee
William M. Walsh	Supervisor, Personal Welfare, Employment Services, and Bishops' Storehouses

Regional Staff

Donald Bailey	Manager, Nephi Bishops' Storehouse; Coordinator, Central Utah
Lloyd Bishop	Manager, Salt Lake Bishops' Storehouse; Coordinator, North Salt Lake and Davis Counties
Arvil W. Dean	Manager, Ogden Bishops' Storehouse; Coordinator, Northern Utah

Clara B. Emmett	Manager, Mesa Bishops' Storehouse; Coordinator, Arizona
Thomas Y. Emmett	Manager, Portland Bishops' Storehouse; Coordinator, Northwest
Jay Grant	Manager, Los Angeles Deseret Industries
Milton Jamison	Manager, Mt. Timpanogos Bishops' Storehouse; Coordinator, Utah County
Moroni Langford	Manager, Cedar City Bishops' Storehouse; Coordinator, Southern Utah
C. Lucius Laudie	Manager, Provo Bishops' Storehouse; Coordinator, Central Utah
Willard Olson	Manager, Jordan Valley Bishops' Storehouse; Coordinator, South Salt Lake County
Delbert Park	Manager, Idaho Falls Bishops' Storehouse; Coordinator, Eastern Idaho
Leland Payne	Manager, Los Angeles Bishops' Storehouse; Coordinator, Southern California
Victor Peterson	Manager, San Francisco Bishops' Storehouse; Coordinator, Northern California
June B. Sharp	Manager, Sugarhouse Bishops' Storehouse; Coordinator, Eastern Salt Lake County and Eastern Utah

APPENDIX G: WELFARE HANDBOOKS

In 1933 President J. Reuben Clark, Jr., wrote a pamphlet titled *Suggestive Directions for Church Relief Activities*. This served as the first handbook to guide bishops and other leaders before the official organization of the welfare program.

In 1944 the *LDS Church Welfare Handbook* was prepared by Elder Marion G. Romney under the direction of President Clark, Elder Henry D. Moyle, and Elder Harold B. Lee. These four brethren met in Grantsville, Utah, in the home of President Clark, to discuss what Brother Romney had written. They asked him to condense it. Some time later, they reconvened in Grantsville to further simplify this handbook. When it was completed it was widely distributed in the Church. It was updated in 1952.

New handbooks were produced in 1960, 1969, 1974, and 1980.

Welfare Publications

Date	Publication
1933	*Suggestive Directions for Church Relief Activities* (pamphlet)
1936	*An Official Statement from the First Presidency* (pamphlet)
1936	"An Important Message on Relief" (statement)
1944	*Fundamentals of the Church Welfare Plan* (pamphlet)
1944	*LDS Church Welfare Handbook*
1946	*The Church Welfare Plan* (Gospel Doctrine course of study)
1948	*Handbook for Relief Society*
1952	*Welfare Plan—Handbook*, revised
1960	*Welfare Plan—1952 Handbook*, revised
1969	*Welfare Plan—Handbook of Instructions*, revised
1974	*Welfare Services Handbook*
1978	*Essentials of Home Production and Storage* (pamphlet)
1980	*Welfare Services Resource Handbook*

New Guidelines That Supersede
Previous Welfare Handbooks

1990	*Providing in the Lord's Way: A Leader's Guide to Welfare*
1991	*Church Welfare Resources for Use in the United States and Canada*

INDEX

Pure Religion